MODERN TARIFF HISTORY

MODERN TARIFF HISTORY

GERMANY—UNITED STATES—
FRANCE

BY PERCY ASHLEY

NEW YORK
Howard Fertig
1970

First published in 1904 by John Murray, London
3rd edition 1920 [here reprinted]

HOWARD FERTIG, INC. EDITION 1970
Published by arrangement with John Murray, London

Library of Congress Catalog Card Number: 68-9645

PRINTED IN THE UNITED STATES OF AMERICA
BY NOBLE OFFSET PRINTERS, INC.

To

MY WIFE DORIS

PREFATORY NOTE TO THE SECOND EDITION

THE first edition of this book, published in 1904, was based upon lectures delivered to the students of the London School of Economics and Political Science in the course of that year. They were an attempt to provide a brief and, so far as possible, unpartisan sketch of the development of tariff policy in Germany, the United States, and France, and of the forces, political and economic, which have determined its course.

The opportunity offered by a second edition has been utilised for an extensive revision. Besides the correction of some errors, typographical and other, the statistics have been re-cast and extended; some additions have been made to the original narrative and the foot-notes; further references have been added, and the bibliographies enlarged. Moreover, since 1904 there have been important developments of tariff policy in all three countries: the new German Commercial Treaties and Tariff entered into effect in 1906, the United States Tariff was remodelled in 1908, and a new French Tariff has come into force in the present year. Fortunately the proceedings in all these cases have taken place in full publicity—this was especially so in regard to the tariff revisions in the United States and France—and it has consequently been possible to give in additional chapters some account of these developments, recent as they are.

It is hoped that in its new form the work may prove to have retained its original character, and to be even more useful to students of economic problems.

P. A.

LONDON,
April, 1910.

PREFATORY NOTE TO THE THIRD EDITION

IN the present edition the character and form of the work remains unchanged, but the narrative has been carried up to the outbreak of the European War of 1914–1918, by the addition of a chapter on the United States Tariff of 1913, and the inclusion of statistics relating to the years 1909–1913. A few notes have been added and a few passages rewritten, and minor changes made in consequence of the time which has elapsed since the publication of the second edition.

The narrative necessarily ends with the commencement of the Great War, which suspended altogether the normal economic life of two of the States whose tariff policy is considered in this book, and for the United States, as for the rest of the world, created trade conditions in which tariff policy played no part.

P. A.

LONDON,
June, 1920.

CONTENTS

PART I

GERMANY

PART II

THE UNITED STATES

PART III

FRANCE

PART I

GERMANY

MODERN TARIFF HISTORY

CHAPTER I

THE FORMATION OF THE ZOLLVEREIN

At the close of the Napoleonic wars Germany was in a state of the utmost political and economic confusion, and the Congress of Vienna did little to remedy the evil. It gave the new Germanic Confederation a constitution vague and impracticable, and it offered no effective means of dealing with the most pressing problem, that of economic reorganisation. One of the worst results of German particularism was the existence of a separate customs system in each of the thirty-nine states, many of them very small, which composed the Confederation; and, moreover, commerce was hampered in every conceivable way, not merely within the boundaries of the Confederation, but also within the larger of its constituent states, such as Prussia. In that kingdom there were nearly sixty different local tariffs with a total of nearly two thousand eight hundred classes of goods:[1] in some of its provinces, particularly in the western part of the monarchy, the importation of foreign manufactures and products was allowed free or on payment of only moderate duties, in others it was either absolutely prohibited or subject to extremely heavy duties. The multiplicity of customs barriers made administration costly and inefficient, and there was much petty smuggling.[2]

The first reforms came in Prussia with the Tariff Act of 1818. Its authors—Bülow, the Minister of Finances, and Maassen, who was responsible for the details of the tariff—were greatly influenced by the

[1] Zimmermann, i. p. 1.

[2] Bowring, p. 2.

economic ideas of Adam Smith, which were at that time making their way in Germany; the internal customs barriers were abolished, and the whole tariff policy reformed in the direction of the establishment of greater liberty of trade and commerce. Under the new system the importation of raw materials was to be free; an average duty of 10 per cent. was imposed on manufactured goods, whilst "colonial produce" and wine were to pay up to 30 per cent.; and there were to be moderate duties on the transit of goods passing through Prussia to other states. The general level of duties was somewhat higher in the eastern provinces than in the western. There was also to be an excise levied on the consumption of certain goods in Prussia itself. The tariff so adopted was more liberal than any continental tariff of the time, and in some ways the new policy was more advanced than that even of Great Britain.[1] Germany was predominantly agrarian, and the north-eastern part (the country of the great landowners), in particular exported substantial quantities of agricultural produce to foreign markets. A considerable part of the agricultural population of Prussia was therefore directly interested in the promotion of foreign trade, and so were also the coast towns on the Baltic with their extensive carrying trade. Manufactures were developing slowly; they had received some stimulus from the "continental system" of Napoleon, but the new tariff gave only a moderate protection to the home manufacturers, who were by no means satisfied with it; and it contained no prohibitions of import except in regard to salt and playing-cards, which were Government monopolies. It had one peculiarity—the new duties were not levied on the value of the imported goods, but consisted of a fixed charge on a

[1] Schmoller, *Grundriss*, ii. p. 611, observes that such a reform was rendered possible only by the fact that Prussia was then an absolute monarchy; in a constitutional state the protectionist influences would have been too strong. He ascribes the new policy to the position of foreign affairs, which rendered anything like a tariff war inadvisable; a desire to avoid causes of friction with the other German states; financial needs; and the influence of the new economic ideas.

given weight or measure of each commodity. These "specific" duties were at first on the average about 10 per cent. on the estimated value of the goods, and remained not at the same percentage, but at the same actual amount, whatever changes occurred in respect of the value. This procedure had the advantage of simplicity; it was not necessary to provide a staff of expert valuers at all the customs stations. On the other hand, there was the distinct disadvantage, which later was severely felt, that there came to be no particular relation between the value of the commodity and the duty; if the value of the given quantity of a particular article declined for any reason, the old duty might become extremely heavy; whilst, on the other hand, if the quality improved, and with it the value, the duty became proportionately so much smaller. So that the duties tended to become much more protective for goods of inferior quality than for the better class of commodities.[1]

The new tariff came into force on January 1st, 1819, and in the same year a policy was inaugurated which was destined to have the most far-reaching results. In the kingdom of Prussia there were no less than thirteen "enclaves,"—petty states or parts of states completely surrounded by Prussian territory. All of these attempted

[1] In the report of Dr. (afterwards Sir John) Bowring, who visited Germany to report on the Zollverein to the British Government in 1840, it is stated that the effect of the fall in prices since 1818 and of some increases of duty had been to make the duties on some kinds of manufactured goods anything from 20 to 100 per cent., so that in some cases they became absolutely prohibitive. These duties had come to be higher on goods of coarse quality than on fine qualities; the actual duties on cotton goods varied from 30 to 120 per cent., and on some classes of woollen goods from 20 to 50 per cent. (pp. 3, 53, and 279). Friedrich List welcomed this effect of the Tariff, because it gave protection to "articles of common use, which every land can best manufacture for itself, and of which the home manufacture, on account of its great amount, is most important for the country" (Schippel, p. 86; *cf.* also Schmoller, *Grundriss*, ii. pp. 6, 12). This system has been commonly adhered to throughout German tariff legislation, as in Great Britain since the middle of last century, mainly because of its superior administrative advantages. For an account and criticism of the alternative method of *ad valorem* duties, see p. 155 *n.*, and pp. 211–212 *infra*.

to maintain customs systems of their own, and as a result came into sharp conflict with Prussia, whose new tariff with its reformed and strict administration against them roused considerable indignation in Germany. It was, however, impossible for them permanently to resist the pressure, and in 1819 the little principality of Schwarzburg-Sondershausen accepted Prussia's offer to take over the administration of its customs, and in return to give it the right of trading with Prussia free from all restrictions, and a proportion of the total joint customs revenue. But the particularist sentiment ruling in most of the German states was in general strongly hostile to such a course, and it was only very slowly that the other enclaves followed the example; in fact, the next instance was not till 1822.

The policy of Prussia, as exemplified in the agreement with Schwarzburg-Sondershausen, was to take the absolute control of any union which might be formed; but it was quite evident that, whatever the small states might do, the larger states would not agree to any such arrangement. All clung to their independence; the small states would not subordinate themselves to the larger, save under compulsion, and scarcely any state was willing to consider the economic interests of the whole Confederation as superior to its own private aims; there was, in fact, an incessant commercial and industrial war. But already there were signs that the people were becoming weary of these conditions. Early in 1819, Nebenius, an official of Baden, issued on behalf of his Government a memorandum on the economic condition of Germany. He pointed out that, though that country suffered from the tariff systems of its neighbours, it suffered still more from the commercial policy of its own component states; the only real remedy was the formation of a league of the German states, the abandonment of their protective policy against each other and the adoption of a common tariff against foreign countries. At the same time it would be necessary for the German states to bring their systems of internal taxation into something approaching uniformity. It is this memorandum which has given Nebenius the credit of being the father of the idea of the later Zollverein, but the idea was not confined to him. In April, 1819, a deputation of manufacturers and others, chiefly from the South German states, appeared at the Federal Diet to urge the adoption of a similar policy: that deputation represented a commercial and trade union, which had been formed two or three years before, largely under the leadership of Friedrich List, and, unlike Nebenius, it was avowedly protectionist in the interests of German industry. Unfortunately, the Federal Diet was hopelessly weak, and exercised practically no influence on the policy of the various states; it could do nothing in the direction proposed, and reform had to come in another way.

The southern states set to work to attain the desired end by treaties among themselves; it was absolutely necessary for them to do something, since they were harassed in the north by the growing Prussian Union and in the south by Austria—both with their transit duties. So there began a series of conferences between the southern states at Darmstadt during the years 1820 to 1823 on schemes to resist Prussia, and to combine on a common tariff policy—conferences which had no practical result, but at their close "offered foreign countries a new and pitiable picture of German confusion, and of the triumph of petty particularist interests over the common good."[1] The failure of the conferences was followed by a new tariff war in Southern Germany, and such a condition of affairs could not long continue. Württemberg in particular was untiring in its efforts to improve the situation; it called a fresh conference at Stuttgart (1823 to 1825), which was again unsatisfactory and produced no immediate result. Recourse was then had to separate treaties. Already in 1824 an agreement had been made between Baden and Hesse-Darmstadt, and also one between Württemberg and the Hohenzollern principalities in its midst. Early in 1825 Württemberg and Bavaria

[1] Weber, p. 34.

had agreed on a scheme of Customs Union under joint administration, and they now tried to get Baden, Hesse, Electoral Hesse and Nassau to join them. These negotiations failed, but in April, 1827, a provisional agreement, confirmed and completed in January of the following year, established a Union of Bavaria and Württemberg on the basis of a common tariff, abolition of duties on commodities passing between the two contracting countries, joint administration of the customs, and division of the net proceeds of the duties according to population.

Prussia had not failed to follow the course of these negotiations, or to learn the lesson which they taught. Until this time, it seems that the Prussian statesmen had not thought of a larger union, except (as already indicated) in the form of a customs system under the direction of themselves alone. They had treated the other enclaves, which had united with them—Schwarzburg-Rudolstadt, Saxe-Weimar, Lippe, Mecklenburg-Schwerin—just as Schwarzburg-Sondershausen; the small states were given no share in the management of the Union. "In the south, on the other hand, Bavaria and Württemburg had fully realised the idea of a union with equality of rights for all its members, including independent administration and complete reservation of all individual rights, without prejudice to the necessary unity of the whole and to the common end in view. Clearly this system must commend itself to the Governments of the minor states rather than the Prussian plan, which involved some loss of independence."[1] The Prussian rulers saw the danger, and changed their policy. In February, 1825, less than a month after the completion of the treaty between Bavaria and Württemberg, and largely because of that treaty,[2] an agreement was made between Prussia and Hesse-Darmstadt, which laid the

[1] Weber, p. 61.

[2] "The political purpose had triumphed over the fears of the Prussian financiers, for, shortly before, on the 18th of January, Bavaria and Württemberg had finally completed their Customs Union" (Zimmermann, i. p. 53).

foundation of the later Zollverein. No changes were to be made without mutual consent, and Hesse kept control of the customs administration within its own area.

Events now moved rapidly. In August, 1828, some of the minor states, including Hanover, Brunswick, and the two Hanse towns, Hamburg and Bremen, formed a Middle German Commercial Union, under the leadership of Saxony, chiefly to resist the pressure of the two existing unions. But the new organisation was inchoate and shortlived; it had no definite policy or purpose beyond that of resistance, and found no means of reconciling the interests of its constituent members. In fact the small states were in an impossible position, and their difficulties were intensified when in May, 1829, an agreement was made between the Prussian Union and Bavaria and Württemberg, on the basis of reciprocal reduction of duties to the extent of 20 to 50 per cent. on many commodities, the approximation of the two customs systems to a common form, and yearly conferences. The Middle German Union was breaking down; its members were showing an inclination to draw near to the Prussian Union or the Southern Union, as suited them best, and in 1830 Saxony intimated to Prussia its desire to enter into negotiations for its entry into the Prussian Union. The collapse was completed when Electoral Hesse joined Prussia in 1831—an event of considerable importance, since the geographical position of that state between the western provinces of Prussia and Hesse-Darmstadt could establish or prevent the real effectiveness of the commercial alliance of these two. The Northern and Southern Unions now drew together, and the final negotiations commenced. They were most delicate and difficult, for there were many diverse interests to be reconciled. In Prussia itself the sea-towns and the agricultural provinces were favourable to freedom of trade, and the manufacturers desired protection; the former, however, had the upper hand. The northern states of Germany, and especially the Hanse towns, supported the liberal policy;

and so did the great commercial centre of Frankfurt-on-Main. In Saxony, the traders of Leipzig inclined towards union with Prussia, since they sympathised with the ideas which underlay her tariff;[1] the manufacturers there were dissatisfied with the amount of protection which the Prussian tariff offered, though there was the compensating advantage of the opening of the Prussian market for their products. The southern states were divided in the same way. Moreover, the manufacturers of Prussia felt that they would be seriously menaced by the increased competition, on equal terms, from the industries of Saxony for example, which must follow a complete union. The division to be made of the proceeds of the tariff was also a difficult matter, for the consumption of "colonial produce" per head was much greater in Prussia than in the south; and, further, some of the smaller states were strongly averse to the surrender of any sovereign rights.[2] The Prussian ministers were by no means optimistic, but the negotiations were carried to a successful issue, partly because of economic considerations, and partly because political motives on the part of Prussia made her conciliatory—these latter were in fact the determining consideration.[3] The work was done by Maassen, now Minister of Finance in Prussia, and Von

[1] In 1822 the inequality of the duties in the eastern and western provinces of the Prussian monarchy had been practically abolished, and the duties themselves reduced. Further reductions had been made in 1825 and 1828 (Bowring, pp. 13–14).

[2] It is curious to observe how indifferent Austria was to these negotiations; Metternich and his colleagues did not regard them as dangerous, and did not believe that they could be successful. They might possibly have drawn the southern states towards Austria by commercial treaties, but the efforts which they made in this direction were scarcely serious, and altogether ineffective. Great Britain, on the other hand, was fully alive to the danger which threatened her position in the German market, and attempted to check the formation of a great German customs area by treaties with various small German states. The treaty completed with the free city of Frankfurt did for some time prevent that city from joining the Zollverein. France made a number of attempts to detach the smaller states, especially those along the Rhine, by the offer of special tariff treatment, but without success (Weber, p. 105).

[3] "The anxiety of the economist had been forced to yield to the hopes of the statesman" (Von Treitschke).

Mieg, who represented Bavaria and Württemberg. On the 22nd of March, 1833, Bavaria and Württemberg joined the Prussian Union, and the example was immediately followed by Saxony.[1] Negotiations had meanwhile been going on with Hesse-Cassel and the Thuringian states, and in May of the same year they also gave their adhesion.

The Zollverein, so formed by a series of treaties, and including seventeen states with a population of some twenty-three millions, came into force on January 1st, 1834. Policy was to be determined from time to time by an annual meeting of representatives of the constituent states, but any change required unanimous approval; this (though probably unavoidable in view of the tenacity with which the several states clung to their independence) was one of the weak points of the organisation—a proposal, approved by all the states chiefly concerned, might be vetoed by one of the least important members of the Union. A common tariff (based in the main on the rates in force in Prussia) against all states outside the Union, and the abolition of all duties on goods passing between the various members, were the fundamental principles; but each state kept its own commercial code, its own patent laws (with the right to tax commodities, coming from other members, which would infringe patents) and its own government monopolies. The proceeds of the customs duties were to be divided amongst the states in proportion to population. The tariff rates imposed moderate duties on manufactured articles, and duties for revenue on colonial produce, and gave freedom of import for raw materials and some manufactured articles re-

1 "In fact, Saxony had scarcely any course to take but to join the Union. She had lost many of her richest provinces by the peace; she was hemmed in by unfriendly tariffs; her manufacturing population found insufficient outlets for their productions" (Bowring, pp. 33–4). "On the whole, Saxony is the portion of Germany which has most profited by the Commercial League, for in Saxony manufacturing industry was most developed, and in the competition with other states of the League Saxony had the vantage-ground. To her especially it has opened a market of 26,000,000 of consumers, and closed the gates to a great extent against foreign rivals" (*ibid.*, p. 37).

quired for industry. Much still remained to be done before the Zollverein became a unified commercial and industrial organisation, but the foundations were firmly laid.[1]

Several important states still stood aloof, particularly the northern states—Hanover, Brunswick, Oldenburg, Holstein, the two Mecklenburgs, the three Hanse towns and Luxemburg—with Baden and the important commercial city of Frankfurt. Some of these did not long remain outside the Union; the accession of the isolated Grand-Duchy of Baden, realised by its Government to be inevitable after the breakdown of the Middle German Union, was delayed only till May, 1835, by the hostility to Prussia of some of its political parties. In the same year Nassau joined the Zollverein, and the example was followed by Frankfurt after long and difficult negotiations at the beginning of 1836. In the next five years a number of small and not very important territories—such as Waldeck-Pyrmont and Lippe-Detmold—were included in the Zollverein without receiving the rights of independent members. Most of the larger states which persisted in their independence continued to act separately, but in May, 1834, Hanover, Oldenburg and Brunswick, whose interests were nearly identical, formed a union of their own, called the Steuerverein.

Almost immediately after the completion of the work of organisation, attempts were made to place the relations of the Zollverein with the neighbouring states on a more satisfactory footing. The diplomatic representation was entrusted to Prussia, but the first efforts were by no means successful. The negotiations with Russia, which pursued an almost prohibitive policy, failed completely, as did those with Austria;[2] whilst the Zollverein was distinctly worsted in a conflict with the Government of Louis Philippe in France.[3] The chief

[1] Schmoller, *Grundriss*, ii. p. 612.
[2] The details of these negotiations can be read in Zimmermann, i. pp. 138–52.
[3] *Ibid.*, p. 162.

treaties actually completed were with Holland and Great Britain. In the former case there was something like a short customs war; the Dutch Government desired a commercial treaty, and to enforce its desire, and partly also to protect Dutch agriculture against German competition, it imposed higher duties on grain in October, 1835. The Zollverein replied by the imposition of higher duties on Dutch sugar, and by the abolition of privileges enjoyed by Dutch vessels on the Rhine. Negotiations for a treaty then began, but broke down over the sugar question, since the growing sugar industry in Germany was strongly hostile to any concessions to Holland in this matter. So at first it was only possible to make an agreement in 1837 in regard to shipping, which put the vessels of the two nations on an equality. Negotiations continued, however, and in the beginning of 1839 a further treaty was completed, which reduced a number of duties on some Dutch dairy produce, sugar and rice, whilst the Zollverein obtained reductions in the Dutch duties on wine, grain, stones, timber, and a number of classes of manufactured goods. But it was speedily felt in the Zollverein that the concessions made to Holland were too great, and certainly there is in this case no sign of the skill which subsequently characterised the conduct of German commercial negotiations. Consequently the treaty was denounced by the Zollverein less than two years later. The treaty with Great Britain, completed in March, 1841, was also limited to the matter of shipping; it exempted Prussia from many of the restrictions contained in the English Navigation Acts, and on the whole was of some benefit to Germany, whilst Great Britain, in return, got the same reduction in the duties on sugar and rice as had been granted to Holland. The treaty was not popular, in the southern states particularly, and came to an end in 1848.

In 1841 the formal renewal of the Zollverein took place. It was perfectly clear that its institution had been of the utmost benefit to the constituent states; industrial and commercial development had been greatly stimulated; many of the causes of inter-state disputes had been removed, and Governments and people alike were on the whole well satisfied.[1] The only difficulty at the renewal was caused by Prussia, for the financial arrangements of the Union had benefited the smaller states, but had reduced the revenues of Prussia, and her statesmen were somewhat dissatisfied, though they recognised fully the advantages which they had gained.[2] But the difficulty was not insuperable, for no one was anxious to break up the Union; certain additional financial arrangements were made, not quite satisfactory to Prussia, but accepted by her, and the Zollverein was renewed on May 8th, 1841, for twelve years. Immediately afterwards there came fresh additions of territory. Brunswick was discontented with the action of Hanover in the Steuerverein, and quitted that organisation in 1842; in the same year it entered the Zollverein. So did Lippe-Detmold and Schaumburg, and, much more important still, Luxemburg, which, though in dynastic union with the kingdom of Holland, was itself a member of the Germanic Confederation. In the last case special arrangements had to be made to prevent the Dutch Government making use of the position of Luxemburg to influence the policy of the Zollverein, and so the representation of the Duchy in the councils of the Union was entrusted to Prussia.

[1] "The Commercial League is, in fact, the representative of a sentiment widely, if not universally, spread in Germany—that of national unity. It has done wonders in breaking down petty and local jealousies, and has become a foundation on which future legislation, representing the common interests of the German people, ay undoubtedly be hereafter raised. . . . The Zollverein has brought the sentiment of German nationality out of the regions of hope and fancy into those of positive material interests" (Bowring, p. 1). For an extremely interesting contemporary criticism of Bowring's Report, see List, *System of National Economy* (translated by Lloyd), chap. xxxiv. (published in 1844).

[2] "Although Prussia does not fail to recognise that its subjects have shared in the general advantageous results of the Union, yet the position is altogether different when viewed from the financial standpoint" (Circular of the Prussian Government, 1839; quoted in Weber, p. 185). It would have been inadvisable to refer to the political advantages accruing to Prussia.

One other important event of this period, which it will be convenient to notice here, was the treaty with Belgium. It was desirable that the relations between that country and the Zollverein should be as amicable as possible, since a great part of the German import and export trade passed over the Belgian railways and through Belgian ports. For the purposes of negotiations, then, the Belgian Government was in a strong position owing to this fact, and also because its geographical situation enabled it to play off France against Germany. The result was the treaty of 1844, by which the Zollverein gave reductions of duties on commodities coming from Belgium, and on some articles of Belgian origin (particularly iron); whilst Belgium, on its side, guaranteed the existing freedom of transit for goods coming from or going to the Zollverein, and established certain preferences for German products. The shipping of the two nations was put on an equal footing. Weber, the chief historian of the Zollverein, holds that the treaty chiefly benefited Belgium, since she gained easier access to German markets with her iron, whilst the Zollverein got no new concession of value, and he adds that Prussia would never have yielded so much but for the fear of a Belgian alliance with France;[1] but the Zollverein had secured freedom of transit for its goods through Belgium, and the establishment of an entrepôt at Antwerp, and these were matters of no small importance.[2]

[1] Weber, pp. 213, 214.

[2] Zimmermann, i. p. 278.

CHAPTER II

THE BEGINNINGS OF PROTECTION AND THE FIRST CRISIS

DURING the early years of the Zollverein there had been only a few increases in the customs duties,[1] but after 1840 there was a marked upward tendency in the tariff rates, owing to a distinct movement towards Protection, which found its scientific expression in the writings of Friedrich List,[2] and particularly in his *System of National Economy*, published in 1841.[3] His doctrine, that Protection is necessary to enable a nation to pass from the purely agricultural condition of society to a higher stage of combined industry and agriculture,[4] that the encouragement of "production" was less immediately important than the development of "productive powers," and that if Germany was to make economic progress in the face of the overwhelming industrial supremacy of Great Britain, a reasoned policy of Protection was essential—this doctrine found ready

[1] *E.g.*, on cotton and woollen yarn from six to eight thalers per centner, and on the finer qualities of bar iron from one thaler to three thalers.

[2] List, "the prophet of our railways, Chambers of Commerce, and Eastern colonisation"; Naumann, *Mittel Europa* (Engl. trans., p. 223).

[3] The best account of List's work and teaching will be found in M. E. Hirst, *Life of Friedrich List* (1909).

[4] "In short, history and statistics alike prove the correctness of the dictum expressed by the ministers of George I.: that nations are richer and more powerful the more they export manufactured goods and import the means of subsistence and raw materials. In fact, it may be proved that entire nations have been ruined merely because they have exported only means of subsistence and raw materials, and have imported only manufactured goods" (List, *System of Political Economy*, trans. Lloyd, p. 218).

acceptance in the industrial circles of the Zollverein. List pointed always to the example of Great Britain, whose long-continued policy, he held, had been to secure the home market for its manufacturers, to encourage the increase of "productive powers" by the free admission, not of foreign goods, but of foreign workmen, and to bear a temporary loss for the sake of an ultimate gain. This policy had laid the foundation of Great Britain's industrial power, and he called on Germany to follow the example.[1]

The practical demand for the application of List's doctrine came from the manufacturers of iron and the cotton-spinners, who had already secured some increases of the customs duties on imports competing with their products; and over this proposal there arose, between 1841 and 1850, the first real struggle between the rival policies of Free Trade and Protection. In the case of the iron producers, the call for increased duties was due largely to over-production in England and the consequent reduction of the prices of English iron in the continental markets to a point at which continental manufacturers could not compete with them. There was a great increase in the importation of iron into Germany, from 0·9 million centner in 1839 to 2·6 millions in 1842, and 4·2 millions in 1843. In 1839 the German iron works produced 78 per cent. of the total amount consumed in Germany, whilst by 1843 their share had fallen to 45 per cent.[2] The cotton-spinning industry had been growing

[1] "If any nation whatever is qualified for the establishment of a national manufacturing power, it is Germany. . . . If any nation whatever has a right to anticipate rich results from a protective system adapted to her circumstances, for the progress of her home manufactures, for the increase of her foreign trade and her navigation, for the perfecting of her internal means of transport, for the prosperity of her agriculture, as also for the maintenance of her independence and the increase of her power abroad, it is Germany. Yes, we venture to assert, that on the development of the German protective system depend the existence, the independence, and the future of the German nationality" (List, *System of Political Economy*, trans. Lloyd, p. 425). For a general statement of List's view see below, pp. 50 *seq.*, and 55-6.

[2] Sering, *Geschichte der preussischdeutschen Eisenzölle von* 1818 *bis zur Gegenwart* (1882).

rapidly in Prussia, Saxony and the south-western states since the establishment of the Zollverein, but it was not yet firmly established, and in 1842 the import of cotton yarn was more than double the home production. The request for protection for these two industries naturally led to a sharp conflict of interests between the producers and the consumers of the two commodities. There was a growing demand for industrial machinery, and the manufacturers were opposed to any policy likely to increase its cost; and to the producers of cotton goods (an industry which had made rapid progress of recent years, and supplied one of the chief exports of the Zollverein) an ample supply of British yarn was an absolute necessity. The division over the question was also territorial. On the whole, the north was in favour of Free Trade. The attitude of the Prussian Government was determined in the main by the agricultural and commercial interests. Large quantities of agricultural produce, chiefly grain and timber, were exported, especially to Great Britain after the repeal of the Corn Laws; and, on the other hand, the landowners needed agricultural machinery and feared an increase in its price as a result of the proposed higher duties; so that the Prussian Conservatives, whose strength lay in the agricultural districts, were, unlike their English contemporaries, strong advocates of freer trade. The Baltic ports—Dantzig, Stettin, Elbing, Königsberg and others—were engaged in the export of grain and timber, and were opposed to anything which might tend to restrict trade.[1] These influences were strong enough to overcome any inclination on the part of the Prussian Government to accede to the demands of the iron producers of the Rhine province. The two great Hanse towns (Hamburg and

[1] Schippel points out that, in the absence of a well-organised railway system, the sea made foreign markets nearer to the lands along the Baltic than were the inland territories of the Zollverein. Even with the development of means of communication this is true of some parts of Germany to-day; for some years before 1914 it was a cause of complaint that British coal could be conveyed to Berlin (by sea and canal) more cheaply than German coal from Upper Silesia (by rail and canal) or Westphalia (by rail).

Bremen) took the same line; both had a large trade with Great Britain and America, exporting linen, timber, minerals, woollens, glassware and wines, and importing manufactured goods, tobacco and colonial produce generally. Frankfurt, which was the great entrepôt for British trade, also stood firmly on the Free Trade side. Saxony was carried the same way by the influence of the traders of Leipzig and the cotton-weavers, whose industry far exceeded in importance that of the spinners. The Thuringian states followed the lead of Prussia and Saxony. Brunswick and Nassau supported Prussia largely because the financial results of the Zollverein had been for them so favourable that they were unwilling to break with her.

The southern states, on the other hand, were distinctly inclined to Protection. Bavaria wavered; it was difficult for its government to decide between the rival spinning and weaving industries, but it was carried into the protectionist movement by the personal authority of King Ludwig I., who seems to have been influenced chiefly by political considerations. Württemberg and Baden, however, were anxious for the protection of the cotton-spinning industry, which had been most successful in those territories; and they were supported by Hesse.

The conflict continued for several years, and was particularly keen at the annual conferences. After the Karlsruhe Conference in 1845 feeling was so strong that Prussia was accused of being unduly under the influence of Great Britain. On the other side, the Prussian Government had declared, as early as 1842, that the southern Governments took too narrow a view of the economic interests of Germany as a whole, and were unduly swayed by the cotton-spinners, who were suffering from bad organisation and the over-hasty development of their industry.[1] Both sides gave way somewhat, and by 1850 the duties had been considerably increased. In 1843 the duty on certain kinds of cotton yarn was increased by 50 per cent.; in 1844 a small duty

[1] Zimmermann, i. pp. 190 and 200.

was imposed on pig-iron, hitherto admitted free, and there were slight increases on iron bars and rails. In the same year the duties on various kinds of woollen goods were increased 33 per cent., and those on gold and silver articles and leather gloves were doubled. In 1846 there were still further increases on all kinds of cotton yarn, linen yarn and twist, and some other commodities. On the other hand, however, there were reductions in the duties on a number of raw materials, and in the transit dues in 1850. It must be remembered also that the changes in the price of commodities (and there had been a very marked fall during this period) had not been followed by any corresponding change in the amount of the duties which, as already pointed out, had been fixed according to the value, thirty years before, of a particular quantity of each commodity. The result was that duties which had been quite moderate originally had now come to be in some cases almost prohibitive.[1] It is impossible to say how much further the movement towards Protection would have gone had it not been for political considerations, and particularly the problem of the relation of Austria to the Zollverein.

The Austrian Government, under Prince Metternich, had paid little attention to the negotiations for the formation of the Zollverein; its attempts to interfere had been unimportant, and its whole action in the matter had been marked by that complete indifference to economic questions which was its peculiar characteristic amongst the Governments of Europe. Its own tariff policy was protectionist, or rather in many cases prohibitive. But after 1833 even Metternich awoke to the danger which threatened Austrian authority in the Germanic Confederation from the growing influence of Prussia, and, as time went on, he realised that the economic leadership of that state in the Zollverein might, without great difficulty, lead to political predominance

[1] Michaelis, *Kommissionsbericht uber den preussischfranzösischen Handelsvertragentwurf*, quoted in Schippel, pp. 135–7; *cf.* note on p. 5, *supra*.

also. In 1841 the Austrian ministers began to consider the possibility of the adhesion of the Austrian Empire to the Zollverein, but came to the conclusion that for the time being, at any rate, it was impracticable, partly owing to the supposed impossibility of abandoning the policy of high Protection, and partly because of the peculiar position of Hungary, which was not in economic union with the rest of the Empire.[1] But from that time onward the problem was always under consideration, and the discussion became vigorous after the renewal of the Zollverein. In Austria itself the manufacturers clung to the protective policy, but in the community as a whole there was considerable dissatisfaction with it; and, further, the Austrian statesmen were more and more impressed by the political necessity of checking the Prussian advance. Consequently, the Austrian efforts were now directed towards forcing an entrance into the Zollverein, or, as a less preferable alternative, towards destroying it. These efforts became much more vigorous after the events of the revolutionary years 1848 and 1849. For one thing, the action of the National Assembly at Frankfurt, in offering to Frederick William IV. of Prussia the Imperial Crown of a Germany from which Austria was excluded, had brought home to the Austrian statesmen the extreme weakness of their position; and further, Metternich had been succeeded by one of the ablest and strongest ministers Austria has ever had, Prince Schwarzenberg.[2] Moreover, the conditions in the Zollverein were not unfavourable. It has already been pointed out that difficulties had arisen between Prussia and her colleagues in 1841 over the division of the customs revenue, and the dissatisfaction then created in the southern states had been increased by the growing preponderance of Prussia. They were therefore not unwilling to admit Austria, partly to keep Prussia in check—thus adopting in the Zollverein that policy of

[1] Weber, p. 244.

[2] Prussian diplomacy had received its severest blow in the Treaty of Olmutz in November, 1850, on the questions of the Elbe Duchies and Hesse-Cassel.

"balance" which had reduced the Confederation to impotence—and partly because they desired support for their protectionist policy. They were, however, hampered by the knowledge that, with the comparatively small consumption of imported goods in Austria, any division of the customs revenues on the old lines would seriously reduce their revenues.[1] In 1849 the Austrian Government began to put forward proposals for the complete economic union of Germany and the non-German territories of the Austrian monarchy. It proposed, that is to say, the establishment of a complete industrial state, including a large part of Middle Europe and a population of over seventy millions; in this state neither the commercial, nor the industrial, nor the agricultural class would be predominant, but a tariff policy was to be adopted which would equally safeguard all three.[2]

The Prussian Government from the first realised the political effect of an acceptance of these proposals, and set itself resolutely to oppose the admission of Austria. The most striking manifestation of this was its action in regard to Hanover. It has already been mentioned that in 1834 Hanover had formed, particularly with Oldenburg and Brunswick, a Steuerverein in the north. Since then there had been constant disputes with Prussia, which continued even after the adhesion of Brunswick to the Zollverein, an event destructive of the effectiveness of the Northern Union, and seriously crippling Hanover by cutting her territory in two. Negotiations had been going on for years between Prussia and Hanover, but without success, owing to the excessive demands made by the latter; but now suddenly Prussia gave way, and concluded in September, 1851, a treaty in which she accepted most of the conditions which

[1] Thus in October, 1851, Beust declared that, for financial and economic reasons, Saxony could not leave the Zollverein; and Bavaria and Württemberg requested Austria to guarantee the maintenance of their existing revenues (Zimmermann, i. p. 358).

[2] The chief Austrian official advocate was Bruck, the Minister of Commerce.

she had hitherto decisively rejected. Hanover received permission to import iron rails free of duty, and a guarantee of a larger share of the customs revenue than she would have received on the basis of population. The treaty was advantageous to Hanover in many ways, since it was clearly impossible for her much longer to maintain her economic isolation; and for Prussia also the results were of great importance. For, in the first place, the alliance with Hanover secured the connection of her territories, even if the Zollverein should break up; and secondly, it strengthened the Free Trade party, as did the treaty between Prussia and Oldenburg early in the following year.[1] But the treaty was with Prussia —not with the Zollverein; it was therefore necessary for Prussia either to force the other states to accept the treaty, or to break up the Zollverein and throw herself into union with the northern states alone.[2]

Negotiations for the renewal of the Zollverein had already begun under the terms of the treaty of 1841, and they were complicated by the simultaneous discussions with Austria. In form, the controversy arose over the procedure to be adopted. Prussia insisted that the renewal of the Zollverein, with the acceptance of the treaty with Hanover and the various modifications of the tariff required by it, or considered necessary after the experiences of recent years, must precede any treaty with Austria. The southern states, on the other hand, wished the negotiations with Austria to be completed before the settlement of the future constitution of the Zollverein, since those negotiations might mean the admission of Austria. It is not necessary to follow in detail the course of the extremely involved proceedings of the various conferences which agitated Germany from September, 1851, to April, 1853. Whilst endeavouring to secure the treaty with the Zollverein as a whole, Austria was secretly preparing the way for the formation of a union to include herself and the South German states,

[1] Neither Hanover nor Oldenburg had any industries to protect.

[2] Weber, pp. 294, 297.

in the event of Prussia refusing to give way and breaking up the Zollverein.[1] The Prussian statesmen, on their side, as we have seen, were preparing for this and planning a new union in the north. Neither side was anxious to take the decisive step; but the current ran strongly against Prussia, partly because of the distrust inspired by her unyielding attitude, and partly owing to the superior statesmanship of Schwarzenberg, until the death of that statesman in April, 1852; after that date the action of Prussia became more decided. At the first conference of all the states of the Union of Berlin in the same month, Manteuffel, the Prussian Minister-President, declared uncompromisingly the determination of his state to settle the question of the new constitution of the Zollverein before making any treaty with Austria. In May the Prussian Ministry published a note, in which it asserted that Prussia had not sought in the Zollverein any financial or political advantage, but simply the promotion of the economic progress of Germany, and expressed its willingness to negotiate with Austria for an extension of that system; but repeated that it was absolutely necessary to determine the area and policy of the Zollverein before any useful action could be taken in that direction. It condemned strongly the methods of the southern states in entering into secret relations with Austria, and lamented the bad impression which the sight of the internal discord of Germany must make on foreign nations. But neither the southern states nor Austria were convinced of the sincerity of the Prussian declarations, and as they persisted in their policy, the Prussian Government thought itself compelled to play its last card, and consequently announced in September, 1852, that it considered the general negotiations for the renewal of the Zollverein at an end, and henceforward would only discuss treaties with separate states.

[1] The conferences between Austria and the Zollverein states began in January, 1852, at Vienna. Prussia and the Thuringian states were not represented; the public negotiations were in regard to the Zollverein treaty with Austria, but at the same time there were private conferences for the formation of a union without Prussia (Zimmermann, i. p. 371).

But by this time both parties were prepared to give way. On the one side, Prussia was not anxious to carry out her threat, and was beginning to realise that her obstinacy had been carried too far; whatever her statesmen might say, they could not fail to recognise the political advantages which the Zollverein had given them, and they could not afford to run the risk of an alliance between Austria and the southern states. Further, it was doubtful whether Hanover was prepared to go the whole way with Prussia, who was more dependent than she cared to admit on the action of that state. On the other side, Von Beust and Von den Pfordten, the Ministers of Saxony and Bavaria and the leaders of the policy of the south, had become aware that the commercial and industrial classes of their states were doubtful as to the advantages to be gained by union with Austria alone, and were not prepared to sacrifice the economic benefits of the Zollverein for the sake of the political aims of the Governments. The conferences with Austria had been by no means satisfactory; the attempts to find a basis of agreement for the rival interests had so far failed. A more conciliatory attitude was adopted on all sides, and Prussia entered into direct relations with Austria without waiting for the settlement of the problem of the Zollverein. Progress then became rapid, and in February, 1853, a treaty between Prussia and Austria was signed for twelve years. The entrance of Austria into the Zollverein was postponed, but it was agreed that in 1860 a joint commission should be appointed to consider plans for her complete admission; meanwhile, the two contracting parties undertook reciprocal favoured treatment of each other. Many commodities, chiefly raw and semi-manufactured goods and manufactures of small value, were to pass between the two contracting states free from any duty; and the duties on such articles as cotton yarn and goods, chemicals, iron and metal goods of all kinds except machinery, glass, agricultural produce, linen yarn, woollen and silk goods, and many other manufactured commodities were reduced 25 per cent. The terms of the treaty were to extend to all states in customs union with Prussia and to the Italian possessions of Austria.[1]

The treaty was a compromise favourable to Austria, since it was the kind of arrangement usually made to prepare the way for a complete union. But Prussia had gained time, and she had secured the renewal of the Zollverein; therefore the treaty on the whole gave general satisfaction in Germany.[2] In the following April the Zollverein was formally renewed by a series of treaties which made various modifications and rearrangements, but in the main continued the old conditions; and Hanover was included.

The years from 1853 to 1860 have been described as the period of the stagnation of the Zollverein. The protectionist movement was satisfied for a time;[3] the treaty with Austria did not greatly develop trade between the two countries,[4] but there was a considerable growth of German industry; and the temporary failure of Prussia to get her own way seemed to put an end to any danger of the adoption of the policy of Free Trade which that state was supposed to represent. The mutual distrust inspired by the conflict left its effects, and in spite of numerous attempts from various sides at the annual conferences, no serious changes were made in the policy or adminstration of the Zollverein. But by 1860 the political and economic conditions had alike changed; it was necessary for Prussia to take decisive action if Austria was to be kept out of the Zollverein. The new commercial policy of the western states rendered a reconsideration of Germany's own policy inevitable, and furnished Prussia with her most effective weapon against her rival.

[1] In the treaty there was a clause which hampered Germany for some time. By Art. iv., if one of the two contracting parties reduced the duty on a commodity coming from a third state, not in receipt of favoured treatment at the date of the treaty, then the other party could impose a duty equivalent to the reduction on all goods of that kind coming from the state which had made the reduction. [2] Weber, p. 335. [3] Schippel, p. 138.

[4] The export of raw materials from Austria to the territories of the Zollverein increased somewhat; the export of manufactured goods remained almost stationary. The increased exports from the Zollverein to Austria were chiefly cotton and woollen yarn, iron and metal goods.

CHAPTER III

THE SECOND CRISIS AND THE COMMERCIAL TREATIES

THE years 1861 to 1864 are filled by the second great crisis in the history of the Zollverein, and in many respects the phenomena of the former crisis were repeated. Economic and political considerations were again involved, and political aims to a large extent again determined commercial policy.[1]

The treaty with Austria had provided for the commencement, about the year 1860, of negotiations for the admission of that state to the Zollverein. But in order that there might be any real prospect of those negotiations being brought to a successful issue, it was necessary on the one side that the finances of the Austrian Empire should be brought into order, so that when the time for negotiations came she might have a free hand, and that her protective policy should be to some extent modified; and, on the other side, that the Zollverein should not follow a policy so liberal as to frighten Austria away.[2] None of these conditions were realised; for the war of 1859 and the loss of Lombardy had again brought Austrian finances into disorder, and, moreover, between 1853 and 1862, the protectionist party had regained strength, and practically none of the reforms contemplated in the treaty of 1853 with the Zollverein had been carried out.[3]

[1] "Justified as was the general course of German tariff policy in the period 1860–1873, it must be admitted that it was determined far more by reasons of home parliamentary and party politics, by considerations of foreign policy, and by a somewhat exaggerated devotion to pure theory, than by any scientific investigation of the actual position or German industry" (Schmoller, *Grundriss*, ii. p. 615).

[2] Lotz, i. p. 10.

[3] Weber, p. 399.

From a purely economic point of view the Zollverein, in its endeavour to secure a large market for its agricultural and industrial products, might adopt either one of two policies. It might adopt the plan put forward long before by the Austrian Minister of Commerce, Bruck, of forming a large area with Austria with freedom of trade within and a strong policy of Protection against all outside. In this way a large home market would be secured, and an economic unity created which would be self-sufficing in many respects. Or alternatively, the Zollverein might adopt a more liberal tariff policy, and establish closer commercial relations with the western states of Europe.

The first of these alternatives was supported by the high protectionists in the Zollverein—that is, by a considerable number of the manufacturers, especially in the iron industries, and by some of the South German states, particularly Bavaria and Württemberg; these had always advocated union with Austria, and represented to some extent in politics that "Greater Germany" party whose ideal was the establishment of a German Empire which should include all the possessions of Austria, even though many of them were inhabited by peoples not of German stock. There were great difficulties in the way of the realisation of this ideal, and the Austrian Government seems to have lost about 1860 much of its earlier interest in the matter; in 1861 it admitted that for the time the obstacles were almost insuperable.[1] The second alternative was supported by the Free Traders, or rather by those classes who desired the lessened restriction of foreign trade, and by the anti-Austrian politicians of Prussia.[2]

In the late fifties there was something approaching to a real agitation for Free Trade in Northern Germany. It found its theoretical expression in the writings of

[1] Weber, p. 383.

[2] An interesting, though discursive, account of the "Greater Germany" and "Smaller Germany" policies and their effect upon tariff discussions will be found in Naumann, *Mittel-Europa*, especially chaps. i., ii., and vii.

Prince-Smith, to whose energy and influence was due the foundation of the German Economic Congress, which gathered together after 1858 all the reforming forces. There was an admitted need for the amendment of the tariff; no readjustment of the specific duties had been made to bring them into a more satisfactory relation to values. But the reformers desired to go further than this; they wished the amendments to be made deliberately in the direction of greater freedom of trade. Much of their political strength continued to depend on the support given to their ideas by the landowners, who wanted cheaper machinery and also the extension of the English market for their grain. Germany was still an overwhelmingly agricultural country—at the beginning of the second half of the century two-thirds of her population were engaged in agriculture,[1] and the proportion declined only slowly up to 1870; much grain was exported from the north, especially to Great Britain.[2] The Free Trade movement took its rise therefore in the agricultural eastern provinces of Prussia, but it was supported also by the weavers, who wanted cheap English yarn, by the middle class and small officials, to whom the cheapness of many commodities was a matter of very great importance, and by the commercial classes and the seaports. On the other side, many of the manufacturers were beginning to feel that they were strong enough to do without much of the protection they had hitherto enjoyed; some of them were already largely exporting (for example, one-quarter of the produce of the woollen industry was sent abroad), and they were anxious to get rid of anything which in any way hampered their relations with foreign markets.[3] Political circumstances in Prussia itself were changing; the moderate Liberals were becoming predominant in the Parliament, and though

[1] Voigt, in *Handels- und Machtpolitik*, vol. i. p. 141.

[2] The average value of the surplus of grain exported over that imported was estimated for 1860–4 at 35 mill. mks. (Lotz, i. p. 11).

[3] Weber, p. 389. In 1859 manufactured goods amounted, so far as values were concerned, to $\frac{4}{7}$ of the total export (Lotz, i. p. 52).

vigorously opposing them on the question of the re-organisation of the army, the Government was quite ready to use their support for its anti-Austrian programme and was therefore favourably inclined towards a commercial policy which commended itself to them, and would repel Austria.[1] It found its opportunity in the necessity of dealing with the situation created by the change which had come over the economic policy of the states of western Europe, and by the altered attitude of France.

It has already been remarked that the trade relations between the Zollverein and France under the Monarchy of July had been greatly strained. A long commercial struggle had now been going on for nearly twenty years.[2] After the failure of negotiations in 1839, the July Monarchy had imposed very high duties on German goods; the Zollverein had replied in 1843 with retaliatory duties—increases on gloves, brandy, etc.—and most of these were still in force. Negotiations up to 1851 had failed, and fresh attempts after 1853 had been equally unsuccessful. In 1860 Napoleon III., by his own personal will and in spite of strong and general opposition in France, had broken with French traditional policy and made a commercial treaty with Great Britain,[3] which "ranks with the treaty which founded the Zollverein, as perhaps the most important international event of the century in the sphere of economics."[4] By the treaty France undertook to impose on an agreed number of British products no duties higher than 30 per cent., and after October, 1864, 24 per cent., *ad valorem :* and Great Britain, on her side, undertook to abandon some duties and to reduce those on French wines. And further, both sides bound them-

[1] *Cf.* Lotz, i. pp. 28–30.

[2] Zimmermann, i. pp. 161–2, 263–5, 393–5.

[3] For details of the Treaty, *vide* pp. 295 *seq.*, *infra.*

[4] Weber, p. 368. It is interesting to notice the failure of this historian's prophecy in the following sentence, written in 1871: "The impetus which this treaty gave to the customs policy of all European countries is still far from ended, is rather becoming stronger, and in all probability will end only by a complete change of the whole customs legislation."

selves to reciprocal "most favoured nation" treatment, that is to say, any tariff advantage granted by one of the contracting parties to any other state was, *ipso facto*, to extend to the other contracting party also.[1] The British treaty inaugurated a series which covered the States of Western Europe as a net. Treaties were made by France with Belgium, Italy, Holland, Switzerland, Sweden, Norway and other countries, and of these the Belgian treaty, with its reciprocal reductions and provision for mutual "most favoured nation" treatment, became the model for all the others. The net result was that France had one general or "autonomous" tariff, which applied to all countries with which special arrangements had not been made; and a treaty or "conventional" tariff, with rates of duty settled by treaty with any one country and then extended to all other treaty countries by the action of the "most favoured nation" clause. Most of the nations which entered into the system were influenced partly by the desire not to let Great Britain secure greater advantages in France than they themselves enjoyed, and partly by the anxiety to do something to compensate for the loss of part of the American market, owing to the United States high protective tariff of 1861.

The inauguration of this treaty system in 1860, and the avowed intention to extend it as widely as possible, made it absolutely necessary for the Zollverein to take action. Great Britain generalised all the reductions which she had made in the French treaty—that is, she extended them to the products of all countries; but France only gave reductions to the treaty states.

[1] "English industry had long reached a point where it had no further need of protection against foreign competition; in fact, the existing protection was rather a burden. Already it was necessary for it to fight in the great world markets with similar products of the great industrial states, and it could therefore easily face their competition in its own country, where all the conditions were favourable to it. It was to be anticipated that this impulse would drive other states to a reform of their strict customs systems, and in this the English industry would assuredly find its benefit. The justice of this calculation has since then been completely established" (Weber, p. 370).

Consequently the British and Belgian manufacturers enjoyed an immense advantage over the Germans,[1] and the trade of Germany with France was at the best only small, for, whilst it imported from that country goods to the value of 154,000,000 francs, it sent her goods worth only 82,000,000 francs.[2] The German manufacturers hoped that by a treaty they would secure a greatly developed market in France for their iron and steel, textiles, leather goods, etc., many of which were practically prohibited by the French "autonomous," as distinct from the "conventional" or treaty tariff. France, on the other hand, communicated early in 1861 her willingness to negotiate with Prussia, which was entrusted with the diplomatic representation of the Zollverein, and Prussia readily accepted the invitation.

It was clear, however, that the proposed treaty must have much wider effects than the mere readjustment of trade relations with France. It must involve a readjustment of the whole Zollverein tariff, and to that there was no particular opposition; in fact, the work of reform had commenced already—in March, 1861, the transit duties were abolished, and also a considerable number of the export duties. But of far greater importance was the probable influence of the contemplated treaty on the relations with Austria. The Prussian statesmen realised at once that the grant of reductions of duties to France, and the establishment of "most favoured nation" terms with that country, would render impossible the continuance of the special relations, under the treaty of 1853, with Austria, and would put an end to the idea of an economic union between Austria and the Zollverein.[3] Free Trade was to be the most potent weapon employed by Prussia in her effort to exclude Austria from the future German Empire.[4] The other states of the Zollverein realised this, and at once a struggle began.

[1] *E.g.*, "Edged tools from treaty states paid a duty into France of 18 francs per 100 kilo., but from the Zollverein 160 francs; the duties on paper were respectively 10 and 160 francs, on iron tools 12 and 60 francs" (Schippel, p. 171).

[2] Lotz, i. p. 37. [3] Weber, p. 373. [4] Schippel, p. 172.

It was, in fact, a repetition of the events of ten years before. The time for the renewal of the Zollverein was drawing near, and, just as on the previous occasion Prussia had made a treaty with Hanover and insisted on its acceptance as a condition of the renewal of the union, whilst the southern states had striven to make the admission of Austria the basis of negotiation, so now Prussia pushed on the completion of the treaty with France in order to repel Austria. And again she insisted that the new treaty should be accepted by the other states if the Zollverein were to be continued. The treaty between Prussia and France was hastened admittedly for political reasons,[1] and was completed on the 29th March, 1862, though the actual ratification did not take place till the following August, after approval had been given by the Prussian Parliament. It was communicated immediately to the other Governments for their acceptance, and was speedily rejected by Württemberg, Hanover, Nassau, and Hesse-Darmstadt; Saxony alone, abandoning her old policy, now threw herself on the Prussian side. The attitude of the opposition was undoubtedly influenced by the proposal put forward in July by Austria for a complete union with the Zollverein, the preliminary condition, of course, being the postponement of any arrangement with France till after that event. To this Prussia would not accede, declaring herself bound, for her own part, to carry out the treaty. The southern states attempted, at the end of 1862, to open direct negotiations with France, but were rejected.[2] Meanwhile conferences on the renewal of the Zollverein were going on, but the difficulties were great. In November, 1862, the Prussian Government had declared definitely that it took the rejection of the French treaty by the southern states to mean their intention not to continue the Zollverein. After the conferences of the first half of 1863 on the Austrian question and the renewal of the

[1] Weber, p. 386.

[2] Schippel, p. 175, quoting Bismarck's speech on the 26th December, 1862.

Zollverein had produced no satisfactory result, the Bavarian Government suggested the formation of a separate union from which Prussia and her allies should be excluded, and which should come to terms with Austria on the basis of the treaty of 1853. But it soon became apparent that only Bavaria and Württemberg were prepared to go so far, and even in those states the Governments were not sure of complete popular support. After further complicated discussions, in which both sides attempted to justify themselves before public opinion, but the Prussian Government was handicapped by the impossibility of stating its real aims, Prussia, on the 17th December, 1863, gave formal notice of the termination of the Zollverein. The other states now yielded, particularly as Austria was now less inclined to push her proposals. The conferences were renewed in February, 1864, and at the same time Prussia began negotiations for a simple treaty with Austria. After some delay, on the 11th April, 1865, a treaty, containing not much more than the guarantee of simple "most favoured nation" treatment, was made with Austria; and in May, after the acceptance in the previous year by the southern states of the French treaty, the Zollverein was formally renewed.[1] In the same year treaties similar to the one with Austria were made with Belgium, Great Britain (including her colonial possessions) and Italy, and the treaty with France, so long under discussion, at last came into force. The Zollverein had followed the example of the last-named country in its adoption of the system of "autonomous" and "conventional" tariffs.

The series of treaties thus completed brought of necessity sweeping changes in the customs tariff of the Zollverein. Already, whilst the negotiations with France were in progress, but without particular reference to them, the transit duties had been abolished, and all the parties to the treaties now bound themselves to maintain this policy for the future. Further, there had been a growing inclination to abandon the idea of helping those industries

[1] Its practical renewal dates from October in the previous year.

for which the raw materials were produced at home by prohibiting or limiting the export of these commodities. In no case was the method very effective, and in some instances, such as the leather and woollen industries, it could be shown to be harmful.[1] Most export duties were now abolished; some remained, but were reduced, as, for example, those on the materials requisite for paper-making. All the contracting parties reserved to themselves the right to prohibit exports, but under strong French pressure the Zollverein agreed not to make use of this power in regard to coal.

Much more important was the reduction of duties on imports, and this presented the greatest difficulties. For the insertion in most of the treaties of the "most favoured nation" clause meant that any reduction granted by the Zollverein to one power would have to be extended to all the others. So the Zollverein in granting to France reductions of duties on the commodities in which that country was especially interested had to consider, not simply their effect on the imports from that country, but also the ultimate effect of the necessary extension of the reductions to similar commodities when imported from the United Kingdom or Belgium, or any other country enjoying "most favoured nation" rights. The reductions made under these conditions represented a deliberate policy of Free Trade, in that they were inspired by the desire not only to promote trade relations with the contracting states, but also to improve the tariff by the removal of anomalies, and by abolishing protection wherever it seemed no longer required. So the tariff was disencumbered of duties which had no protective or financial results (as that on zinc, of which the Zollverein exported none and imported much);[2] the duties introduced for retaliatory purposes (usually without effect) and no longer important—as the surtaxes on French goods imposed in 1842 and the duty on Russian tallow—

[1] Lotz, i. p. 43.

[2] By 1914 the production of zinc had become one of Germany's most important metallurgical industries.

were abolished; and all the raw and semi-manufactured materials of industry were admitted free.[1]

On none of these matters was there much conflict of opinion, but the case was different in regard to manufactured commodities; some of the industries, such as the iron trades and the cotton spinners, still clung to Protection, and had strongly opposed the treaties for that reason. But their resistance was overcome, and a great number of reductions were made—the treaty with France alone had provided for 161 changes in the tariff, mostly in regard to manufactured goods. Thus the duties on cotton goods were reduced by 40–80 per cent., on silk 50 per cent., on silk goods 45 per cent., on pig-iron 25 per cent., on leather 60 per cent., on leather goods 50 per cent., on sewing needles 80 per cent., on woollen cloth 60–80 per cent., on fine iron goods 80 per cent., on pressed glass 33 per cent.[2] These changes, however, were not made on any definite plan—the tariff had never yet undergone a complete and systematic revision; that might have followed, but the rapidity of the subsequent movement towards Free Trade rendered any rearrangement of the tariff necessary, by almost destroying it.

[1] Lotz, i. pp. 42–4.

[2] Weber, pp. 441–3.

CHAPTER IV

THE ZOLLVEREIN AFTER THE TREATIES—THE COMPLETION OF FREE TRADE AND THE REACTION

It is a striking testimony to the strength of the Zollverein and its hold upon Germany that during the war of 1866, when the constituent states were fighting each other, the joint customs administration went on without interruption.[1] After the speedy termination of the struggle and the destruction of all prospect of Austrian predominance in Germany, there came a reform of the constitution of the Zollverein by the treaty of 1867 between the North German Confederation on the one side, and Bavaria, Württemberg, Baden and Hesse on the other.[2] The system of a union of independent states, each possessing the right to veto any proposal, was replaced by an organisation in which matters were decided by a majority of votes—a change generally felt to be necessary on account of the innumerable difficulties and delays which the old method had called forth. The Zollverein, thus reconstituted, now included all the German states except Hamburg and Bremen. The Customs Union Council (Zollbundesrath) consisted of fifty-eight members, of whom Prussia had seventeen, and represented the old general conference; but to it was added a Customs Parliament (Zollparlement) composed of members of the North German Parliament and repre-

[1] Weber, pp. 462–3.

[2] It should be noted that Hanover, Electoral Hesse, Nassau, and Frankfurt, hitherto independent states of the Zollverein, had become part of the Prussian Kingdom; and the Zollverein area was extended by the inclusion of Schleswig-Holstein, also added to Prussia.

sentatives of the South German states.[1] The position was somewhat peculiar, for many of the states were largely dependent on the customs revenue, and this was controlled by the Customs Parliament. Consequently, while each separate state could fix its expenditure at whatever it pleased, it could not control the chief part of its revenue—a fact which gave great impetus to the movement for complete union.

In 1871 the Franco-German War, and the patriotic enthusiasm it evoked, brought the establishment of the Empire, and at last political as well as economic union was attained.[2] In the Empire, legislation concerning customs and trade was to be a matter for the Imperial Parliament; the proceeds of the customs duties were to go to the imperial exchequer, and not to be divided between the state exchequers as before; the duties were to be collected by officials of the separate states, but under the control of the Emperor as executive official of the Empire. The new machinery speedily showed itself to be effective, and the old wearisome negotiations between the states on every proposal for a change of economic policy were at an end.[3]

The wars of 1866 and 1871 necessarily made considerable changes in the commercial relations of Germany with Austria and France. Austria was inclined to a less strongly protectionist policy, partly because her statesmen, in the reorganisation of the Empire, were compelled to pay more attention to the interests of Hungary, which was mainly agrarian, exported grain and other agricultural produce, and was distinctly sympathetic to freer trade. In the treaty of 1868 between Austria and the Zollverein there were reductions made on both sides; by Austria on manufactured goods, by Germany especially on wine and iron.[4] In the case of France, there were fears that she

[1] Weber, p. 467.

[2] There were some slight modifications of this—Hamburg and Bremen were, at this time, in the Empire, but not in the Customs Union; Luxemburg remained until 1919 in the Union, but was never part of the Empire.

[3] Zimmermann, ii. pp. 71, 72.

[4] Lotz, i. 86–8.

might refuse to renew the treaty with Germany whilst continuing her arrangements with other states; and it was also likely that, should Thiers remain in power, she would adopt a strongly protective policy. All that could be obtained was secured in the peace Treaty of Frankfurt in May, 1871, but it was little more than the guarantee of perpetual "most favoured nation" treatment; it did not establish any system of conventionalised duties for a term of years, as the old commercial treaty had done. Other treaties of the same nature were made in March, 1868, with Spain and her possessions in Cuba, Porto Rico, and the Philippines; and in the following year with the moderately protective Switzerland, with Mexico and Japan.

The Franco-German War had consequences of great importance for the economic development of the German Empire. The acquisition of Alsace-Lorraine greatly increased the competition which German spinners and textile manufacturers had to meet, without bringing any corresponding development of the home market. In Germany, in 1868, there were 3,000,000 cotton spindles and 37,000 weaving looms, whilst in the same year there were in Alsace-Lorraine 2,131,000 cotton spindles and 48,536 looms.[1] There was much discussion and uncertainty in Germany as to the policy to be adopted in regard to the new imperial lands; but finally it was found necessary to admit them completely into the Union, and the prosperity which followed immediately after the war made the new competition less felt than it would otherwise have been.[2] The new provinces also possessed great resources, as yet little developed, of iron ore, the utilisation of which, in consequence of the discovery of new metallurgical processes, was to give a remarkable stimulus to the German iron and steel industry, and large deposits of potash salts which, added to the deposits of the Stassfurt area, were to give Germany almost a world monopoly of those products.

The policy pursued by the Zollverein after 1866 was

[1] Zimmermann, ii. p. 81. [2] *Ibid.*, pp. 81–5.

in the direction of Free Trade, and under the guidance of Delbrück the movement progressed with great rapidity. In 1868 the reductions made in the treaty with Austria were generalised; some duties were abolished, and there were reductions on certain kinds of cotton goods, linen yarn, pig-iron, unwrought steel, drugs, fine leather goods, and other commodities.[1] Then came the further reform in 1870, which simplified the tariff, reduced still further the duties on iron and steel, and freed altogether a number of articles, particularly chemicals. Finally, in 1873 there were still more changes, and the completion of the general policy of the reduction or entire abandonment of protective duties, and the adoption of duties for revenue purposes only.[2] The changes thus made were not to come entirely into force before the 1st January, 1877, and by that date the duties on iron, except on fine goods, were completely abolished, as on most other classes of imported goods. Only a small group of highly finished commodities remained liable to duties; the German Empire had become very nearly a free-trading state.

As the duties on iron form about the best illustration of the line of movement, it may be useful to set them out here.

	Rates of Duty in Mks. per 100 Kilo.						
Commodity.	1839.	845.	1865.	1868.	1870.	1873.	1877.
Pig-Iron ..	0	2	1·50	1	0·50	0	0
Bar-Iron ..	6–18	9–18	5–7	5–7	3·50–5	2	0
Iron Plates ..	9–24	18–24	7–15	7–15	5–7	2	0
Coarse Cast-Iron Goods	6	6	2·40	2·40	2·40	2	0
Coarse Iron Goods ..	36	36	8–16	8–16	8	5	0
Fine Iron Goods	60–300	60–300	24–60	24–60	24–60	24–60	24–60

The establishment of this policy was the result of mingled economic and political forces. The landowners

[1] Schippel, p. 185.

[2] Schippel, p. 186, remarks that the tariff legislation of these five years was altogether in the spirit of the financial reforms of Peel and Gladstone.

of the eastern provinces were still free traders, and so in a more moderate way were the commercial class and many of the manufacturers.[1] The opposition came, as always, from the heavy iron manufacturers and the spinning industries, championed chiefly by the governments of the southern states. The Free Trade movement, which was so strong that Government proposals to protect petroleum and raise the duty on tobacco for financial reasons were rejected,[2] found its political opportunity in the facts that there was at the time no compact Conservative party, and that Bismarck was relying on the moderate Liberals for support in his schemes for the organisation of the Empire. Unwilling to accept many items in their political programme, he disarmed their hostility by the adoption of their economic policy; but he left commercial matters largely to Delbrück and Camphausen.[3]

The practical completion of the Free Trade policy by the cessation of the iron duties was followed by an immediate and sharp reaction. The representatives of the iron and cotton industries had never ceased their agitation against the reduction of the tariff, and in conjunction with the manufacturers of chemicals, sugar, linen and leather, they, in 1876, formed the Central Union of German Manufacturers, which commenced to work for a return to Protection. They were aided by the conditions of German industry after 1872, but still more by the changes which were coming over German agriculture and by the financial needs of the Empire.

In the history of German trade after 1871 the dominant fact is the payment of the war indemnity of nearly six milliard francs (including interest) by France;[4] much of it was paid in bills of exchange, but a great amount in gold.

[1] Lotz, i. pp. 91, 92. [2] Zimmermann, ii. pp. 219, 220.

[3] Zimmermann, (ii. p. 230) complains that the whole policy at this time was a slavish imitation of the action of Great Britain, without any regard to the difference in geographical and economic conditions.

[4] The fullest discussion of the form and effects of the indemnity is in A. Wagner's article on German Imperial Finance in Holtzendorff's *Jahrbuch für Gesetzgebung*, 1874.

The results were a great increase of imports, whilst exports remained almost stationary; a very rapid rise in prices, as a result of the large influx of gold; and considerable impetus to industry from the high prices and also from the expenditure by the Government on railways and other public works. There followed the usual results—excessive development of factories and mills, over-capitalisation, and over-production. In June, 1870, there were in Prussia 410 joint-stock companies with a total capital of three milliard marks; by the end of 1874 the number had increased to 2,267, with a capital of seven and one-third milliards.[1] But already in 1873 a reaction had commenced; it was widespread and general, not merely in Germany, but outside. There followed a rapid fall in prices and general depression; and for a time the low level of prices in Germany kept serious foreign competition away. Then, however, the situation gradually improved; markets became steadier, and prices began to rise. But just at that time Great Britain entered upon a period of depression; agricultural difficulties, due to bad harvests, affected the whole country; there was a drop in the home demand for iron and textile goods, and the British manufacturers, who were overproducing as a result of the impetus given by the unusually high prices of 1872 and 1873, now sent large quantities of goods abroad at extremely low prices, that is to say, they "dumped." This counteracted the tendency of the German market towards a rise in prices, and seriously hindered the recovery of the German manufacturers; hence came the renewed demand for Protection, strongest in the case of the textile and iron industries.[2]

Moreover, a very important change was coming over the opinions of the landowners. With the development of means of transport and especially the growth of the

[1] Blum, p. 158, quoting Max Wirth's *Geschichte der Handelskrisen.*

[2] Dietzel, in *Quarterly Journal of Economics*, May, 1903. *Cf.* Lotz, i. pp. 122–37.

American railways, the Russian and even American competition in the supply of grain to the European markets was beginning to be severely felt; the German landowners were not only ceasing to be exporters, but were severely threatened even in the home market. Further, the movement of population to the towns had commenced in Germany, and the more attractive conditions offered by industrial employment were beginning to deprive the landowners of their labourers. They had ceased to have any further direct interest in the promotion of Free Trade; in fact, they were themselves beginning to desire some measure of Protection. And even some of those observers who believed that it would be a mistake to attempt to shut out the foreign and cheaper supplies of foodstuffs, were yet, like Conrad, willing to establish a moderate amount of Protection for grain, by a scale of duties limited in duration and gradually diminishing, to enable the agriculturists to transfer their attention to other branches of production.[1]

How far this joint protectionist movement of agriculture and industry would have been successful, if left to itself, is doubtful; the determining factor in the situation was the condition of the imperial finances. The expenditure of the Empire was increasing rapidly, and to Bismarck it seemed impossible to continue to raise the revenue required by direct taxation, which was becoming extremely burdensome. It was felt that a rearrangement of the imperial finances was absolutely necessary, both on economic and political grounds, and Bismarck resolved that his best policy was to have recourse to indirect taxation in the form of customs duties, and to substitute the proceeds of these for the contributions to the imperial exchequer from the separate states—contributions which they raised by direct taxes. The demands on the states were steadily rising; in 1874 they were 51,400,000 marks, whilst by 1878–9 they had risen to over 70,000,000 marks. The Chancellor was much influenced by these considera-

[1] Dietzel, *loc. cit.*

tions, and as a member of the landowning class he was not insensible to its demands; the position of affairs in home politics had changed, and he could afford to break with the Liberals. In October, 1878, 204 members (*i.e.*, a majority) of the Reichstag signed a declaration in favour of the reconsideration of fiscal policy.[1] And another fact which had considerable weight with the Chancellor was the growth of Protection in the neighbouring countries, particularly in France in the tariff of 1878.[2] The policy which Bismarck now adopted had three objects in view. First, he desired to establish (to use his own words) "a customs system which secures to the entire home production a preference before foreign production in the home market, whilst keeping within the limits imposed by financial interests." Secondly, there was to be a reform of the railway system and railway rates, to promote the transport of German goods, and to put an end to the preference given on many of the railways to foreign products; he wished to obtain an imperial railway system, and when that proved impracticable, he resolved that the Prussian railways, at least, should become the property of the state. And thirdly, he was anxious for the re-arrangement of the imperial finances.[3]

The argument for the new policy was set out in a letter addressed by the Chancellor on 15th December, 1878, to a committee appointed by the Bundesrath to consider the revision of the tariff. The financial object

[1] Blum (p. 310) quotes from the Circular: "In view of the commercial policy of most of the countries bordering on Germany, with the knowledge of the absence of a German customs tariff and the evil effect of this on national well-being, and on account of the continuance of the crisis in German industry and agriculture (the signatories) believe a reform of the tariff, based on the result of careful investigations and expert balancing of interests, to be absolutely necessary. . . . Although holding diverse views as to commercial policy, the signatories are agreed on this fundamental point—that the difficult problems of German commercial policy cannot simply be solved by phrases about Free Trade and Protection, but that it is much more necessary to reconcile the real and supposed conflicts of interests by the exercise of a scientific, patriotic, and reasonable spirit."

[2] Lotz, i. pp. 146–9.

[3] Blum, pp. 305, 306; *cf.* Dawson, pp. 47–54.

of tariff reform, according to this memorandum, was to be the reduction of direct and the increase of indirect taxation; and the Chancellor calculated that if the future import duties were to average 5 per cent. *ad valorem*, the increased revenue would amount to about seventy million marks, or almost exactly the amount which in the year 1878–9 was contributed by the separate states to the imperial exchequer. To secure this result it was necessary to return to the principle of the liability to taxation of all foreign products crossing the frontier, with the exception of those materials for industry which Germany either did not produce at all, or produced only to an inadequate amount. This proposal the Chancellor proceeded to justify on the ground of the economic interests of the nation. "I leave undecided the question whether complete mutual freedom of international commerce, such as is contemplated by the theory of Free Trade, would not serve the interests of Germany. But as long as most of the countries with which our trade is carried on surround themselves with customs barriers, which there is still a growing tendency to multiply, it does not seem to me justifiable, or to the economic interest of the nation, that we should allow ourselves to be restricted in the satisfaction of our financial wants by the apprehension that German products will thereby be slightly preferred to foreign ones." Protective duties for particular industries he thought likely to cause difficulty and arouse hostility, but a customs system protecting the whole home production would "in no way appear partial, because its effects would be more equally spread over all the productive circles of the land than is the case with a system of protective duties for isolated branches of industry. The minority of the population, which does not produce at all, but exclusively consumes, will apparently be injured by a customs system favouring the entire national production. Yet if by means of such a system the aggregate sum of the values produced in the country increase, and thus the national wealth be on the whole enhanced, the non-producing parts of the population—and especially the state and communal officials who are dependent upon a fixed money income—will eventually be benefited." He therefore proposed the maintenance of the existing duties and their possible increase, and the introduction of new duties; and he held that, except in cases where the foreign commodity was not produced in Germany and was indispensable, the greater part, if not the whole, of the import duty would be borne by the foreigner. And in any case a small duty of from 5 to 10 per cent. would only be one of the forces affecting prices; it would probably not do the consumer any harm, and would do the home producer some good. In regard to agriculture, the Ministry, in the memorandum which accompanied its definite proposals, declared that the duties were so small that they could not be regarded as protective to any considerable extent, and would not diminish, and still less exclude, the import of foreign grain; but they would check the swamping of the German market by the surplus products of other lands, and make German agriculture better able to hold its own, even if the general price of grain should fall. Even granted that the result of the new duties would be an increase in the price of the necessaries of life, the Government asserted that this would be corrected ultimately by the increase of home production and by the greater demand for labour and consequent rise of wages.[1]

The Chancellor was supported by the iron and textile industries and their allies, and by the landowners and the agrarian party generally. He was opposed by the exporters, who feared retaliation (though this opposition was somewhat weakened by the growing tariffs of foreign powers); by the two great seaports, which dreaded the dislocation of their trade; and by the municipalities, which, on the great Municipal Day at Berlin, where seventy-two town councils were represented, protested strongly against any policy likely to cause an increase in the price of food.[2] The National Liberals led the opposi-

[1] See passages quoted in Schippel, pp. 230–2. [2] Blum, p. 330.

tion, but they were a declining party, and they had no hold on the workmen; the Socialist movement was growing rapidly, but its leaders seem to have been disinclined to take any vigorous action. Thus in 1876, the Socialist Congress at Gotha declared that "the Socialists of Germany are indifferent to the controversy raging in the proprietary classes as to Protection and Free Trade; the problem is a practical one, and must be so considered in each particular case." And some of the Socialist leaders were apparently inclined to take the line that a protective tariff might increase the demand for labour in the home market, and consequently bring some benefit to the workmen, though, on the other hand, they disapproved of proposals which tended to raise the price of food.[1]

In spite of a considerable amount of opposition, the tariff proposals were carried,[2] not, however, before the agrarian party, which held the political balance, had forced the Government to increase considerably the duties originally proposed on agricultural produce. The tariff ultimately adopted dealt with forty-three groups of commodities, and retained in the main the system of specific duties, that is to say, duties levied on a given quantity of each commodity, and not changing with the changes in value of that quantity. The rate of duty on wheat, rye and oats was 1 mark per 100 kilogrammes; on barley and maize 50 pfennigs; on flour 2 marks; on meat 12 marks; on oxen 20 marks each, sheep 1 mark, and pigs 25 marks. Raw materials for industry, such as cotton, flax, hemp, wool, hides and coal were admitted free; on pig-iron the rate of duty was 1 mark per 100 kilogrammes; on iron and steel "semi-manufactured goods" the rates were from 2 to 2·5 marks, and on other iron and steel goods they ranged from 7·5 to 15 marks; on machinery they varied from 3 to 8 marks. On yarns and textiles the duties were from 15 to 30 per cent. *ad valorem.* The whole tariff system was inelastic, defective, and un-

1 For a sketch of the Socialist attitude towards the problems of tariff policy, see Schippel, pp. 323–52.

2 The details of the controversy may be read in Zimmermann, ii. pp. 271–300; and Lotz, i. pp. 163–74.

scientific; in particular it did not take sufficient account of the complications of industry, and lacked adaptability.[1] The new policy was based on the principle of moderate Protection for agriculture and industry alike. The British protective system, up to 1846, had been maintained chiefly for the sake of agriculture; the German protective system from 1848 to 1860 had been dictated by the interests of manufacturers; now an effort was to be made to harmonise the two, and to give a fair measure of Protection to all. And at this point it will be convenient to examine the attitude of the German economists towards national fiscal policy.

[1] Schumacher, in *Verhandlungen*, pp. 157, 158.

CHAPTER V

THE ATTITUDE OF THE ECONOMISTS

AT the outset of a survey of the movement of economic opinion in Germany in the last century, it is necessary to remind ourselves of two very important influences which have dominated the whole of German political thought during that period. The first of these is the idea of the paternal state—an idea based on the historical fact that the Prussian State is the creation of a series of strong rulers, such as the Great Elector, Frederick William I., and Frederick II., working by means of a powerful and highly centralised bureaucracy. For centuries the nation looked for impetus and initiative in all departments of national life to the monarchs, and on the whole it rarely looked in vain. The second great influence is that of the desire for national unity—a desire disappointed after the War of Liberation, but ever growing in strength, attempting to realise itself in the abortive movements of 1848-9, and at last triumphant in 1870. The effect of these two ideas has been a general sympathy on the part of all German writers on economics and politics towards State action, and an inability amongst economists to keep their discussions free from political considerations.

Most of the German economists of the early years of the nineteenth century were followers and interpreters of Adam Smith, and the most important representatives of this school were Rau, whose *Lehrbuch* was published between 1826 and 1832, and Nebenius, the official of Baden, who, it will be remembered, played a considerable part in the foundation of the German Zollverein.[1] But

[1] See p. 6.

as early as 1809 a note of revolt against the doctrines of Adam Smith was sounded by Adam Müller, whose *Elemente der Staatskunst* was published in that year. His criticism of Adam Smith was based chiefly on his own conception of the State as representing the "totality of national life." Too much regard, he held, is paid by Adam Smith to the individual and to the immediate production of exchange values; and he complained that the collective interests of the community, the maintenance of collective production in the future, and the social well-being of the workers are almost entirely ignored, and that Adam Smith neglects to point out "the necessary counterpoise and completion of the division of labour," namely, the principle of the "national combination of labour." For Great Britain Adam Smith's individualistic economics might be adequate, and probably were; for Germany and the continental states generally a different theory of economic action and of the relation of the State to commerce and industry was absolutely necessary.

Much more important and much more influential was the work of Friedrich List (1789-1846), who published his *Nationale System der Politischen Oekonomie* in 1841—a book which owed its wide-reaching success partly to its power of argument and abundance of historical illustration, and partly to its fervid patriotism and its appeal to that growing desire for national unity which animated the vast majority of the German people.[1] It is less an economic argument than a great political appeal, and its title gives the key to its contents. Like Müller, List lays great emphasis on the distinction between "private economy" and "national economy."[2] National unity

[1] "He drew up plans for a German railway and canal system; he advocated in the thirties and forties a unified German currency, postal service, and patent law, a unified German industrial law, a German Consular system, a German navy, the inclusion of the Hanse towns in the Zollverein, a comprehensive scheme of German colonisation. . . . The whole of modern German science is more or less influenced and pervaded by his ideas" (Schmoller, *Was ist uns Friedrich List?* in *Charakterbilder*, 1912.)

[2] List, *National System of Political Economy* (translated by Lloyd), chap. xiv. "The foreign trade of a nation must not be

is the first essential of individual well-being, and "private economic interests, like all others, must be subordinated to the maintenance, completion, and strengthening of a nationality." Like Müller again, he emphasises the fact that it is not to the production of wealth alone that the economic policy of the nation should be directed, but to the creation of many-sided productive powers, and the harmony and balance of the three branches of national economic action—agriculture, manufacture, commerce. In this latter idea of the balance of the three departments of economic activity we may detect traces of the influence of one of the most remarkable works of Fichte, whose *Geschlossene Handelsstaat*, published in 1800, sets forth a scheme of a self-contained socialistic state, in which perhaps the most important task of the Government is to maintain the balance between the producers of food and raw material, the producers of manufactured goods and the merchants, and to prevent the predominance of any one group over the others; from this ideal state foreign trade must be excluded, because it is certain to tend to destroy such a balance. But whilst he desired to maintain agriculture, List also held most strongly that industrial development is essential to any community which desires to attain to the highest possible level of civilisation.[1] To

estimated in the way in which individual merchants judge it, solely and only according to the theory of values (*i.e.*, by regarding merely the gain at any particular moment of some material advantage); the nation is bound to keep steadily in view all those conditions on which its present and future existence, prosperity, and power depend" (chap. xii.).

[1] "Manufactories and manufactures are the mothers and children of municipal liberty, of intelligence, of the arts and sciences, of internal and external commerce, of navigation and improvements in transport, of civilisation and political power. They are the chief means of liberating agriculture from its chains, and of elevating it to a commercial character and to a degree of art and science, by which the rents, farming profits, and wages are increased, and greater value is given to landed property. The popular school has attributed this civilising power to foreign trade. . . . If, however, trade in the manufactures of far-distant lands exercises admittedly so beneficial an influence on our agricultural industry, how much more beneficial must the influence be of those manufactures which are bound up with us locally, commercially, and politically" (List, chap. xii.).

enable industries to grow up, Protection by tariffs and all possible forms of governmental action is necessary until such time as the manufactures are strong enough to stand alone and to contend effectually with foreign competition. This is the "infant industries" argument for Protection; but it will be noticed that even List did not contemplate the maintenance of Protection as a permanent policy—the ultimate ideal for each state is (in his doctrine) that by these "educational tariffs" it should at last become strong enough to cast off trade restrictions.[1] But in spite of the increase of prosperity and growth of industrial activity in Germany since the establishment of the Customs Union, Protection could reasonably, at the date of List's book be thought necessary to enable the rising industries to develop in face of the overwhelming industrial power of Great Britain.

Two years after the publication of List's great book, there appeared the first work of the school which was to exert the most potent influence on German economic thought for the remainder of the nineteenth century—the historical school. In 1843 Roscher published his *Grundriss*, and this was followed in 1848 by Hildebrand's *Die Nationaloekonomie der Gegenwart und Zukunft*, and in 1853 by the book of Karl Knies entitled *Die Politische Oekonomie von Standpunkte der geschichtlichen Methode.* These various works formulated the general principles on which the new school has worked, and the principles have been applied since that time by an ever-increasing army of students and investigators, who have devoted themselves chiefly to historical inquiry and the collection of the facts of economic history, and to the deduction from the results so obtained of principles which may serve as a guide for the economic action of communities, and particularly of their own country.

The historical school has on the whole always thrown its weight on the side of Protection, at least for Germany. It does not regard either Free Trade or Protection as an ideal, except in so far as universal Free Trade is a

[1] See below, pp. 55-6.

far-off goal, desirable, but only to be reached when the whole political character of the world is changed. Both Free Trade and Protection have their uses in the different stages of national development. "The fundamental propositions," set forth by Knies and adopted by all the historical school, "are that the economic constitution of society at any epoch on the one hand, and on the other the contemporary theoretic conception of economic science, are results of a definite historical development; that they are both in vital connection with the whole social organism of the period, having grown up along with it and under the same conditions of time, place, and nationality; that the economic system must therefore be regarded as passing through a series of phases correlative with the successive stages of civilisation, and can at no point of this movement be considered to have attained an entirely definite form; that no more the present than any previous economic organisation of society is to be regarded as absolutely good and right, but only as a phase in a continual historical evolution; and that in like manner the now prevalent economic doctrine is not to be viewed as complete and final, but only as representing a certain stage in the unfolding or progressive manifestation of the truth."[1] Given the particular conditions of Germany, most of the writers of the historical school have held that their country was at the time of the Bismarckian tariff legislation of the late seventies in the stage where protection and vigorous State action in regard to commerce and industry were necessary, and their general views are best represented by the greatest of German economic historians, Professor Gustav Schmoller. In his *Mercantile System*, published in 1884, Professor Schmoller has given a clear exposition of this theory, though in an elaborate historical setting.[2]

[1] Ingram, *History of Political Economy*, p. 203.

[2] A masterly survey of the history of the tariff policies of the principal European countries, and of the United States of America, from Professor Schmoller's particular point of view, will be found in his *Grundriss*, ii. pp. 558–651.

He traces the development (with special reference to Germany) of the economic unit from the village through the town and the territory to the state; "political organisms and economic organisms are by no means necessarily conterminous; and yet the great and brilliant achievements of history, both political and economic, are wont to be accomplished at times when economic organisation has rested on the same foundation as political power and order."[1] Like Müller and List, and like all the members of the historical school, he emphasises the moral element, and the need for the consideration of the general interests of society. "All economic and political life rests upon physical mass movements, mass sentiments, and mass conceptions, gravitating around certain centres."[2] "The idea that economic life has ever been a process mainly dependent on individual action—an idea based on the impression that it is concerned merely with methods of satisfying individual needs—is mistaken with regard to all stages of human civilisation, and in some respects it is more mistaken the further we go back."[3] So the municipal economic policy of the Middle Ages, in spite of its local partiality and prejudices, was fully justified so long as the towns were the most important forces on the side of civilisation and economic progress. Later the place of the towns was taken by the territories, striving to make themselves into self-contained and self-conscious economic units. "What to each in its time gave riches and superiority, first to Milan, Venice, Florence, and Genoa, then later to Spain and Portugal, and now to Holland, France, and England, and to some extent to Denmark and Sweden, was a *state* policy in economic matters, as superior to the territorial as that had been to the municipal. . . . It was not only a question of state armies, fleets, and civil services; it was a question rather of unifying systems of finance and economy which

[1] Schmoller, *The Mercantile System* (translated by W. J. Ashley), p. 3.

[2] *Loc. cit.*, p. 61.

[3] *Loc. cit.*, pp. 3–4.

should encompass the forces of millions and whole countries and give unity to their social life."[1] And this is the true conception of mercantilism; it is, in fact, a great policy of national construction, "state making and national economy making at the same time. . . . The essence of the system lies not in some doctrine of money or of a balance of trade; not in tariff barriers, protective duties, or navigation laws, but in something far greater:—namely, in the total transformation of society and its organisation, as well as of the state and its institutions, in the replacing of a local and territorial economic policy by that of the national state."[2] And so to Professor Schmoller the practice and theory of the European states in the first half of the nineteenth century, as expounded by List, had a truer relation to their actual economic conditions than had the theories of Adam Smith.[3]

But this doctrine of Protection is a very relative one; it all depends on the particular condition of a country at a given time. The policy of Bismarck in his tariff legislation may, on this reasoning, have been a sound one for Germany at the time it was adopted, when it was necessary to take all possible steps to consolidate the Empire and promote its economic development. It is defensible on precisely the same principles as those which led Adam Smith to defend the old Navigation Acts; but this very fact would condemn merely protective tariffs as a permanent policy. There is a higher stage of development, when the infant industries have become adult and are able to fight their own way in the world. To give them permanent protection is to keep them in perpetual tutelage. List himself wrote that "a nation which has already attained manufacturing supremacy can only protect its own manufacturers against retrogression and indolence by the free importation of the means of subsistence and raw materials, and by the

[1] *Loc. cit.*, pp. 48–9. [2] *Loc. cit.*, pp. 50–1.
[3] *Loc. cit.*, p. 60.

competition of foreign manufactured goods."[1] England, he argued, had by 1841 reached the highest stage of development, and for her Free Trade was the right economic policy.[2] So also Professor Schmoller writes: "That age could begin to think and act in the spirit of Free Trade which had left so far behind it the toilsome work of national development that it regarded its best results as matters of course";[3] and most of the other members of the modern German historical school seem to regard German industries as having reached the stage in which they no longer have need of what List called "educational tariffs" (Erziehungszölle).[4] Where they did defend the maintenance of the tariffs against the importation of agricultural produce and manufactured

[1] List, *loc. cit.*, chap. xv. The previous passage is interesting: "England will then give up the idea that she is designed to monopolise the manufacturing power of the whole world. She will no longer require that France, Germany, and North America should sacrifice their own manufactures in consideration of the concession by England of permitting the import, duty free, of agricultural products and raw material. She will recognise the legitimacy of protective systems in those nations, although she will herself more and more favour Free Trade," for the reason given above. He adds that England will cease to urge foreign nations to become Free Traders; "she will herself permit competition without regard to the foreign systems of protection."

[2] "Finally, history teaches us how nations which have been endowed by nature with all resources which are requisite for the attainment of the highest grade of wealth and power, may and must—without on that account forfeiting the end in view—modify their systems according to the measure of their own progress: in the first stage, adopting Free Trade with more advanced nations as a means of raising themselves from a state of barbarism, and of making advances in agriculture; in the second stage, promoting the growth of manufactures, fisheries, navigation, and foreign trade by means of commercial restrictions; and in the last stage, after reaching the highest degree of wealth and power, by gradually reverting to the principle of Free Trade and of unrestricted competition in the home as well as in foreign markets, that so their agriculturalists, manufacturers, and merchants may be preserved from indolence, and stimulated to retain the supremacy which they have acquired" (chap. x.). He adds that Great Britain alone appeared (in his time) to have reached this final stage.

[3] Schmoller, *loc. cit.*, pp. 61–2.

[4] *Cf.* Schacht, "Inhalt und Kritik des Zolltarifentwurfs" in Schmoller's *Jahrbuch*, 1902; and Wagner, *Agrar- und Industriestaat*, 2nd ed., p. 223.

commodities, they did so, as we shall see later, on entirely different grounds.

The German historical school has taken up also an altogether different attitude towards State action from that adopted by the older English economists. It allows a very large sphere of action to the State, and the term applied to so many of its representatives—"Socialists of the Chair"—means that they go a considerable way towards that form of socialism which in its origin is associated with the name of Ferdinand Lassalle. As a philosophic doctrine, however, it is much older than that writer. Fichte had opposed to the "security" theory of the State the proposition that "it is the duty of the State to give each man that which is his due, then to establish him in the actual possession of his property, and then to safeguard him therein."[1] Many of the followers of Hegel, whose philosophic teaching tended "to glorify existing institutions, to see in Church and State the objective embodiment of the Absolute Idea,"[2] had regarded the Prussian State as the instrument appointed to bring about the social reformation. The term "state socialism" was adopted in Germany to indicate the antithesis to revolutionary socialism, and to mark a policy of reform, not by the destruction, but by the utilisation of the existing state organisation. So in Professor Wagner's articles on "Finanzpolitik und Staatsozialismus," published in 1887, it is asserted that "the chief aim of the State at present—in taxation and every other form of its activity—ought to be to alter the national distribution of wealth to the advantage of the working class. All politics must become social politics; the State must turn workman's friend."[3]

This does not mean merely the protection of the worker by factory legislation and his relief in time of poverty by the Poor Law system: it includes the ownership of railways and other industrial enterprises (such as mines)

[1] Fichte, *Der Geschlossene Handelsstaat*, bk. i., chap. i.
[2] Russell, *German Social Democracy*, p. 2.
[3] Rae, *Contemporary Socialism*, p. 387.

by the State, the undertaking by the State of whatever enterprises are desirable, but cannot be, or are not likely to be, undertaken by private individuals or companies, and the establishment of State-aided compulsory insurances against sickness and accident, and State systems of old-age pensions. This State socialism found its expression in the social legislation of Prince Bismarck, which was inspired partly by a genuine interest in social reform, and partly by a desire (not in the least successful) to outbid the Social Democrats for popular favour.[1]

A most important and beneficial influence was exercised on the industrial development of Germany by the new railway policy. The older State action in this matter had taken the form of subventions to private companies, and the purchase or direct construction of railways to only a limited extent. In 1875 eight lines were owned, and eight others were managed, by the Government, and thirty were privately owned and managed. The constitution of the Empire provided for the imperial control and supervision of railways, the building by the Government of railways "considered necessary for the defence of Germany or for the purpose of general commerce" and the settlement of railway rates. An Imperial Railway Board was set up in 1873, and Bismarck secured the passage through the Prussian Parliament, of a law enabling the Government to transfer the railways of that state to the Empire. This was intended to set an example, but the smaller states would not take the same line; and consequently, with the exception of those in Alsace and Lorraine which, came into the possession of the Empire, the railways remained the property of the several states. The Prussian Government then set to work to buy up the lines in its own territory; between

[1] For a detailed description of the early stages of this policy, see Dawson, *Bismarck and State Socialism*; and for a full account of the development of compulsory insurance the same author's *Social Insurance in Germany*, 1912. The principal original enactments were the Sickness Insurance Law of 1883, with its complement the Accident Insurance Laws of 1884 and 1885, and the Old Age and Infirmity Insurance Law of 1889.

1879 and 1882 about six thousand miles were bought. Thereafter the policy of State ownership was persistently pursued, so that by 1912 the Imperial and State Governments owned in all railways over 37,500 miles in length.[1] This policy was from the financial standpoint highly beneficial, and it also enabled the Governments to establish a scientific and coherent system of railway rates, including through rates, combined railway and shipping rates,[2] and special rates for export, which have undoubtedly been of great assistance in promoting German foreign trade.

Other developments during this period were the commencement of German colonial expansion by the acquisition of territories in East Africa, South-west Africa, and South-east Africa, of Kaiser Wilhelm's Land and the Bismarck Archipelago; and the inauguration of a policy of steamship subsidies.

[1] *Statistical Abstract for the Principal and Other Foreign Countries* (1914), p. 387.

[2] The German-Levant and German-East Africa combined tariffs are the most conspicuous examples.

CHAPTER VI

GERMAN COMMERCIAL POLICY TO 1894

For some years after the adoption of the new tariff in 1880, German foreign trade expanded only very gradually; after steadily advancing up to 1883, it fell off again during the three following years. The following table shows the movement of German imports for home consumption and exports of domestic produce (exclusive of the precious metals) for the period 1880–91:[1]

Year.	Imports for Home Consumption.		Exports of German Produce.	
	All Kinds.	Manufactured and Partly Manufactured Articles.	All Kinds.	Manufactured and Partly Manufactured Articles.
	Million £.	Million £.	Million £.	Million £.
1880	138·6	38·4	142·4	82·1
1881	145·7	40·6	146·4	86·1
1882	153·9	42·7	156·8	92·5
1883	160·5	47·3	160·9	96·5
1884	160·3	45·0	157·5	98·9
1885	144·7	41·3	140·6	88·5
1886	142·0	41·7	146·8	95·6
1887	153·6	40·9	154·2	100·7
1888	161·8	43·1	157·6	102·0
1889	197·5	48·8	155·7	103·2
1890	204·6	48·2	163·6	105·6
1891	204·0	44·5	156·1	100·7

It will be observed that for the five years 1880 to 1884, the average value of the total imports was 151·8 million pounds, whilst the average for the next four years was 150·5 million pounds, or about 1¼ million

[1] *British and Foreign Trade and Industry* (Cd. 4954, 1909), pp. 62–3.

pounds a year less; the average of exports was for 1880 to 1884, 152·8 millions, and for 1885 to 1888, 149·8 millions, or about 3 million pounds less. After 1888 the figures are not altogether comparable, because of the inclusion of Hamburg and Bremen, which though long under negotiation, had been delayed by the return to Protection.[1] It will be noticed further that after 1888 there was a sharp rise in imports, whilst exports remained at about the same level, and the excess of imports over exports became relatively very large.

For the Imperial exchequer the effects of the new customs system seem to have been altogether satisfactory. In 1877-8 the net revenue from the customs was 103·7 million marks, or 2·4 marks per head of population; by 1883–4 the amount had risen to 189·7 million, or 4·2 marks per head; and in 1889–90 a total was reached of 357·7 million, or 7·3 marks per head. The contributions to the Imperial exchequer from the separate states, which had reached 70 million marks in 1878-9, sank rapidly until in the year 1882–3 the customs revenue not only supplied an amount equal to the old contributions, but provided a surplus which could be distributed amongst the states; and in 1884–5 nearly 41 million marks were available for this purpose.[2]

After 1880 the most noticeable feature in the history of the German tariff is the increase of the duties on agricultural products, coincident with the growth of the political power of the agrarian party. It is true that there were some slight increases in the duties on manufactured commodities, but these were not very important, and against them must be set some small reductions.[3] The agrarians complained of growing competition, and urged the necessity of protecting the food supply of the empire against the dangers of war; and they secured increases, of which the more important are shown in the following table:[4]

[1] Zimmermann, ii. p. 98.
[2] Blum, p. 306.
[3] Lotz, i. p. 177.
[4] *British and Foreign Trade and Industry* (1909), pp. 210–11.

Commodity.	Rates of Duty per 100 Kilo.			
	1879.	1881.	1885.	1888.
Wheat	1 mk.	—	3 mk.	5 mk.
Rye	1 ,,	—	3 ,,	5 ,,
Barley	·5 ,,	—	1½ ,,	2¼ ,,
Flour	2 ,,	3 mk.	7½ ,,	10½ ,,
Meat of all kinds ..	12 ,,	—	20 ,,	—

As regards Germany's foreign trade, the exporters had feared at the time of the establishment of the new protective tariff that they might be hampered by retaliation on the part of foreign nations. Fortunately their fears in this direction were not realised, since the administration of Prince Bismarck was able, in most cases, either to make new treaties, or to secure the maintenance of the existing treaty relations. Political influence enabled Germany between 1880 and 1888 to establish, with such Eastern Powers as China, Japan, Corea and Siam, and also with Servia and Roumania, treaties which bound those Powers to reduce some of their existing duties, or, at least, not to increase the duties on German products, without imposing any corresponding obligation on Germany herself. Of another kind were the treaties with Italy, Spain, Greece and Switzerland, in which the reductions of duties were mutual, although on the German side they were not, except in the case of Switzerland, of marked importance. With other states, such as Austria-Hungary, Belgium, the Netherlands, Sweden and Norway, all that could be obtained was a continuance of "most favoured nation" treatment, the importance of which for Germany was enhanced by the fact that France had made treaties with the other countries, which gave her certain reductions of duties, and that under the "most favoured nation" clause in the Frankfurt Treaty Germany enjoyed the same advantages. In Great Britain, under the treaty of 1865, Germany continued to receive the same favourable treatment—a privilege which was extended to her also in the British Colonies.[1]

[1] Lotz, ii. pp. 60–3.

As regards Russia and the United States the condition of affairs was by no means so satisfactory, for both those nations were particularly interested in the export of agricultural produce, and therefore came into sharp conflict with Germany over the new tariff, which they not unnaturally regarded as directed specially against themselves. Russia had always refused to bind herself by treaties, even of the simplest kind, and from 1877 onwards her tariff wall was steadily rising—a fact which was not without influence on the movement of the German tariff between 1880 and 1890.[1] Germany's relations with the United States had long been based on reciprocal "most favoured nation" treatment, but this had been of little value; the situation was now very strained, and the German policy in regard to agricultural products must be counted as one of the strong motives for the high protective policy established in the United States by the McKinley Tariff.

On the whole Prince Bismarck was disinclined to the old policy of conventional tariffs; he seems to have been opposed to anything which would bind the hands of the Government in its defence of the commercial interests of the country. He adhered, with certain slight exceptions, to the simple system of the autonomous tariff; but by 1890 a considerable change had come over the political conditions of Germany, marked by the dismissal of Prince Bismarck and the appointment of General Caprivi as his successor. In home affairs the chief features of the new system were the abandonment of anti-socialist legislation and the attempt towards a "labour policy," illustrated by the international conference at Berlin; in parliamentary politics the important development was the rise of the Centre or Catholic party and the decline of the National Liberals.[2] In

[1] *Cf.* Schmoller, *Grundriss*, ii. pp. 623-6.

[2] In 1887 the National Liberals were the largest party in the Reichstag with 99 members, the Centre came next with 98, and the Conservatives next with 80; at the election of 1890, 106 members of the Centre were returned and 73 Conservatives, while the National Liberals fell to 42.

foreign policy, the independent attitude was abandoned, and the most striking example was furnished by the Anglo-German arrangement with regard to East Africa, under which Great Britain was given a free hand there and in Zanzibar, in exchange for the surrender of Heligoland to Germany. Commercial policy was now to be modified in the same way as the result of a number of converging influences.

The question of the food supply had suddenly become serious. The following table shows the movement of wholesale prices for wheat and rye in Prussia and Bavaria for the period 1880 to 1891:[1]

AVERAGE WHOLESALE PRICES.

Year.	Wheat (per Imperial Quarter).		Rye (per cwt.).	
	Prussia.	Bavaria.	Prussia.	Bavaria.
	s. d.	s. d.	s. d.	s. d.
1880	46 10	52 7	9 8	10 0
1881	47 1	53 3	10 1	10 5
1882	44 7	50 2	8 0	8 11
1883	39 7	45 3	7 4	7 7
1884	37 0	42 4	7 4	8 0
1885	34 8	39 11	7 2	7 9
1886	33 7	40 10	6 9	7 3
1887	35 2	40 1	6 3	7 1
1888	37 3	42 3	6 9	7 8
1889	39 2	43 6	7 9	7 11
1890	41 2	46 6	8 6	8 8
1891	47 6	50 4	10 5	10 2

It will be observed that, as a result of a number of causes, the agricultural duties did not prevent a continued fall in prices until 1886 and 1887, but after the latter year there was an upward movement which became extremely sharp with the failure of harvests in 1890 and 1891. This was particularly the case in regard to rye, which is the chief bread stuff for a very large part of the German population. In 1891 the Russian Government found itself compelled, in view of the acute economic

[1] *British and Foreign Trade Industry* (1909), pp. 195 and 200. *Cf.* Dade, pp. 27–8.

distress in Russia, to prohibit the export of wheat and rye and other agricultural produce. At the same time the difficulties of the German exporters were increased by the adoption of the McKinley Tariff in the United States and by the marked movement towards higher protection all over Europe. Most of the nations with which Germany had treaties either gave notice of their termination, or were inclined to do so, and France was also about to denounce the treaties which she had made with various countries, and by which Germany had profited.

It had become necessary for Germany to readjust her policy. It was believed to be clearly impossible for her to continue in the old way and to make no effort to influence the tariffs of her neighbours. It was therefore decided to endeavour to continue the existing reciprocity arrangements, but to elaborate them into a new series of treaties, which should return to the old principle of reciprocal reductions of duties; the German Empire was thus to imitate the example of France in 1860, and take the lead in a readjustment for a definite period of the economic relations of the European states. The agrarian party clung to the protection of the autonomous tariff, and were opposed to any modifications; but under the prevailing circumstances they were not unwilling to see a temporary reduction of the duties. What they did object to was anything which would establish those reductions for any considerable number of years. On the other hand, the growth of industry not only rendered an abundant and cheap food supply desirable, but made it necessary that everything possible should be done to secure a large and assured foreign market for German manufactured products. The latter was the dominant consideration, but if German manufacturers were to export freely, foreigners must be allowed to have easier access to the German market.

"The conclusion of new international treaties with simple 'most favoured nation' treatment, without the settlement of tariffs, would indeed give Germany the possibility of securing an internal market for its own manufactures by means of an arbitrary protective tariff, but would provide not the slightest guarantee for the maintenance of that foreign market which is so essential for our export trade. In face of the world competition of the economically developed states, becoming ever fiercer with the rapid increase of production and its aids, permanent intercourse between them is conceivable only in the form of a reasonable exchange of commodities, and this presupposes again a deliberate reciprocal limitation of free action in regard to tariffs. Under the present commercial conditions Germany cannot count on the maintenance of its export, unless by such limitations on its own side it secures to other nations the possibility of paying for its goods, wholly or in part, by their own products."[1]

The home producers, both agricultural and industrial, must consent to some sacrifices, for "concessions at the hands of agricultural nations, such as Austria-Hungary, Italy, and Russia, were to be obtained only by the reduction of certain duties on agricultural commodities; concessions at the hands of manufacturing nations, like Belgium and Switzerland, by the reduction of certain German duties on manufactured products."[2] The manufacturers as a whole supported the new policy, since they were anxious for the growth of the export trade, and did not fear foreign competition in the home markets so much as formerly; the working classes also gave their support to it, and the opposition was in the main confined to the agrarians, who were called on to make the chief sacrifices, and were unwilling to do so for any length of time.[3]

The new policy was inaugurated in December, 1891, by the commercial treaty with the Austro-Hungarian Empire, which for some time had been desirous of entering into closer relations with Germany, since the latter country was its most important market, taking on an average over

[1] Government Memorandum, quoted in Lotz, i. p. 87.
[2] Dietzel, p. 367.
[3] A suggestive short discussion of the aims and effects of the commercial policy initiated under Caprivi will be found in Harms, *Deutschland's Anteil an Welthandel*, pp. 170 *seq*.

one-half of the total Austro-Hungarian exports.[1] But at the same time, only about 10 per cent. of the German exports went to Austria-Hungary, and her imports from that country were only about 14 per cent. of the whole, so that for the purposes of negotiations Germany was in much the stronger position. Hungary was particularly interested in the reduction of the German agrarian duties, and in Austria itself there was a reaction against the protective policy of recent years. Following the treaty with Austria came others with Italy, Belgium, and at the beginning of 1892 with Switzerland. They were all to remain in force till the 31st of December, 1903, and unless then denounced were to continue indefinitely, but were to be terminable at one year's notice from either side. The bases of all these treaties were the same—reciprocal "most favoured nation" treatment and reduction of duties. The most important changes on the German side were in respect of the duties on agricultural products, which were reduced below the level of 1888, but in no case to the rates of 1885; thus the duties on wheat and rye were lowered from 5 to 3½ marks per 100 kilog., on barley from 2¼ to 2, on flour from 10½ to 7¼, on pork from 20 to 17, and on other fresh meat from 20 to 15; the cattle duties were also reduced. As regards manufactured articles moderate reductions were made in the import duties on joinery, glass and earthenware, some iron goods, textiles, paper, leather manufactures, and others. In all, it was estimated that articles of the classes affected by these reductions and by some abolitions of unimportant duties had been imported from the four countries concerned to the amount of 260 million marks on an average for the years 1888 to 1890.[2] On the part of the other contracting states there were general reductions of duties on German manufactured goods; and in a number of cases where reductions were not made, the contracting states bound themselves not to make an increase. The German exporters were by no means satisfied, for they had hoped to obtain greater reductions of hostile tariffs, and they over-

[1] Wuttke, p. 415. [2] Lotz, ii. p. 83.

looked the fact that they had, at any rate, prevented any further advances for a considerable period. They were, however, willing to accept the treaties, and though the agrarians made strong opposition on certain points, they were not powerful enough to secure the rejection of the Government policy.

Then, however, agricultural conditions changed, and there was a fall in prices, due partly to improved harvests at home, and partly to the increase of imports into Germany from the United States and Roumania. The following table shows the movements of prices from 1891 to 1894:[1]

AVERAGE WHOLESALE PRICES.

Year.	Wheat (per Imperial Quarter).		Rye (per cwt.).		Wheat Flour (per cwt.).	Barley (per Imperial Quarter).
	Prussia.	Bavaria.	Prussia.	Bavaria.	Cologne.	Baden.
	s. d.	s. d.	s. d.	s. d.	s. d.	s. d.
1891	47 6	50 4	10 5	10 2	15 6	30 6
1892	40 6	43 9	8 11	8 7	13 1	27 7
1893	32 6	35 9	6 9	7 0	11 1	28 2
1894	28 11	30 5	5 11	6 1	9 7	24 9

The result was that the Government had much more difficulty in carrying the second series of commercial treaties in the latter part of 1893 with Servia, Spain, and especially Roumania. The last-named country was coming to be one of the most important sources of Germany's food supply, particularly during the conflict with Russia. In 1889 5 per cent. of the German supply of wheat came from Roumania, but in 1893 the amount had risen to 20·4 per cent., and to an even higher point in the case of rye.[2] The agrarian party were therefore strongly hostile to anything which would encourage the increase of the quantities imported from Roumania, whilst, on the other hand, the manufacturers, who sent, it was estimated,

[1] *British and Foreign Trade and Industry* (1909), pp. 195, 197, 200, 202; *cf.* Dietzel, p. 369.

[2] Lotz, ii. p. 110.

100 million marks worth of goods a year to that country, desired a treaty which would still further develop their market. The new treaties, although supported by the whole force of the manufacturers, were confirmed by the Reichstag only after a most strenuous opposition from the agrarians. The conflict reached its height over the treaty with Russia, which was in some ways the most important of all. It has already been remarked that the commercial relations between that country and Germany had for some time been distinctly strained, but the trade between the two was, nevertheless, very considerable. In 1890 Russia imported from Germany goods to the value of £10,300,000—30 per cent. being for manufactured goods—and exported to her goods to the value of £27,000,000—95 per cent. of these latter being foodstuffs, raw materials, and unfinished goods.[1] In 1891 Russia sent into Germany more than one-half (53 per cent.) of the latter's total import of cereals, and this quantity taken by Germany amounted to about one-sixth of the total Russian export of the kind. Germany sent to Russia iron and steel goods, chemicals for use in manufactures, coal and coke, porcelain and cement, and a very large quantity of flour. Moreover, she had a large transit trade with that country, for a considerable proportion of Russia's supplies of raw cotton and wool came to her through Germany.

Germany had two grounds of complaint against Russia. The highly prohibitive tariff, which, after eight increases of duties between 1881 and 1891, culminated in the latter year in a new general scheme of duties and reached the highest point in Russian protective policy since 1850, affected all nations equally; but the discrimination against land-borne in favour of sea-borne goods hindered the competition of Germany with Great Britain in the supply of coal and iron, and in the carrying trade. Russia had hitherto stood apart from the treaty system, in her unwillingness to bind her customs tariff for any definite time, but now she was not disinclined to modify her policy, particularly as the treaties already made by Germany put

[1] Wuttke, p. 419, and *Foreign Office Report*, p. 41.

her in an extremely difficult position. Those treaties had given reductions of duties on agricultural produce to other nations, who thereby enjoyed a distinct advantage over Russia. After the conclusion of the first series of treaties, Russian corn paid a duty 43 per cent. higher than that imposed on the products of the favoured nations—Austria-Hungary, Italy, Switzerland, Belgium, by the treaties,[1] and the United States, Argentina, Servia, Bulgaria, and Turkey, under the "most favoured nation" clause. Roumania was also about to be included.

Negotiations between the two Powers had commenced towards the end of 1891, by Russia proposing that Germany should grant her the terms of the conventional tariff in regard to most agricultural products, together with free entry for a number of raw materials, and offering in return to make some concessions, but not on metals, textiles, chemicals, or sugar. The German Government replied that the proposals were inacceptable, since they secured to Russia reductions on 80 per cent. of her exports, and gave practically nothing in return; it suggested, therefore, that Russia should remove the obstacles to commercial intercourse on the frontier by simplifying the customs regulations, equalise the duties on sea and land-borne goods, and reduce the duties on about four-fifths of the tariff groups of commodities. Negotiations were continued after the control of Russian commercial policy had passed into the hands of M. Witte, who proposed to establish a minimum and maximum tariff—the minimum to be a slightly modified version of the tariff of 1891, for the benefit of those states which gave Russia "most favoured nation" treatment, and the maximum to be the same tariff increased in various cases and against various countries. In October, 1892, Russia offered to admit German goods under the minimum tariff, and to abolish the preferential treatment of sea-borne trade; and in March of the following year the German Government replied with its final proposals. It offered the conventional tariff terms in return for considerable reductions on

[1] *Foreign Office Report*, p. 42.

the Russian minimum tariff, and the promotion of trade by a modification of the customs regulations. On the refusal of the Russian Government to consider these proposals and the failure of an attempt at a conference of experts, the actual tariff war began. From August 1st, 1893, German goods imported into Russia became subject to the maximum tariff, which imposed on them surtaxes amounting to at least 30 per cent. on manufactured goods and 20 per cent. on semi-manufactured articles. In the same month Germany replied by imposing surtaxes of 50 per cent. on all Russian goods liable to customs duties—one result being that the duty was about 115 per cent. higher on Russian bread stuffs than on those imported from America, Hungary, Roumania, and Argentina. In return, the Russian Government again increased the tariff against German produce by 50 per cent., and raised the shipping dues against German vessels. It extended these measures to Finland; and the German Government consequently applied the 50 per cent. surtaxes to goods imported from the Grand-Duchy also. All these various increases had been made by the 16th of August, but the strain on both sides was very much too severe; early in September fresh negotiations were opened, and on October 16th the first conference was held at Berlin.

"The statistics published by the German Government show that after the outbreak of the tariff war, the German export trade to Russia had been partially paralysed. The export of locomotives ceased; the export of wrought iron was one-third of the average in the preceding year, and of cement less than one-half. And in addition to the losses of the German exporters and manufacturers, it became apparent that a large number of Germans lived by the import and handling of Russian products, and they were, of course, severely affected. The railways, which are State property, were run, on certain branches, at a loss. German ships were practically excluded from Russian ports, and the German coast towns, interested in the carrying trade, were heavy sufferers. . . . With the approach of winter the situation became worse, as the

Baltic ports were closed by the ice. The large trade in extra-European goods, which had been carried on through Germany, was crippled. The transit of raw cotton through Germany for the Russian market was, in 1893, only one-half of what it had been in the preceding year. And in addition to the economical losses, a grave danger was imminent. There is ample proof that the tariff war, as it proceeded, was regarded by both responsible parties as likely to lead to a state of things dangerous for the peace of Europe."[1] On the other side, Russia was suffering from the injury inflicted on her agricultural exports, particularly after the good harvest of 1893. The following table shows the movement of imports and exports between the two countries for the years 1889 to 1894 inclusive.[2] It will be remembered that the acute struggle was in the latter half of 1893.

Year.	German Imports from Russia.	German Exports to Russia.
	Million £.	Million £.
1889	25·6	8·6
1890	25·7	9·0
1891	28·5	7·1
1892	18·8	6·4
1893	17·3	6·7
1894	21·6	8·4

Both sides were now anxious to come to terms, and political motives combined with economic interests to bring about this result. Russia desired a treaty with Germany as a first step in a series of such treaties, and Germany was anxious to do something to counterbalance the growing Russo-French alliance. The outcome of this less hostile disposition on both sides was the treaty signed on February 10th, 1894. The German Government declared that German trade, commerce, and shipping were profoundly interested in the reduction of the Russian

[1] *Foreign Office Report*, p. 46.

[2] *Statistical Abstract for the Principal and Other Foreign Countries* (1900), pp. 166–170; the figures have been converted at the rate of 11·8d. to the mark.

duties, and that, on the other hand, the freer importation of Russian grain would not seriously affect German agricultural interests, since the really dangerous menace was from the United States, Roumania and other countries which already enjoyed treaty privileges. The agrarian party fiercely resisted the treaty, but it was carried after a hard struggle.

It was a compromise. Russia received "most favoured nation" treatment, which gave her the benefit of the lower grain duties; she also secured the abolition of duties on some of her products, such as flax, oil-seed and wool, and an advantage over the United States in the duty on oil. Germany, for her part, obtained a reduction of duties on 120 articles—as, for instance, 20 per cent. on leather goods, 17 to 20 per cent. on unwrought iron, 18 per cent. on iron machinery, 17 to 20 per cent. on pottery, 17 per cent. on paper, 12 to 30 per cent. on woollen tissues. Both parties bound themselves for ten years not to increase the duties on certain specified goods. The treaty also provided that Russia should abandon the distinction between sea-borne and land-borne goods, whilst Germany undertook that Russian goods should not be subject to higher rates than domestic goods for carriage on the Prussian State railways. The following table shows the movement of trade between the two countries after 1894:[1]

Year.	German Imports from Russia.	German Exports to Russia.
	Million £.	Million £.
1894	21·6	8·4
1895	27·9	10·2
1896	30·9	11·4
1897	34·7	13·2
1898	36·1	14·9
1899	31·2	19·0
1900	31·7	17·1
1901	33·5	16·2
1902	38·9	16·1

Thus Germany had returned to the system of the "autonomous" and "conventional" tariffs; the former

[1] *Statistical Abstract for the Principal and Other Foreign Countries* (1908), pp. 204–7.

applied against all those countries which had not made with her a commercial treaty providing for reciprocal reductions of duties, and the latter containing all the lower rates of duty established by treaties and generalised to treaty powers by the force of the " most favoured nation" clause. But it is important to note that the system adopted differed from that then employed by France; there the Government could increase the minimum (" conventional ") as well as the maximum (" autonomous ") rates at any time, whilst the German Government, in its treaties, bound itself not to increase the tariff rates for a term of years.

The Russian treaty seems to have been satisfactory in its effect, but this was by no means the case with all the others, and in particular the settlement of Germany's commercial relations with the Austro-Hungarian Empire was not followed by results equal to the expectations of the German exporters. They had hoped for a great expansion of the Austrian market, but their export of textile manufactures actually declined for some time.[1] There was an increase in respect of metals, but in the early years at least, after the conclusion of the treaty, the development of trade between the two countries was only very gradual. The following table shows its course for the years 1893-1902:

Year.	Exports of German Produce and Manufactures to Austria-Hungary.	Imports into Germany of Austro-Hungarian Produce and Manufactures.
	Million £.	Million £.
1893	16·7	28·1
1894	17·3	28·1
1895	18·4	25·2
1896	19·6	26·9
1897	19·9	29·6
1898	20·9	30·8
1899	22·1	35·2
1900	23·9	34·6
1901	22·8	33·6
1902	23·6	34·2

[1] The average import of textiles into Austria-Hungary from Germany from 1892–4 was 33·8 million kronen; 1897–9, 30·8 million kronen (Wuttke, p. 439).

The Austrian Empire sent chiefly agricultural produce to Germany, and the general effect of the treaty (allowing for the fall in agricultural prices after 1891) seems to have been to increase the competition which the German agrarians had to meet, without securing any considerable increase of the market for the manufacturers.[1] The negotiations with Spain brought Germany into yet another tariff war. In 1893 a treaty had been signed between the two countries, which was accepted by the German Parliament, but rejected by the Spanish. Thereupon the German Government withdrew the "most favoured nation" treatment of Spanish goods, and subjected them to the autonomous tariff; the Spanish Government did the same for German goods. Germany, in her turn, imposed a surtax of 100 per cent. on all commodities coming from Spain. Spain then proposed in 1896 that both sides should make use simply of the lowest rates of the autonomous tariff—terms which Germany accepted. But inasmuch as France, England, Switzerland, and other countries enjoyed in Spanish markets preferences over Germany, the Government of the last-named country soon became anxious to obtain more satisfactory terms, and at the time of the purchase of the Caroline Islands, in the beginning of 1899, a fresh treaty was signed, securing reciprocal "most favoured nation" treatment.[2]

A word must be said as to the commercial relations of Germany to two other countries, the United Kingdom and the United States. Ever since the treaty of 1865, Germany had enjoyed the advantages of the "most favoured nation" clause in the United Kingdom and in all its colonial possessions. In 1897 the Canadian Government granted a reduction of duties on British goods alone, and Germany immediately protested against this on the ground that it violated the terms of the treaty of 1865. The British Government, therefore, gave a year's notice of the renunciation of the treaty, but suggested that it would be willing to undertake negotiations for a fresh

[1] Wuttke, p. 458. [2] Zimmermann, ii. pp. 308, 309.

arrangement. Germany then decided to continue the existing arrangement so far as concerned the United Kingdom and those of her colonies which did not discriminate between British and German goods; but against Canada she applied her autonomous tariff, to which Canada replied by the imposition of a surtax of 33⅓ per cent. on German goods. The arrangement as to the United Kingdom was renewed, for periods of two years, by legislative enactment from time to time, and was in force up to the outbreak of the Great War in 1914.[1] With the United States German relations had almost always been far from satisfactory. By the Saratoga Convention, signed in 1891, Germany abandoned many of the restrictions on the import of American meat, and gave the United States a right to participate in certain reductions of duties, whilst she received in return "most favoured nation" treatment for her sugar products. But this was not of much use to her, since the United States subsequently imposed surtaxes upon all bounty-fed sugar, and in spite of all its efforts the German Government could not secure preferential treatment.[2]

[1] By a provisional agreement made in February, 1910, the tariff war between Canada and Germany came to an end; the former country remitted the surtax on imports from Germany, and Germany granted to Canada the benefit of the conventional rates on certain commodities (including grain, rough timber, meat, and some fruits).

[2] A few other treaties were made towards the end of the century, the chief being the agreement with Japan in 1896.

CHAPTER VII

THE REVIVAL OF THE PROTECTIONIST MOVEMENT, AND THE NEW GENERAL TARIFF

COUNT CAPRIVI had succeeded in carrying the commercial treaties, but he had incurred the fierce hostility of the agrarians, and soon after the conclusion of the Russian treaty they were strong enough to secure his overthrow and his replacement by Prince Hohenlohe. The period from the latter's succession to office until the close of the century was characterised chiefly by the revival of the protectionist agitation, particularly amongst the agrarians. But before noticing the causes of this agitation and its results, it will be well to review some of the features of the industrial development of Germany in the first three decades after the foundation of the Empire.[1]

The population of the Empire increased from 41 millions in 1872 to 59·5 millions in 1904, and continued thereafter to increase at the rate of some 850,000 persons a year.[2] The following table shows the development of Germany's foreign trade:[3]

[1] See *Statistisches Handbuch für das deutsche Reich*, 2 vols., 1907; "Veritas," *The German Empire of To-day;* W. H. Dawson, *The Evolution of Modern Germany;* Eltzbacher, *Modern Germany;* W. J. Ashley, *Progress of the German Working Classes; British and Foreign Trade and Industry* (1909).

[2] *Cf.* Troeltsch, pp. 10–11.

[3] The strict comparability of German trade statistics over a long period of years is limited by a number of considerations: (i.) The statistics are very incomplete for the earlier years; (ii.) Hamburg and Bremen were not included in the Zollverein till 1889; (iii.) the value of ships and of the improvement trade for home account has been included only since 1897; (iv.) the free port areas of Hamburg and three smaller ports have been included in the *Wirtschaftsgebeit* only since March 1, 1906.

Period.	Average Annual Value of Imports for Home Consumption (Merchandise only).		Average Annual Value of Exports of German Produce (Merchandise only).	
	Total.	Manufactured and Partly Manufactured Goods.	Total.	Manufactured and Partly Manufactured Goods.
	Million £.	Million £.	Million £.	Million £.
1872–4 ..	*	*	113·7	*
1875–9 ..	*	*	132·3	*
1880–4 ..	151·8	42·8	152·8	91·2
1885–9 ..	159·9	43·2	151·0	98·0
1890–4 ..	198–9	44·0	152·5	98·6
1895–9 ..	232·8	49·1	181·3	116·9
1900–4 ..	287·0	57·0	235·6	154·2

* Cannot be given.

The total imports thus increased from £3 7s. 2d. per head of population on the average for 1880-4 to £4 19s. on the average for 1900-4, whilst the total exports increased during the same period from £3 7s. 8d. to £4 1s. 3d.

The average annual production of coal rose from 31·8 million tons in 1870-4 to 110·7 millions in 1900-4,[1] whilst the average annual output of pig-iron rose in the same interval from 1·8 to 8·9 million tons.[2] The average production of crude steel was only 0·3 million tons for the quinquennial period 1870-4; for 1900-4 it had risen to 7·3 million tons.[3] The home production of zinc averaged 60·3 thousand tons, and the consumption 33·8 thousand tons, in 1870-4; by 1900-4 the amounts had risen to 174·6 and 160·4 thousand tons respectively.[4] The average annual production of lead was in the earlier period 57·6 thousand tons, and the consumption 37·4 thousand; thirty years later the average production had risen to 133·6 thousand tons, and the consumption to

[1] *British and Foreign Trade and Industry* (1909), pp. 166–7.

[2] *Loc. cit.*, pp. 168–9. The great development of the German iron industry was rendered possible by the discovery by an Englishman, Thomas, of a process for the utilisation of phosphorific ores, which constitute the great bulk of Germany's native supplies.

[3] *Loc. cit.*, pp. 170–1.

[4] *Statistisches Handbuch für das deutsche Reich*, i., p. 489.

165·6 thousand.[1] The number of spindles employed in the cotton industry increased from an average of 4,262,000 for the four years 1871-4 (it will be remembered that the number was greatly increased by the acquisition of Alsace-Lorraine in 1871) to an average of 8,450,000 for the quinquennium 1900-4,[2] and the average annual consumption of raw cotton rose from 2·2 million cwt. in the former to 6·8 millions in the latter period.[3] The estimated annual consumption of raw sheep and lambs' wool averaged 174·5 million lbs. in 1875-9, and 345·3 million lbs. in 1900-4.[4] The net tonnage of the German mercantile marine (vessels of 17½ gross tons and upwards) increased from 982,000 tons in 1870 to 2,353,000 tons in 1904; the annual net tonnage of vessels built and added to the register advanced from 32,600 tons in 1878 (the first year for which statistics are available) and an average of 50,345 for the period 1880-4 to an average of 113,463 in 1900-4.[5] The length of railways open to traffic increased from an average of 21,719 miles in 1880-4 to an average of 32,232 in 1900-4, whilst the average weight of goods annually conveyed rose from 187 million tons in the former to 370 million tons in the latter period.[6] In the application of science to industry, notably in the chemical trades (including the manufacture of synthetic dye-stuffs and drugs and of fine chemicals) and the chemico-metallurgical and electrical trades, Germany had very remarkable achievements to her credit—aided by an educational system which on the technical and scientific side was undoubtedly then, and in some respects probably is still, superior to anything existent elsewhere, and by an enlightened policy on the part of the manufacturers. Much aid has been given to the industrial development of the country by a well-conceived railway transport policy, facilitated by the State ownership of railways.

1 *Loc. cit.*, p. 490.
2 *British and Foreign Trade and Industry* (1909), p. 157.
3 *Loc. cit.*, p. 159. 4 *Loc. cit.*, p. 165.
5 *Loc. cit.*, pp. 114–6 and 121.
6 *Loc. cit.*, pp. 127–8.

There was a very marked improvement in the condition of the working classes.[1] Wages were rising fairly steadily throughout this period, and particularly in the last decade of the nineteenth century; in spite of marked fluctuations, the prices of foodstuffs showed a pronounced downward movement until about 1894–6, and though after that date an upward tendency became manifest, there was no return to the old level. A gradual reduction in the hours of labour; the establishment of old age and invalidity pensions, and of compulsory sickness and accident insurance; greater attention to housing reform; an enlightened municipal policy; and the growth of trade unionism, all combined to bring about a substantial amelioration of the conditions of life for the great masses of the German people.

It is important to observe also that the industrialisation of Germany was marked by the same general features as the economic history of England after the industrial revolution. There was the same rapid growth of the towns (an increase as astonishing as that of the American cities),[2] and the same decline in the agricultural population. In 1871 the "urban population"—*i.e.*, in communes having over 2,000 inhabitants—was 36 per cent. of the total population; by the census of 1905 the proportion had increased to 57 per cent. Agriculture remained, however, still a very important occupation, though in the interval between the industrial censuses of 1895 and 1907 it had lost the foremost place. In 1895 the number of persons returned as engaged in agriculture and kindred occupations (including fishing) was 8,293,000 and by 1907 this number had increased to 9,883,000; but

[1] On the rise of wages, see Ashley, *Progress of the German Working Classes*, pp. 82–106; and R. Kuczynski, *Die Entwicklung der gewerblichen Löhne seit der Begrundung des deutschen Reiches.* On Food Prices, see *British and Foreign Trade and Industry* (1909), pp. 193–205; and the *Statistisches Handbuch für das deutsche Reich*, i. 474–480. For much information as to the conditions of life of the German working classes, see the Board of Trade Report on *Cost of Living in German Towns* (1908).

[2] *Cf.* Shaw, *Municipal Government in Continental Europe*, chap. v.

meanwhile the numbers engaged in industry and mining rose from 8,281,000 to 11,256,000.[1]

At the same time, and as a natural consequence, there has been an increasing tendency towards dependence on foreign food supplies,[2] as appears from the following table:[3]

AVERAGE ANNUAL CONSUMPTION (FOR ALL PURPOSES) OF WHEAT AND RYE.

Period.	Wheat and Wheat Flour.		Rye.	
	Home Grown (Production less Domestic Export).	Foreign (Imported for Home Consumption).	Home Grown (Production less Domestic Export).	Foreign (Imported for Home Consumption).
	1,000 Cwt.	1,000 Cwt.	1,000 Cwt.	1,000 Cwt.
1880–4 ..	42,247	11,910	109,712	14,412
1885–9 ..	47,315	9,317	114,861	14,507
1890–4 ..	52,490	19,238	136,618	12,394
1895–9 ..	57,537	28,650	162,310	17,056
1900–4 ..	65,194	38,072	176,239	15,870

The prices of agricultural produce, though there were marked fluctuations, showed throughout the greater part of this period, until about the middle of the last decade of the nineteenth century, a pronounced downward tendency; thereafter the fall was arrested, and an upward tendency began to manifest itself. There still remained a considerable difference between the various parts of the Empire, largely because of the distance in many cases of the markets from the place of production and the difficulties of transport, in spite of the growth of German railways and canals.[4] The main distributing centre for the grain-producing provinces of Eastern Prussia was Danzig, whilst foreign wheat from Roumania and Southern Russia, as well as from North

[1] *Statistisches Jahrbuch für das deutsche Reich*, p. 14. *Cf.* Troeltsch, p. 25.

[2] *Cf.* Voigt, "Deutschland und die Weltmarkt" (in *Handels- und Machtpolitik*), pp. 154–79.

[3] *British and Foreign Trade and Industry*, pp. 178 and 180.

[4] Troeltsch, pp. 29 and 30.

and South America, entered chiefly at Cologne and Mannheim, by way of the ports of the Low Countries. The level of wheat prices was consequently appreciably lower in the eastern and central parts of Germany than in the west and south.[1]

Thirdly, imports greatly exceeded exports. In the Free Trade period, from 1872 to 1879, the average annual imports were valued at £190,000,000, and the exports at £130,000,000; and although the latter were admittedly under-estimated, there yet remained a considerable excess of imports over exports. After 1879 the statistics were improved, and at first the new protective system acted as a drag. The import trade declined for a time, and in 1880 exports were slightly in excess of imports. From then till 1888 the two were in practical equilibrium, but after 1888 and the inclusion of the Hanse towns, the turn came, and the following table shows the "special trade" of Germany between 1890 and 1904:[2]

Period.	Average Annual Value of Imports for Home Consumption.	Average Annual Value of Exports of German Produce.	Average Annual Surplus of Imports over Exports.
	Million £.	Million £.	Million £.
1890–4	198·9	152·5	46·4
1895–9	232·8	181·3	51·5
1900–4	287·0	235·8	51·4

During the same period there was a marked increase in the import of manufactured articles. The following table gives the figures for the fifteen years from 1890 to 1904:[3]

[1] *Cf.* table in *Statistisches Jahrbuch*, 1909, p. 271.

[2] *British and Foreign Trade and Industry* (1909), p. 63. The amount of German capital invested abroad was estimated in 1905 at from £1,300,000,000 to £1,500,000,000.—Professor Arndt, in *The Statist*, October 14, 1905; and *cf. Die Entwicklung der deutschen Seeinteressen*, published by the German Admiralty, 1905 (pp. 135–200).

[3] *British and Foreign Trade and Industry* (1909), p. 63.

Period.	Average Annual Value of Imports of Manufactured Goods (*Fabrikate*).
	Million £.
1890–4	44·0
1895–9	49·1
1900–4	57·0

It should be added that German industry has been characterised more than that of any other country, with the exception of the United States, by the rise of trusts, or by their practical equivalent in economic effect, the Kartels, which were very numerous, and, though strongest in the coal and iron industries, gradually extended themselves over a very large part of the whole range of German industry. "They are combinations for maintaining prices (and more or less for the joint marketing of the produce) by a number of concerns which retain their own independence as producers.[1] And these Kartels have notoriously sought to relieve the German market in times of depression by sending abroad below the domestic price. . . . The Kartels have, however, advanced considerably beyond the point of lower foreign prices; they have devised a plan whereby export is assisted and encouraged by the grant of bonuses by the several syndicates to their members and customers. This plan appears to have been first introduced in 1891, and it would seem to have been more systematically established in 1897. In the period of expanding trade which soon followed, it was quite unnecessary, but in 1901 the reaction again came."[2] Finally, it must be

[1] It is in this respect that the Kartels chiefly differ from the American trusts.

[2] W. J. Ashley, *The Tariff Problem*, pp. 120–1. For a detailed description of the organisation and working of the Kartels, see Raffalovich, *Trusts, Cartels et Syndicats*, and the Consular Reports for the Frankfurt District, 1903, 1906, and 1908. On one special feature of the Kartels, see Morgenroth, *Die Exportpolitik der Kartelle*. Much useful information is contained in the Report of the Imperial German Commission on Kartels, and in the monthly review entitled "*Kartell-Rundschau.*"

pointed out that neither the tariff nor the Kartels (though it is one of the commonest claims of the latter—and of the American trusts—that they can regulate industry and give it a more equable course) have been able to guard Germany against recurring periods of reaction, such as that through which the country passed between 1901 and 1903, and the more pronounced depression of 1908.[1]

It has already been remarked that the closing years of the nineteenth century witnessed the revival of protectionist movements, arising chiefly amongst the agrarians. We have observed that after 1891 there was a somewhat rapid decline in the price of agricultural produce, particularly grain. This was due in part to the effects of the treaties, which opened the German market more than before to foreign grain, and partly to the good harvests. The agricultural party ascribed the fall solely to the tariffs, and until 1896–7 their great cry was the fall of prices;[2] but then a turn came. The table on p. 85 illustrates the movement of prices from 1894 to 1903. It will be seen that there was a pronounced rise between 1894 and 1898.[3]

After about 1896 they raised the new cry of "Leutenot," declaring that the rapid development of industry was denuding the land of labourers, and that the agricultural interest was suffering from low prices because of the reciprocity treaties made for the sake of the industrial exporters, and at the same time was hampered by the

[1] The nature and extent of the first of these depressions, which alone falls within the period under consideration in this chapter, have been fully examined in the volumes published (1903 *seq.*) by the *Verein für Sozialpolitik* under the title *Die Störungen in deutschen Wirtschaftsleben wahrend der Jahre* 1900 *ff.* The extent and duration of the depression varied with the different industries (it seems to have been most pronounced in the engineering and electrical industries, where there were for a time large reductions in the numbers employed, whilst in the cotton and linen industries recourse was had only to short time), and some were practically unaffected. In no case does an industry appear to have received a serious set-back.

[2] Lotz, ii. p. 134.

[3] *British and Foreign Trade and Industry* (1909), pp. 195, 197, 200, and 202. *Cf.* Dietzel, p. 369.

withdrawal of labourers from the rural districts, which increased the agricultural cost of production. The agrarian party therefore denounced the "export orgy," and the policy which furthered the exportation of manufactured articles by the importation of agricultural produce. They put forward a demand for duties protecting all branches of agriculture—grain, cattle, garden products, etc.[1]

AVERAGE WHOLESALE PRICES.

Year.	Wheat (per Imperial Quarter).		Rye (per Cwt.).		Wheat Flour per Cwt.).	Barley (per Imperial Quarter).
	Prussia.	Bavaria.	Prussia.	Bavaria.	Cologne.	Baden.
	s. d.	s. d.	s. d.	s. d.	s. d.	s. d.
1894	28 11	30 5	5 11	6 1	9 7	24 9
1895	30 0	32 4	6 1	6 6	10 1	25 0
1896	32 9	35 9	6 1	6 6	10 8	26 11
1897	35 5	40 5	6 4	7 4	12 0	27 7
1898	39 10	42 6	7 3	7 6	13 2	30 4
1899	33 2	36 5	7 2	8 4	11 1	28 11
1900	32 1	35 7	7 2	7 9	10 11	27 9
1901	34 8	37 8	7 1	7 8	11 0	27 4
1902	35 2	37 1	7 2	7 5	10 10	27 3
1903	33 2	35 10	6 7	7 4	10 10	27 1

Moreover, the time for the renewal of the treaties was approaching, and it became necessary for the Government to prepare for negotiations. It proposed to do so by the adoption of a new tariff which should contain higher rates of duty, and should also be much more specialised and detailed than the tariff of 1879. It believed that the higher the rates of the tariff, the better would be the terms which could be obtained from foreign nations, and also that it was desirable to introduce greater specialisation into the tariff schedules in order to enable reductions to be made on any one article, without this involving reductions on a number of others.[2] The

[1] Dietzel, pp. 370–3; *cf.* Lotz, ii. p. 137.

[2] "It frequently happens that another nation lays stress on securing a reduction of rates on certain specialities, and is disposed to pay for this concession with one equally advantageous to us. But if now the Customs Act be made up too summarily, and these

basis of the scheme was to be the simultaneous protection both of agriculture and manufactures; but the strong agrarian movement, which had been going on since 1893 and found its representation in the *Bund der Landwirte*, directed the new policy mainly in the interests of the large landowners. The new Tariff Bill introduced by the Imperial Government in 1901 was consequently the subject of a fierce and protracted Parliamentary conflict, and was not finally enacted until December, 1902. In view of the proposed negotiations for the renewal, with modifications, of the commercial treaties, it was not, however, to come into force until such time as the Government should appoint.

The tariff so enacted was the "general tariff"; that is to say, the rates of duty which it contained were to be levied on goods coming from all countries which should not conclude treaties with the German Empire providing for reciprocal reductions of duties, or should not, by virtue of the "most favoured nation" clause in any treaty, be admitted to the enjoyment of such reductions as Germany might make in the new treaties. The result of the extension of the reductions made in favour of any one country to all the other contracting powers by the "most favoured nation" clause would be to create a scale of duties—the "conventional tariff"—which would be lower than the "general tariff." But there was one important provision, which was the main cause of the prolonged conflict; whilst in respect to all other commodities the reductions which might be made in the treaties to be negotiated with other Powers were un-

---

specialities are bunched together with many other articles under one head, we must lower the rate on the whole group for the sake of one article. The result of that would be that third nations, having the advantage of 'most favoured nation' clauses, would profit by the reduction of the duties on the other commodities included in the same group, without having to pay an equivalent of their own therefor. The more specialised the Customs Act, the more compensation material there would be for treaties; and the more general, the less there would be" (Dietzel, p. 376, summarising the argument of the Imperial Minister of the Interior).

limited, as regards rye, wheat and spelt, malting barley, and oats, there was in each case a specified minimum below which reductions might not be made. These minimum rates were considerably higher than the old treaty tariff rates, as appears from the following table:

	Rye.	Wheat and Spelt.	Malting Barley.	Oats.
	s. d.	s. d.	s. d.	s. d
Rates of Duty per Cwt. as fixed by the Treaties of 1892	1 9	1 9	1 0	1 4¾
Minimum Rates prescribed by Law of 1902	2 6	2 6	2 0	2 6

On this the remarks of a German critic may be quoted: "These four tariff classes form 7 per cent. of our total imports. If, however, we consider these four in relation only to the amount of imports liable to duties—as must be done, since we can consider only those articles which can be used for concessions—they form one-seventh of the import; and if we exclude further all colonial produce liable to duty and some other articles which are of no use in negotiations with the treaty states . . . we perceive how much is lost to us, so far as negotiations are concerned, by the fixing of the minimum tariff for grain."[1] There were increases on other agricultural produce (maize, dead meat, live cattle, sheep and pigs), but no minima were fixed for these.

As regards the duties on manufactured goods, the principles of the new tariff were (1) "the maintenance of the existing exemption of raw materials so far as these are not produced at all in Germany, or are only produced in insufficient quantity or of inferior quality"; (2) the imposition on semi-manufactured goods intended to be worked up for export of only such rates of duty as would not interfere with the export trade; (3) the increase of the duties on manufactured goods.[2] Thus raw materials, or

[1] Schacht, in Schmoller's *Jahrbuch*, 1902, part ii. p. 342.
[2] Schacht, p. 309.

materials only in the early stages of manufacture, were to be admitted free or at low rates; for example, raw silk and single-twisted silk were to be exempt from duty, the duty on silk yarn was reduced by nearly two-thirds, the duties on woollen and cotton yarn and cotton thread either remained at the old level or were reduced. The duties on goods in a more advanced stage of preparation and on finished goods were increased; thus the rate on double-twisted silk was increased 43 per cent., on silk tissues imported in the piece the increase was 50 per cent., and on silk tissues finished off the duty was doubled. On woollen and half-woollen goods there were increases of from 15 to 30 per cent., on cotton manufactures from 57 to 80 per cent., on leather goods 50 to 100 per cent.[1] The rates on all kinds of iron were advanced considerably, as also on tools and all manner of machinery, with an elaborate reclassification. Of the general tariff as a whole the critic above quoted has pointed out that its main tendencies were towards the increase of duties on agricultural produce generally, and also towards the raising of the cost of half-finished goods. There was also a higher taxation of many manufactured goods, on the assumption that the greater the amount of labour expended on a particular commodity, the higher should it be taxed. These principles, he added, were due to a complete misunderstanding of the productive power of Germany; the tariff proposals would promote the pro duction of grain and of half-finished goods, but would harm small farming and manufactures. Yet these latter were the most important factors in the economic life of modern Germany. The main economic problem was the question of population, and work could be provided for the rapidly increasing numbers not by the "extensive" industries of grain-growing and the manufacture of half-finished goods, but by the "intensive" industries of small farming and the manufacture of finished goods. It was essential, then, that nothing should be done to hamper

[1] *Germany—New General Customs Tariff* (Board of Trade, 1903).

German industry in any way; " we dare not adopt a policy which makes competition more difficult for us by increasing the cost of raw and semi-manufactured materials, and reduces our labourers' strength by raising the price of the necessaries of life. But that is the policy of the tariff, and thereby it not only misunderstands the real foundations of German economic life, but lays a direct burden upon the lower classes."[1] And Professor Schmoller, whilst not agreeing in all points with his contributor, concurred with Dr. Schacht in the opinion that the officials entrusted with the preparation of the tariff were much too protectionist, and far too much inclined to consider every new duty as a sign of progress; and he agreed also that those interests which were well organised and best represented had exercised an unduly great influence upon the shaping of the tariff.[2] He still held, however, that a moderate protection for agriculture, and even a slight increase of some of the agricultural duties, was desirable, and hoped that the tariff, in spite of defects, might, in the hands of a skilful diplomacy, offer adequate opportunities for negotiations with foreign Powers.

The opposition to the tariff proposals, which, as already indicated, was concentrated mainly upon the minimum rates of duty upon grain, came in part from the industrial and mercantile interests, but in part also from the smaller agriculturists, who were interested chiefly—though not entirely—in cattle-rearing, dairy-farming and the production of crops other than grain; and was based upon anticipations as to the probable course of the treaty negotiations. Of the countries with which treaties were to be attempted, several of the more important—Russia, Roumania, Austria-Hungary, Switzerland—would be interested primarily in the reduction of the duties upon agricultural products; and Russia and Roumania would find that their principal article of export—grain—was to be subjected inevitably to higher rates of duty than before. Hence the smaller agriculturists (*Nebenagrarien*) feared that reductions of duty in those countries, such as

[1] Schacht, p. 351. [2] Footnote to Schacht, p. 353.

were desired in the interest of the German export trade in manufactured goods, would be obtained only at the price of the reduction of the German duties on those agricultural products in which they were mainly interested, since the great landowners (the *Hauptagrarien*) were secured by the minimum rates. The manufacturers and exporters, on their side, feared the increased cost of production which they anticipated might arise from an advance in the cost of foodstuffs; believed that the higher minimum duties on grain would hinder the attempt of the German Government to secure reductions of foreign duties on German manufactured goods, and would in particular restrict the trade with Russia and Roumania; and contemplated with some alarm the prospect that the Government might be unable to conclude the treaties by means of the agricultural duties alone, and so, to escape tariff wars, would be forced to lower some at least of the duties on manufactured goods also. Moreover, foreign nations, particularly Austria, Russia, and Switzerland, were preparing for the negotiations by devising new tariffs with increased rates of duty. The task which the German Government had to face was consequently full of difficulty both at home and abroad.

CHAPTER VIII

THE ECONOMISTS AND THE NEW TARIFF POLICY[1]

In the long controversy which raged during the preparation of the tariff and the passage of the law through the Reichstag, it was natural that the economists should play a very conspicuous part, and they may be divided into three main groups. The thoroughgoing Protectionists were so mainly in the interest of agriculture; they approached the subject from different standpoints, but they were represented chiefly by Professor Adolph Wagner. Then there was what may be called the Middle School, led by Professor Schmoller; and finally there was a small Free Trade group, whose most conspicuous member was Professor Brentano of Munich.

The agrarian group were all in favour of increased duties on agricultural produce in order to help the landowners and farmers, whose complaints, as we have seen, have been similar to those with which we are familiar in Great Britain. But it is important to observe that scarcely any amongst them cared to base their arguments solely on the economic distress of the agrarian interests. They all advanced other considerations, and their general position was summed up in a dictum of their chief economic representative, Professor Wagner: "An adequate protection for agriculture, higher than the present, would be in

[1] It has been thought undesirable to modify the sketch given in this chapter of economic discussion in Germany at the time of the tariff legislation of 1902, and it appears therefore substantially as in the first (1904) edition of this book, though some notes have been added. In reading it, the date of the discussion (1901–3) must be borne constantly in mind.

the general interest of the whole community, even if by its means the industrial development of the state and possibly also the growth of population should be, not entirely stopped, but certainly slackened, in the general interests of the workers and of the economic organisation of Germany. The maintenance of a capable German agriculture means the maintenance of the German people now and for the future."[1] The argument on which this conclusion is based is elaborated in Professor Wagner's book entitled *Agrar- und Industriestaat*, and an attempt must be made here to indicate its chief propositions. There was a group of extreme agricultural Protectionists, but apparently they found it convenient to accept Wagner's arguments, at least for the present. Professor Wagner viewed with the greatest anxiety what he regarded as the excessive industrialisation of Germany, and his views on this matter were shared by many others, such as Professor Oldenburg and Professor Pohle (Frankfurt).[2] The maintenance of the industrial state presupposes three conditions: (1) that other countries are willing and able to supply agricultural products, both as food and raw materials, cheaply; (2) that these supplies can be safely conveyed to the industrial state; and (3) that the manufactured goods of that state can be assured of an adequate market in the countries which supply the food and raw material.[3] And in regard to all three of these necessary conditions there were believed to be considerable dangers. In the first place, several countries, hitherto content to remain in the agricultural stage of development, are turning their attention to industry; thus not merely is the United States (on which Great Britain, for example, had so long depended for the greater part of its food supply) becoming preponderatingly industrial, but Russia, Canada, Australia, Italy, and Roumania are all striving to make themselves into industrial communities. And

[1] Wagner, *Agrar- und Industriestaat*, 2nd ed., pp. 1, 2.

[2] See the Report of Professor Pohle, and the speech of Professor Oldenburg in the *Verhandlungen des Vereins für Sozialpolitik*, vol. xcviii., pp. 183 *seq.* and 230 *seq.*

[3] Wagner, *loc. cit.*, pp. 143 *seq.*

this means not only that they will sooner or later consume most of their own supplies of raw material (it is, for instance, inevitable that the United States should itself ultimately make use of the greater part of its production of raw cotton), but that further, as these states become more industrial their populations will greatly increase, and they will make greater demands on their own food supplies. They will thus tend to use for their own purposes most of their production of food and raw material; they will have less to export, and the older industrial states, which have based their organisation entirely on the assumption that these supplies are permanent, will find themselves hopelessly crippled. Secondly, even if the supply continue, it will always be liable to be cut in time of war. To guard against this as much as possible, the industrial nations find themselves bound to incur ever-increasing expenditures on naval armaments, and a growing burden of taxation.[1] Thus between 1898-9 and 1903–4, the expenditure on the German navy advanced from six million pounds to ten and a half million pounds, and the British expenditure from twenty-four millions to thirty-five millions. And thirdly, even though the supplies of food and raw material continue quite unchecked, the growth of industrial competition on the one hand, and the attempt of various nations to supply their own industrial wants on the other hand, must make it ever more difficult for a manufacturing nation to dispose of its manufactured goods abroad, except by constantly cutting down its prices. These general propositions Professor Wagner supported by an elaborate examination of the sources of the German supply of food and raw material, illustrating its growing dependence on foreign countries; and by a most detailed investigation of the movement during the previous forty years of the British export industry, which, he held, was tending to become almost stationary, or at any rate to expand only at the

[1] Hence the strong advocacy of a powerful German navy by a group of economists in *Handels- und Machtpolitik* (ed. Schmoller Sering and Wagner).

cost of very great efforts. He regarded the whole foundation of the industrial state in the form which it has taken in Great Britain, and which it seemed likely to assume in Germany, as altogether unsound. So also Professor Pohle wrote: "The rule of the system of industry for export cannot long endure. That system, as Roscher already recognised, contains an element truly of temporary brilliancy, but of permanent outward and inward peril. It is an idle dream to believe that the economic future of Germany can be permanently based on the production of industrial commodities for foreign nations."[1]

The remedy was to make Germany as independent as possible of foreign nations. Not that foreign trade should be cut off, but attention must be paid more to the balance between the manufacturing and agricultural interests of Germany.[2] Production for the home market must be the primary consideration; the condition of agriculture must be improved before the decline has gone so far as to be irremediable, the agricultural population recruited, and the rush to the towns checked. This might mean a slackening in the rate of the increase of the population, but that would not be unwelcome. The best way to attain these ends was to give agriculture the stimulus of greater protection. "It is not to be denied that, like all the great things which a nation needs—armaments, civil administration, justice, a system of education, arrangements for the care of the economic interests of the community, etc.—so also the maintenance of the permanent economic and numerical strength of the nation in an adequate and sturdy agrarian population requires sacrifices. But we believe these sacrifices, in this case as in the others we have named, are necessary for that higher object which we have in view."[3] And Professor Wagner, whilst recognising that the increased duties which he advocated on the importation of agricultural produce might, and very possibly would, mean an increase in the cost of living to the lower classes of the community,

[1] Pohle, *Deutschland am Scheidewege*, p. 10.
[2] Wagner, *loc. cit.*, pp. 42 and 43. [3] Wagner, *loc. cit.*, p. 36.

yet held that compensation could be given for this by employing the proceeds of the new duties in further State grants to the various pension funds.[1] Other economists, sharing the same general opinions, took the same line in regard to the union of tariff legislation and social reform; " it appears to be beyond dispute that increased duties on grain would result in higher prices for bread, and therefore the working-class population, amongst whom the expenditure on foodstuffs may amount to 75 per cent. of their income (whilst in the case of the most prosperous class of the community the amount may fall to 20 per cent.), must in every case, as Sering claims, receive an equivalent compensation by the extension of social legislation and the reform of the imperial taxes with more attention to social needs (*im sozialem Sinne*)."[2]

We may take the criticism of these last points first. As Professor Lotz has pointed out,[3] Wagner failed to demonstrate that higher protective duties are the sole means of improving agriculture and checking the decline of the agricultural population. The fact that in spite of their existing protection the German landowners were in a bad way, was partly at least to be ascribed to their own defects, to their lack of enterprise, their want of money, and consequent disinclination and inability to make improvements. The value of agriculture to the national life is, no doubt, considerable; but it would be extremely hard to demonstrate that a reduction in the number of industrial workers and an increase in the number of the peasantry and rural labourers would tend to raise the general level of civilisation in the community. So Conrad wrote: " There can be no doubt that an increase of the

[1] It may be noted that under Section 15 of the Tariff Act the yield of duties on certain commodities (including wheat and rye) in excess of the average yield of the duties on the same commodities in the years 1898–1903 was to be applied to the establishment of a pension fund for widows and orphans, or, failing the establishment of such a fund, to the assistance of the existing invalidity funds.

[2] Von Halle, *Volks- und Seewirtschaft*, p. 11.

[3] *Verhandlungen des Vereins für Sozialpolitik*, vol. xcviii. p. 121 *seq*.

well-being at home, and the remunerative employment of the growing population with which we have to deal, can only be expected from industry and commerce. And consequently, it is beyond dispute that our tariff policy must have in view chiefly their interests."[1] And, as Lotz again pointed out, while it is desirable to lessen the pressure upon the towns and to remove large masses of people from conditions which do not make for physical efficiency, there are ways of doing this without taking them back to agriculture. It is certain that the development of means of transport and transit will, before very long, enable Great Britain and Germany to carry out, if they choose to do so, great schemes of industrial redistribution which will spread the workers over larger districts, and put an end to much of that density of population in limited areas, which is at present one of the most painful characteristics of our industrial societies. As to the growth of population, it was argued by Wagner's opponents that for Germany, situated as she was, and compelled to be a great military power, it was essential to have as large a population as possible, and that such a population can be maintained only by persisting in the policy which she had so successfully followed, the policy of industrialism; and Wagner's reply, that the strength of a population does not depend so much on its numbers as on its efficiency, hardly meets the case. In regard to the corn duties, Wagner did not carry even all the protectionist economists with him; Schmoller was not particularly favourable to any increase (unless it would not unduly raise the cost of living to the workers), whilst Conrad was decidedly hostile. The latter was in favour only of the raising of the duties on cattle and cattle products; apparently he held that the grain duties had even harmed the landowners, by rendering them less awake to the need of improvement in their methods.[2] Moreover,

[1] Conrad, *Jahrbücher*, February, 1902, p. 189.

[2] Conrad, "Die Stellung der Landwirtschaftlichen Zölle" (*Verein für Sozialpolitik*, vol. xc.). *Cf.* Von Halle, *Volks- und Seewirthschaft*, pp. 10–13: "If they regard a higher duty on grain as a panacea . . . the result for the agricultural classes of East

there is not wanting evidence that the agrarian protective duties affected the cost of living in Germany disadvantageously. The following table shows the average prices of wheat in England and Prussia for quinquennial periods from 1871 to 1905:[1]

Period.	Average Price of Wheat per Imperial Quarter.		Prussian Price less or more than English.
	England.	Prussia.	
	s. d.	s. d.	s. d.
1871–5	54 8	50 4	−4 4
1876–80	47 6	45 3	−2 3
1881–5	40 1	40 7	+0 6
1886–90	31 5	37 3	+5 10
1891–5	27 11	35 11	+8 0
1896–1900	28 7	34 8	+6 1
1901–5	27 11	35 2	+7 3

It will be seen that since the establishment of the tariff policy inaugurated by Bismarck, the Prussian prices had become much higher than the English. And on the question of food prices in general it was remarked in 1903 that

Germany will be as fatal as the clinging to an out-of-date economic system was, fifty years earlier, to the planters of the southern states of the American Union; for the whole state it would, in view of the geographical position of Germany and international relations, be even more fatal."

Cf. also Naumann, *Mittel-Europa*, 1915 (English translation), pp. 226–7: "I maintain that the increase in German agricultural production has not been essentially affected by the new tariff which came into force on April, 1906, but would, on the whole, have gone its own way upward even if the old Caprivi duties had been retained. The rise in price was very desirable in the individualistic economic interests of those concerned, but it has ushered in no new epoch from the standpoint of national economics. There has been a relatively small increase in the area harvested, but the product per hectare has kept on its previous line, which was already rising (with variations according to the year's harvest). The same is true of cattle-raising, only here it is allowable to think that our stock of cattle available at the beginning of the war might have been still greater under a system of cheaper fodder imports, without our own production of fodder being any less in consequence than it is at present. Comparison with duty-free agriculture in Switzerland, Belgium, Holland, and Denmark shows that the improvement is at least as great in the duty-free countries as in those with protective tariffs."

[1] *British and Foreign Trade and Industry* (1909), pp. 194–5. The English prices are the "Gazette Averages"; the Prussian prices are mean market prices. *Cf.* Conrad, *loc. cit.*, p. 125.

"there is in Germany no longer anything said about the great cheapness of food" (as compared with other countries). "Whilst Germany had up to the seventies cheaper food than France and England, to-day in the south-west of Germany it is not only dearer than in Free Trade England, but sometimes even dearer than in France, though that country has a higher tariff on wheat than Germany, and much dearer than in America."[1] The sharp rise in prices (very conspicuous in the case of meat) which occurred in 1905 and 1906, still further emphasised the change.

The arguments as to the bases of the industrial state are more serious, but on the whole not more convincing. After all, it is possible to take too long a view, and to carry speculation too far. It may be perfectly true that a time will come when the whole food supply of the world will be consumed by the countries that produce it—that is to say, that unless some of the now chiefly industrial states return in some degree to agriculture, the supply of foodstuffs will not keep pace with the world's demand. But this prospect will scarcely seem very near to those who have been told so much of the unlimited resources of Canada, who remember the almost untouched possibilities of Argentina and Uruguay and other South American states, of Egypt and Northern Africa, of Russia and Siberia (under an intelligent economic policy), of Asia Minor and Mesopotamia.[2] Similarly, in regard to the exhaustion of raw material, it is, of course, possible that ultimately the United States will consume all its own cotton. But there are great possibilities of the production of cotton in other lands, as yet almost undeveloped, as, for example, in the British possessions

[1] Weile, *Der Einfluss der Deutschen Schutzzollpolitik auf die Entwicklung der Industrie und Handwerkschaft*, p. 22. For a detailed comparison of the relative cost of living for working-class families in the two countries, so far as it can be statistically measured, and subject to definite limitations, see the Board of Trade Report on the *Cost of Living in German Towns* (1908).

[2] *Cf.* Sir R. H. Rew's remarks on the relative growth of the world's population and wheat supply in *Agricultural Statistics for* 1908, vol. xlvii., part iv., pp. 360–1.

in Africa.[1] It must be a very long time before the alarming condition of things which Professor Wagner foresees is realised, and, in any case, that condition can only come about very gradually, and as it comes there will be a gradual transference back to agriculture of the labour for which industry cannot provide employment.[2] As to the question of markets for manufactured products, there is no evidence that they are declining. As a matter of fact, they are increasing even in protected countries. If we take Germany herself, the growth of her export trade meant a corresponding growth in her import trade, and this increase was not merely of imports of food and raw materials, but in manufactured goods also. As civilisation advances with the development of the industrial state, the standard of life rises, the wants of the community increase, commodities which were once luxuries come to be regarded as necessaries, and, in spite of tariffs, they are imported from abroad. Wagner recognised that this would always be the case, but seemed hardly to realise the extent of the process. The following table sets out the movement of the import of manufactured goods into certain European countries during the period 1892–1911:[3]

Country.	Average Annual Value of Imports of Manufactured Goods for Home Consumption.			
	1892-6.	1897-1901.	1902-6.	1907-11.
	Million £.	Million £.	Million £.	Million £.
Russia	12·3	19·7	19·4	31·4
German Empire ..	43·8	53·0	64·2	87·1
Holland	24·0	30·2	38·8	47·7
France	23·4	29·8	34·4	51·2
Switzerland ..	10·9	13·9	16·7	22·1
Italy	10·2	12·5	18·2	31·8
Austria-Hungary	16·6	19·0	22·9	30·8

[1] *Cf.* Report to the Board of Trade of the (British) Empire Cotton-Growing Committee, 1920.

[2] *Cf.*, for the above criticism of Wagner and for further discussion of the problem, Dietzel, "The German Tariff Controversy," in the *Q. J. Economics*, May, 1903, especially pp. 405 *seq.;* and Brentano, *Die Schrecken des überwiegenden Industriestaats.*

[3] *Statistical Abstracts for the Principal and Other Foreign Countries*, 1908, pp. 81–9, and 1914, pp. 99–108.

"Why should the result in the future be any different? Why should the decline of our export industries, taken as a whole, set in, in case Russia, Canada, Central and South America, Eastern Asia, Cape Colony, and Australia should develop manufactures at some future time? If to-day a more extensive division of labour is taking place within the industrial realm, and a comprehensive interchange of products between countries like England, France, and Germany (that is lands, all of which lie in the temperate zone, all on about the same plane of social and economic development), is it not probable that such a division of labour and such intercourse will not only continue, but extend even further, when it includes not only the industrial states of to-day on the one side, but Russia and others on the other side? For between the former and the latter there is a much greater diversity of natural as well as social conditions than exists between England, France, and Germany."[1] And the number of countries which can ever become largely industrial is comparatively limited, and in the others, notably the tropical and semi-tropical countries, the market for manufactured goods will always be very large, and mostly free from home competition. It is true that competition in those markets will become more and more keen, but this simply means that no one country is likely to have in the future such a complete industrial predominance as Great Britain used to enjoy.

There is one other point in Professor Wagner's argument which should be noted. The English theory of international trade as expounded by Torrens, Ricardo and Mill has never had much influence amongst continental economists, and Wagner attacks it on the ground that the greatest relative advantage, which it presupposes as the reason why a country should devote itself to the production of a particular commodity or group of commodities, may work extremely badly for the community as a whole. It may mean that a country will find itself limited to the production of one commodity only,

[1] Dietzel, *loc. cit.*, p. 403.

and hence will lose all the advantages which come from the possession of diverse industries and a variety of technical skill; or it may mean that a country will be compelled to devote itself more and more to the production of commodities in which its advantage over its competitors is of the worst kind, namely, cheapness arising not from efficiency of method or abundance of materials, but from ill-paid and sweated labour.[1] As to the first of these alternatives, it can only be said that there is no evidence in any industrial country of any such process taking place to any appreciable extent; but on the contrary, new industries requiring great technical skill are rising in all industrial communities. The second point will be familiar to English readers in Mr. and Mrs. Webb's work on *Industrial Democracy*. They will remember that in Appendix II. of that work this argument against Free Trade—that it may, according to that pure theory of international trade which has been adopted by most British economists, lead to the dependence of this country on sweated and ill-paid industries—is elaborately stated; but they will remember also the contention that no system of protection would remedy this, but that safeguards against it must be sought elsewhere.[2] The admitted truth of the

[1] Wagner, *loc. cit.*, pp. 32 *seq.* *Cf.* Pohle, p. 218: "In regard to a great part of this industry (the manufacture of clothing) we are entitled to say that Germany's ruling position in the world-market can be maintained only at the expense of the workers' standard of living. Of the conditions of work which prevail in that industry we may fairly use the English expression that wages are only enough to keep 'body and soul together,' and that the hours of labour are as many as the hours of the day. In a great part of these branches of industry home employment is still prodominant. The miserable condition of the home workers of the Erzegebirge, the Fichtelgebirge, the Thuringian Forest, and other German hill districts, is well known; and all these work largely, if not chiefly, for export. There are still worse conditions ruling among the home industries of the towns, and particularly in the different branches of the clothing trade."

[2] "But though the existence of parasitic trades knocks the bottom out of the argument for *laisser faire*, it adds no weight to the case for a protective tariff. . . . The advocate of a protective tariff aims at excluding imports; the opponent of 'sweating,' on the other hand, sees with regret the rapid growth of par-

facts alleged only implies the necessity of State action to put an end to the conditions which render "parasitic industries" possible; it is difficult to see how any policy, which aims simply at restraining the growth of industry and at stimulating the development of agriculture, would be likely to remedy the evil.

We pass now to the Middle School, which, in the main, followed the lead of Professor Schmoller. With the general attitude of that group towards Free Trade and Protection we are already familiar;[1] to them "the tariff problem admits of only relative solution"—all depends on the particular conditions of time and place. They were not hostile to Free Trade, but they believed it to be only one of various policies to be applied according to circumstances. Neither were they Protectionists; in fact, their advocacy of the use of tariffs for the purposes of promoting international exchange was incompatible with any doctrine of high Protection. Professor Schmoller held that for the purposes of negotiation agrarian and industrial duties were alike necessary, and believing that agriculture was suffering, he would encourage cattle-rearing by duties on foreign cattle and meat, but would support duties on bread stuffs only when they did not raise the price of bread unduly—

---

ticular exports, which imply the extension within the country of its most highly subsidised or most parasitic industries. Hence, whatever ingenious arguments may be found in favour of a protective tariff, such a remedy fails altogether to cope with this particular evil. If the expansion of the industries which England pursues to the greatest economic advantage—say, for instance, coal-mining and shipbuilding, textile manufacture and machine-making—is being checked, this is not because coal and ships, textiles and machinery, are being imported into England from abroad, but because other less advantageous industries within England itself, by reason of being favoured with some kind of bounty, have secured the use of some of the nation's brains and capital, and some of its export trade. . . . In short, the absolute exclusion by each country of the imports competing with its own products would not, any more than Free Trade itself, prevent the expansion within the country of those industries which afforded to its wage-earner the worst conditions of employment" (Webb, *Industrial Democracy*, ed. 1897, ii. pp. 865–6).

[1] See above, Chapter V.

whatever that qualification might mean. Agriculture was, in fact, to be maintained and developed by duties so arranged as to raise prices without increasing greatly the cost of living, and without removing the pressure which low prices put upon the farmers to reduce their cost of production by improvements in method.[1] It is not apparent that Professor Schmoller regarded this ideal as being in any way attainable; and in fact to him the tariff was important chiefly as a weapon. "I believe that we may draw this lesson from history, that all protective movements are closely connected with national sentiment, strivings after international authority, efforts towards the balance of power, and therefore will continue to exist so long as amongst the fully developed states there are others striving after economic development, and so long as the peoples for economic purposes have need of every weapon which stands ready for their use."[2] He pointed out that the increases of the tariff in the eighties were used by Bismarck in this way, and that the Bismarckian idea had now been taken up again. But the negotiation tariff was not to be a high protective tariff; it was supported by him only in order to give Germany a better position in commercial negotiations. Schmoller held that the "neo-mercantilism" of the early years of the twentieth century had arisen out of the successful nationalist movements of the preceding century and was based not on List's theory of "educational

[1] "Man wird für Deutschland in der Agrarzöllfrage sagen müssen: wir wollen möglichst unsere Landwirtschaft erhalten, die Masse der selbstwirtschaftenden Grundeigentümer und Pächter vor dem Bankerott schützen; wir müssen als Kompromiss die Zollhöhe so bemessen, das ohne starke Verteuerung der Lebensmittel und ohne Erhöhung der Grundrente doch die Landwirte bestehen können, und zugleich durch den bleibenden Preisdruck ein gewisser Impuls erhalten bleibe, durch technische Fortschritte besser und mehr zu produzieren. Wir werden am leichtesten eine solche Zollpolitik rechtfertigen können, wenn die Regierung durch starke bäuerliche Kolonisation zeigt, dass die Zollerhöhung nicht wesentlich im Dienste der reichen Grossgrundbesitzer geschieht" (Schmoller, *Grundriss*, ii. p. 646).

[2] *Verhandlungen des Vereins für Sozialpolitik*, 1902, p. 265. This and the following quotations are from Schmoller's speech, pp. 264–71.

tariffs" (*i.e.*, the infant industries doctrine), but on the desire to possess an "international weapon" (Machtmittel). "The new period of Protection, this neomercantilism, has come, not because the theorists and statesmen were incapable of understanding the lofty arguments of Free Trade, not because everywhere some monopolists and large manufacturers control the Government, but out of natural nationalist tendencies, particularly in those countries with the most liberal and democratic constitutions. It is based not alone or even chiefly on the doctrine of 'educational tariffs,' but arises out of an instinctive, rather than reasoned, motive that the tariffs are an international weapon which, skilfully employed, can be of the utmost use." A strong tariff was particularly needed to enable Germany to fight the extreme protectionist policy of Russia and the United States. These views were shared by a very considerable number of the younger German economists, the most distinguished, perhaps, being Dr. Schuhmacher, head of the great Commercial High School at Cologne.[1]

But this policy of tariffs to be employed as a means of fighting other nations which pursue a policy of exclusion, has certain serious dangers. We have seen that the application of the policy against France under the Monarchy of July, against Spain and other powers, did not always produce satisfactory results. The increase of the agricultural duties by Bismarck in the eighties did nothing to promote exchange with Russia for a number of years—in fact, by the admission of the German Government itself, German trade with Russia declined steadily between 1880 and 1890; the conflict with Russia in the nineties was short and sharp, and if, on the whole, in that case the policy was justified, the risks run were very great. Moreover, these tariffs for negotiation are like armaments; when one country increases them, others do the same. As soon as the proposals for the new German tariff were published, Austria and Switzerland

[1] See his long report in the *Verhandlungen des Vereins für Sozialpolitik*, 1902.

proceeded to revise and increase their tariffs, in order to be ready to fight Germany. And further, when protective duties are once granted, whatever the original purpose may have been, a vested interest in their maintenance is created, and the producers so protected are sure to oppose any proposal to reduce the duties in the effort to obtain concessions from foreign Powers. So, as we have seen, the agrarian interest in Germany fiercely opposed any treaty reductions of the grain duties. Schmoller himself recognised that "admittedly this neo-mercantilism frequently overlooks the fact that these weapons may as often be used unskilfully and mistakenly as rightly. The agitation of the interested classes commonly fails to see that excessive protection as a whole does more harm than good. So Russia, the United States, and France have fallen into a high protective system, and sometimes into a commercial policy which, though it aims at international power, is of a worse kind, and hinders the economic development of these countries instead of promoting it." And elsewhere (as has been pointed out) Schmoller observed in regard to the latest German Tariff that the officials who planned it were much too favourable to Protection pure and simple, and that those interested groups, which were well organised and skilfully led, exercised far too great an influence upon it.[1]

Another moderate view was that of Professor Conrad, of Halle. Whilst holding that industrial protection had gone far enough, he would protect agriculture so far as that policy did not involve the depression of the standard of living for the working classes. He would have retained for a time the duties on foodstuffs, but only at their pre-1906 level, because of the critical condition of German agriculture, but the only duties he would increase were such as would promote the development of special branches, such as cattle-rearing and dairy-farming. Professor Sering, of Berlin, favoured the increase of the agricultural duties only in the belief that

[1] Schmoller's *Jahrbuch*, 1902, part ii. p. 353.

they will help agriculture over a transition period in which radical changes must be made, if the condition of the eastern provinces was not to be a serious social menace to Germany. He supported the heightened grain duties only if they were to be regarded as part of a social programme which should include the reduction of duties on such commodities as coffee, petroleum, etc., the gradual prohibition of the invasion of the eastern provinces by the cheaper Slave labour, and the transformation (by a national system of land purchase) of the large estates of the eastern provinces of Prussia into peasant holdings. Unless these steps were to be taken to maintain the peasantry, in whom he believed the strength of Germany to lie, he would be opposed to the new duties.[1]

It will have been noticed that none of the economists quoted were inclined to defend increased duties on manufactured goods; the small Free Trade school naturally demanded their abolition, not at once, but gradually. It recognised fully that educational tariffs may be of use to a country in some periods of its economic development —it was prepared to defend their application in the past—but it was opposed to "maintenance tariffs" (Erhaltungszölle).[2] Such tariffs not only hinder the territorial division of labour, which has the same effect on production as labour-saving machinery; they not only prevent or delay a reduction in the national cost of production and the attainment of "a greater total product from a given expenditure of labour, and a higher national dividend than before,"[3] but they also strengthen the industrial combinations, and enable them to maintain artificial prices in the home market by eliminating competition from outside. This party accepted entirely the industrialisation of Germany, and believed that in the stage of that country's economic development which had been reached by 1901 "the real protection of

[1] *Verhandlungen des Vereins für Sozialpolitik*, 1902, pp. 244–7. None of the conditions had been fulfilled by the time of the commencement of the European War in 1914

[2] Brentano, *Das Freihandelsargument*, p. 15.

[3] Dietzel.

national labour is Free Trade."[1] The material progress of Germany depended on the extension of her manufactures and the completion of the division of labour between the industrial communities of the world. The agricultural duties were to be condemned, since they not only increased the cost of food by limiting the supply from countries where it was produced more cheaply than in Germany, but also by limiting imports reduced the market for German exports, which were chiefly manufactured goods, and so in two ways hampered the growth of industry.[2] They also pointed to the experience of Germany as an illustration of the fact that duties once imposed are much more likely to increase than to decrease. Some of their criticisms of Wagner and his allies have already been indicated; and it is unnecessary to state their more general argument, since it follows the lines of traditional English economic thought.

On the whole, then, so far as German economists in the past have been advocates of Protection, their arguments have been based largely on the political need of securing the development of German economic strength as a basis for political power. When that condition had been realised, the argument of Protection was shifted on to another ground; it was alleged that the development had been too one-sided, and that the comparative neglect of agriculture had become a source of weakness to the Empire. Yet for more than twenty years agriculture had received a large measure of protection, and one is forced to believe that if, in spite of that, it had not held its ground, the reasons were to be sought in causes over which tariffs have little control. As to the other argument for Protection—the need for negotiation tariffs—no economist has shown that the results could not have been obtained in another way; if they are to be used at all, it may be argued that a system of occasional duties —such as that established by the Sugar Convention and employed in the United States under the McKinley Tariff[1]—would be preferable to the imposition of a general

[1] Brentano. [2] *Ibid.*, pp. 16, 17.

tariff on manufactured goods, which might, or might not, be reduced. Tariffs for negotiation are at best, as even their defenders in Germany readily admitted, a dangerous weapon; the policy can only be successful where the country making use of them is not dependent on supplies drawn from, or a large market in, the country against which they are employed, whilst the latter is so dependent upon the former. And, finally, it must be borne in mind that tariffs are, after all, only the crudest form of State action, and are not necessarily the only or most efficient means of promoting the economic well-being of a nation; and the safest lesson to draw from the experience of Germany is the simple fact that changes in tariff policy were only one, and commonly not the most important, amongst the many causes of her economic progress.

[1] See pp. 227-8.

CHAPTER IX

THE COMMERCIAL TREATIES AND THE CONVENTIONAL TARIFF OF 1906—ECONOMIC DEVELOPMENT OF GERMANY TO THE EUROPEAN WAR—CONCLUSION

THE commercial treaties in force with Austria-Hungary, Belgium, Italy, Roumania, Serbia and Switzerland were terminable at one year's notice, on or after the 31st December, 1903, and early in that year, immediately the adoption of the new general tariff law provided a basis, the German Government opened negotiations for the conclusion of new treaties. As already indicated, the task was full of difficulties. The legislative limitation of the extent to which tariff concessions in respect of agricultural produce could be made, and the desire to maintain the "sanitary" restrictions on the importation of live animals, particularly over the eastern borders, tied the hands of the German Government in its dealings with those foreign states whose export interests were mainly agricultural. Another guiding principle was the maintenance or increase of the existing protection given to certain special branches of industry—as, for example, machinery, and this impeded negotiations with a country like Belgium, whose export interests were chiefly industrial.[1] Whilst Belgium and Italy, which also had little or no interest in the export of agricultural produce to Germany, used their existing tariffs as a basis for negotiation, Austria-Hungary, Roumania, Russia and Switzerland had all prepared for the discussion by revising their tariffs and increasing substantially the rates of

[1] Roghé, *Weltwirtschafts-Politik* in *Die Weltwirtschaft* (ed. von Halle), 1906, i. p. 16.

duty on manufactured goods, particularly of those classes in which German trade was interested.[1] It should be added that on both sides material for concession was found not only in the tariff schedules, but also in the customs administrative regulations.[2]

The negotiations with Belgium were brought to a close in June, 1904; in the other cases they were more protracted, but the series was completed with the conclusion of the treaty with Austria-Hungary in January of the following year. The Reichstag gave its approval, with some opposition in the case of the Austro-Hungarian and Russian treaties, in February, and, due notice having been given, the new general tariff, and the "conventional" tariff as determined by the treaties, came into force on the 1st March, 1906. The terms of the treaties were by no means generally approved in Germany, for the commercial and industrial classes were in considerable doubt as to the effect of the new arrangements upon their particular interests; but there was a widespread desire to terminate the long-continued uncertainty, and to return to a definite basis of commercial relations. The new treaties were to continue in force until the end of the year 1917, and after that were to be subject to one year's notice on either side; in the case of the Dual Monarchy, having regard to the nature of the commercial relations between Austria and Hungary, provision was made for a possible termination at the end of 1915.

The treaties provided for reductions in the rates of duty imposed by the general tariff on a large number of classes of commodities; and in many other instances the "general" rates were "conventionalised"—that is, the German Government bound itself not to increase them, or impose duties where none existed, so long as the treaties should remain in force. As regards agricultural produce, Austria-Hungary, Roumania and Serbia ob-

1 The Serbian Tariff had also been revised, and on the whole increased, though not with the same direct purpose.

2 *Cf.* Roghé, *loc. cit.*, pp. 13–15.

tained the reduction or conventionalisation of duties in respect of grain, oil-fruits and seeds, vegetables, fruit and timber; Russia in respect especially[1] of grain and timber; Switzerland of fruit; and Italy of vegetables, fruit, "southern fruits," olives, olive and castor oil, wine and vermouth. With regard to manufactured goods or raw materials, concessions involving the reduction or conventionalisation of the rates of duty contained in the general tariff were made (for example) in respect of chemicals for Austria-Hungary; worsted yarns for Austria-Hungary, Belgium, and Switzerland; silk goods for Switzerland and Italy; woollen tissues, cotton yarns, and manufactures thereof for Switzerland; linen yarns for Austria-Hungary and Belgium; boots and shoes for the same countries and Italy; leather wares for Austria-Hungary, Belgium and Switzerland; gloves for Italy; straw-plait for Switzerland and Italy; furniture for Austria-Hungary; glass and glass-ware, iron and iron alloys, copper and copper alloys for that country and Belgium; some steam-engines and machinery, ventilating machines and pumps for Belgium; knitting machines, electrical appliances, and clocks for Switzerland; toys for Austria-Hungary; and marble, granite, and stone-cutters' work for Italy.[2]

All the treaties contained guarantees of the continuance of reciprocal "most favoured nation" treatment, both as to general facilities for the conduct of trade and commerce in Germany, and as to rates of duty, so that the reductions made by Germany in favour of any one nation were *ipso facto* extended to all the other contracting states, the result being the creation of a conventional or "minimum" tariff, with rates of duty in many instances lower than those of the general tariff, incapable of increase in any case during the existence of the treaties, and applicable to goods coming from any country entitled to

[1] Russia also obtained an increase in the number of swine for immediate slaughter, which might be sent weekly from Russia into Upper Silesia.

[2] Full details are given in the *New German Tariff as Modified by Treaties* (Board of Trade, 1905).

"most favoured nation" treatment in Germany. With regard to the effect of the "most favoured nation" clause, it should, however, be pointed out that its force may be, and often is, diminished by the fact that though reductions of the rates of duty on particular classes of goods made by one country in favour of another are necessarily extended to any third party entitled to "most favoured nation" treatment, they may be actually of little value to this third country, because it does not produce goods of identically the same character. One of the primary purposes of the elaborately detailed classification contained in the German tariff, and of other continental tariffs framed on the same model, is to provide opportunities for the special treatment of particular states without any dangerous extension of such privileges by reason of the "most favoured nation" clause.

The new conventional tariff, under which the great bulk of Germany's foreign trade was thereafter carried on until the outbreak of the great European War of 1914–1918, marked a very distinct advance as compared with the previous tariff in the amount of protection afforded to agriculture, with increases on the principal grains, cattle, sheep, pigs, fresh meat, bacon, animal fats, meal of all kinds, margarine, vermicelli, etc.; but as regards the effect of the changes of the rates of duties upon manufactured goods, it is by no means easy to arrive at any very definite conclusion, especially as the numerous and minute reclassifications render comparison between the old and new rates of duty almost impossible except for the experts of the particular trades affected. On the whole, the general level does not seem to have been seriously raised.[1] Thus there were increases in the rate of duty on candles, varnishes, cotton-yarns (the higher counts), linen and jute yarns (the higher counts), boots

[1] The Board of Trade estimated (*British and Foreign Trade and Industry*, 1903, p. 171) that the General Tariff did not involve any appreciable increase in the burden of duties upon German imports from the United Kingdom.

and shoes, gloves, indiarubber wares, some joiners' wares (window-frames, doors, stairs, mouldings, etc.), upholsterers' furniture, mechanically-prepared pasteboard, wood-pulp, paving-stones and machinery. On the other hand, there were decreases in the rates of duty applicable to timber for industrial purposes, condensed milk, refined petroleum, benzine and gas-oils for motor purposes, caustic soda, liquid extracts of dye-woods, mohair and alpaca yarns, raw silk, certain silk tissues, cotton-yarns (the lower counts), linen and jute yarns (the lower counts), felt hats, some saddlers' wares, straw-plait, lithographic stones, and pig-iron. The duties on tea and cocoa were reduced, but that on roasted coffee was raised; and as regards building materials, there were advances in the duties upon roofing-slates and bricks, but reductions in respect of building timber and fireproof bricks.

It has already been observed that several of the continental states had revised their tariffs and increased the rates of duty leviable thereunder in preparation for the treaty negotiations; and though Germany had ultimately obtained the renewal of the commercial treaties and the recognition of the higher rates upon agricultural produce fixed by the tariff law, she had been compelled, for her part, to acquiesce in substantial increases of the duties levied by her neighbours on some articles of importance to her export trade. Thus in Switzerland the new rates of duty were higher than the old in the case of cotton textiles, silk goods, some classes of woollen goods, brushes, furniture, wines, cigars, and shoes of fine leather, whilst the reductions were noticeable only as regards aniline dyes and hops. Austria-Hungary raised the duties on rye and hops, cotton-lace, some half-silk textiles, rough wooden wares (furniture and parts thereof), machines for metal-working, varnished leather, colour-prints and photographic paper; Russia on some cotton textiles, sewing-machines, machines for wood-working, locomotives, fine brass wares, cooper's wares, colour-prints and chromo-lithographs, some perfumery and cosmetics, and fireproof clay; Roumania on a number of classes of cotton and woollen goods, sewing-machines and similar machines, automobiles, the heavier classes of machine tools, glove-leather, colour-prints and lithographs; and Serbia on certain cotton and woollen textiles, woollen yarns, some wrought-iron goods, fine and varnished leather, and glove-leather. The decreases in the rates of duty obtained by the German negotiations were in all these countries of relatively small importance. As in the case of the new treaty with Bulgaria (which came into force in January, 1906), Germany again was not able to obtain any appreciable reduction of the high duties established by the revised Bulgarian tariff, there appeared to be some justification for the complaint of the German manufacturers and merchants that the use of the new general tariff for the purposes of negotiation had not been markedly successful, and that, in fact, whilst the agrarian interests had been safeguarded, the German export industry had been subjected to new and severe handicaps.[1]

It will be convenient at this point to indicate briefly the nature of Germany's commercial relations with countries other than those mentioned in the preceding paragraphs. It has already been stated[2] that, in the absence of any commercial treaty, the United Kingdom continued to enjoy " most favoured nation " treatment by virtue of a German law which was periodically renewed; the same treatment was extended to all the British Dominions except Canada. When in 1897 Canada first accorded to the United Kingdom preferential tariff treatment, Germany protested that such action was repugnant to the provisions of the commercial treaty of 1865 between the British Government and the Zollverein. That treaty, which provided for reciprocal and complete " most favoured nation " treatment, applied to all the possessions of the British Crown. The British Government accordingly denounced the treaty: German goods were consequently subjected to the general (as contrasted with the preferential) tariff of Canada,

[1] Roghé, *loc. cit.*, pp. 15–17. [2] *Vide supra*, p. 76.

and Canadian goods imported into Germany were subjected to the general rates instead of the conventional rates of the German tariff. As Germany persisted in refusing to recognise the principle that the tariff relations between any two parts of the British Empire were a matter of purely domestic concern, Canada in November, 1903, imposed a surtax of one-third over the general rates of duty. As the Canadian market grew in importance this differentiation became increasingly obnoxious to Germany, and informal negotiations at Ottawa led to an agreement in February, 1910, whereby Canada abolished the surtax on German goods, and Germany granted to Canada the conventional rates of duty upon wheat, barley, oats, fresh fruit, a variety of agricultural products, wood-spirit, certain classes of leather, and a few other commodities.

The commercial relations between the German Empire and France remained regulated by the article of the Treaty of Frankfurt, which bound France to accord perpetual " most favoured nation " treatment, which is voluntarily reciprocated. In the case of Spain there existed, from 1899 onwards, an agreement giving the two contracting countries reciprocal " most favoured nation " treatment; this was denounced in 1905 by the German Government, and would have terminated in June, 1906; but the termination was postponed, first for six months, and subsequently for an indefinite period. With Portugal a treaty of a somewhat unusual character was signed in 1908, but ratified only in 1910; under its provisions the rates of duty of the existing Portuguese tariff were conventionalised for the duration of the treaty (eight years), except in the case of certain specified articles, in respect of which Portugal reserved the right to increase the duties within prescribed limits on condition that so soon as such increases were enforced the duties on other specified German goods would be reduced, the reductions so to be made being also set out in the treaty.[1] With Greece a treaty had been in force since 1884, which limited

[1] See *Board of Trade Journal*, June 17 and 24, 1909.

the duties on currants and valonia imported into Germany. In 1906 a treaty was concluded with Sweden, whereby that country obtained the advantages of the conventional tariff, and reductions on a number of commodities (such as wooden window-frames, paving stones, stone-cutters' work, and some dairy machinery). Finally, Holland enjoyed "most favoured nation" treatment in Germany under a treaty of 1851, as did Norway and Denmark by virtue of ancient treaties, or rather (since it is doubtful to what extent such treaties can be regarded as binding), by an understanding not to disturb long-established relations.

As regards non-European countries, the most important matter was the attitude of the German Empire towards the United States. Under an agreement of 1900 the latter granted to the former the reductions in the rates of customs duties provided for by Section 3 of the Dingley Tariff Act (the most important, in this instance, being those on wines),[1] and in return for this were admitted to the advantages of the German minimum tariff. This arrangement was terminated when the new German tariff came into force in 1906; but in the following year a fresh agreement was reached, whereby in return for the same concessions on their part the United States obtained most, but not all, of the German minimum rates. The revision, in 1909, of the United States customs tariff, brought in its turn the necessity of terminating the agreement, and after some uncertainty, and for a time the prospect of a tariff war, the two states agreed to extend to each other the advantages of their minimum tariffs. With all the other American States except Brazil, Chili, Peru and San Domingo, Germany had treaties with secured reciprocal "most favoured nation" treatment, without any specific reductions of duty on either side.[2] Similar arrangements existed since various

[1] *Vide infra*, pp. 229.

[2] Under a treaty of 1908 with Hayti, however, Germany admitted certain Haytian products at the minimum tariff rates, and obtained reductions of duty on some of her imports into Hayti.

dates with Liberia, Abyssinia, Turkey, and Persia; whilst in treaties with Egypt, Japan, China, Corea, and Siam, there were included schedules of rates of duty which might not be increased so long as the treaties were in force.[1]

There are some other matters connected with German tariff legislation which should be noticed here. The first is the extent to which the system of *drawbacks* was adopted. On the exportation of articles in which cocoa is an ingredient, a drawback was allowed equal to the import duty leviable on the amount of cocoa beans used in their manufacture; and similar reimbursements of customs or excise duties were made in respect of exported spirits, products containing spirit, and tobacco and manufactures thereof. A somewhat different arrangement existed in regard to the products of flour and malt mills; the exporters of such commodities received certificates enabling them to import free of duty grain corresponding to the amount of foreign grain utilised in the preparation of the exported products, and a similar plan was adopted in regard to the products of oil factories, according to the amount of foreign oil fruits and seeds which have been employed in the preparation thereof. Other drawbacks related to salt and re-exported timber for building and industrial purposes.[2] A connected matter was the duty-free admission of materials and articles (the list of which might be increased from time to time by decree) required for the construction and outfit of sea-going vessels.

[1] The various commercial treaties to which reference is made in this chapter were in force at the outbreak of the Great European War in 1914: the principle that a state of war automatically terminates treaties between the belligerent states—though they may, of course, be revived by the treaty of peace—put an end to the commercial treaties between Germany and the following states (as the number of her enemies gradually grew): Russia, Serbia, Belgium, Canada, Italy, Roumania, Portugal, Greece, the United States, Guatemala, Honduras, Nicaragua, Panama, Peru, Uruguay, Japan, China, Siam, and Liberia.

[2] Detailed information is given in *Reports of H.M. Representatives Abroad on Bounties* (*other than those on Shipping and Navigation*), 1904.

A second point is the provision made for the "Improvement Trade." "The free import of goods for the purposes of manufacture, of completion or repair, with the object of their re-exportation (the so-called active improvement trade), is permitted if this promises material advantage to the industries concerned, and if it entails no injurious consequences to other home industries; further, it is permitted even when some small disadvantages exist, if these are outweighed by benefits so much greater as to conduce, on the whole, to the furtherance of German economic prosperity. The free importation of goods exported from the country for improvement (the so-called passive improvement trade) shall . . . only be permitted in exceptional cases, and only when the improvement in question cannot at the time be made in Germany, either at all, or only insufficiently, or in an inferior manner; further, when it applies to experiments made for the purpose of attaining new manufacturing methods or new patterns. . . . The separate Federal States have the right of independent decision in individual or temporary cases of improvement traffic. If the question, however, should be the establishment of a permanent improvement traffic not yet permitted within the German customs system, the consent of the Federal Council is necessary before the permit can be granted."[1]

Finally, it may be pointed out that in Art. 15 of the Tariff Law of 1903 it was enacted that the *per capita* yield of the duties on rye and wheat, cattle, sheep, poultry, dead meat, bacon and flour, in excess of the corresponding average annual yield for the six years 1898–1903, was to be set aside to form a fund to facilitate the establishment of a national scheme of provision for widows and orphans. In the event of such a law not being in force at the commencement of 1910, the fund and the annual surpluses were to be handed over for the same purpose to the institutions existing under the Invalidity Insurance Laws.

The tariff of 1906 came into operation in the midst of

[1] *Consular Report for Berlin for the* Year 1906, p. 63.

a period of great industrial and commercial activity throughout the world, which continued until the latter part of 1907, when a reaction was hastened and accentuated by the far-reaching financial crisis in the United States. The period of expansion up to the end of 1907 was accompanied by a fairly general upward movement, both in rates of wages and in earnings, which was, however, in part at least, counterbalanced by the rapid advance in the prices of almost all important articles of food, notably wheat and rye, bread and meat (especially pork); and it does not appear that the reaction of 1908 was accompanied by any appreciable fall of the prices of these commodities.[1] How far the sharp rise of prices in 1906 and 1907 was due to the influence of the increased customs duties, and how far it was the expression of purely economic forces (agricultural conditions, increased earnings, and consequent enhanced demand) are problems which it does not appear possible to solve in any very definite manner, but there can be no reasonable doubt that in an appreciable measure it was the outcome of the increased protection which German agricultural interests had procured for themselves.

In this connection it may be pointed out that of the total customs receipts in 1912, amounting to 896 million marks, over three-fifths (555 million marks, or 62 per cent.), was derived from duties on food, drink, and tobacco; raw materials and semi-finished goods provided 19·4 per cent., and "finished goods" 16·5 per cent. The average *ad valorem* rate of duty (*i.e.*, proportion of duties collected to the value of the dutiable goods) was in that year in the case of foodstuffs, etc., 21 per cent., whilst for raw materials and semi-finished goods and "finished goods" it was 15 per cent. and 16 per cent. respectively. Dutiable commodities constituted 19 per cent. of the value of raw materials and semi-finished goods imported, 56 per

[1] For evidence of the upward movement of prices, see *British and Foreign Trade and Industry* (Cd. 4594, 1909), pp. 193, 195, 200, 204; the *Reports of H.M. Consul-General at Berlin for* 1906 (pp. 11–13), 1907 (pp. 12-15), and 1908 (pp. 40–41); and the *Report of H.M. Consul-General at Frankfurt for* 1908 (pp. 14–33).

cent. of the "finished goods," and 89 per cent. of the foodstuffs, etc. The following table shows the average yield of the customs duties per head of population for a series of years:[1]

Average Yield of Customs Duties per Head of Population.			
	s. d.		s. d.
1890–4 ..	7 6	1905–9 ..	10 3
1895–9 ..	8 6	1910–12 .. (three year average)	11 6
1900–4 ..	9 0		

This is not the place to discuss in detail the financial difficulties which perplexed the Government of the German Empire, and in a lesser degree the Governments of the several states, in the decade before the European War, or the political effects of the attempts to find a solution of the problem. It must suffice here to point out that the failure of the revenue to keep pace with the rapid increase of expenditure, and the consequent doubling of the Imperial Debt within twelve years,[2] were due in part to bad financial administration, and in part to the exigencies of political policy. The first defect was

[1] In 1912 the duties on grain and other cereals yielded 4·04 marks per head of population, unmanufactured tobacco 1·80, coffee 1·52, petroleum, etc., 1·36, wine 0·43, meat and meat extract 0·23 (an abnormally high figure), "southern fruits" 0·21, tobacco products 0·21, lard and similar fats 0·20, cocoa 0·17, butter and margarine 0·17, rice 0·10, cheese and oil-seeds 0·08 each. The highest average yields for manufactured commodities were supplied by iron and steel goods and cotton manufactures with 0·13 mark per head; then came cotton-yarn and twist with 0·10, woollen goods with 0·9, silk goods 0·8, and machinery 0·8. Tobacco, beer and spirits, sparkling wines, sugar and salt are subject to customs and excise duty; but the yield of the customs duties on these articles (except tobacco) is quite small.

[2] The permanent debt of the German Empire was £106,000,000 in 1896, and £212,000,000 in October, 1908; by 1912 it was £243,000,000. This was the debt borne by the Imperial Government. The total of the State debts in 1912 was approximately £780,000,000. Against these debts there were, however, some substantial assets, especially the State railways.

generally recognised; there was a widespread demand for reform. As regards policy, in order to placate the states, to prevent financial demands which might cause them to strain against the federal bond, the Empire deliberately confined itself in the main to indirect taxation, and then handed over to its constituent states the major part even of the revenue derived from the kind of taxation which it reserved for itself. Thus on the one hand it limited its own resources, and on the other it encouraged (indirectly, but not the less effectively) expenditure by the states.[1] When the development of Imperial expenditure made it necessary for the Empire to call upon the states for large contributions towards Imperial purposes, the financial position of the states was not such as to enable them to meet the demand.[2] The Imperial Government felt it necessary in 1908 to devise means of obtaining some £25,000,000 a year of additional revenue, and inasmuch as there was in some quarters a strong desire to prevent, so far as possible, the intrusion of the Imperial Government into the sphere of direct taxation, the preserve of the states,[3] and as its proposals for the introduction of an estate duty and monopoly of the retail sale of spirits were rejected, it was ultimately reduced to the introduction or extension of taxation upon articles of general consumption (beer, spirits, sparkling wines, tobacco, coffee, tea and matches), upon incandescent lamps and burners, mantles and carbons, and upon a number of commercial instruments

1 Details of the financial history of the Empire will be found in *Denkschriftenband zur Begründung des Entwerfs eines Gesetzes betreffend Änderungen im Finanzwesen*, issued by the German Government in 1908.

2 The cumbrous system under which all the customs revenues in excess of £6,500,000 a year was divided among the separate states, which in turn paid to the Empire matricular contributions towards its expenditure, was convenient for the States so long as they received more than they paid; but when the situation was reversed after 1899, they found themselves in grave difficulties.

3 To some German politicians, as to those of other federal states, the exclusion of the central Government from the sphere of direct taxation appeared as an essential safeguard of the federal principle.

(real property transfers, dividend coupons, securities, bills of exchange and cheques).

The salient feature of the long and complicated parliamentary history of the discussions on financial reform was the revival of the hostility between the "industrial" and "agrarian" interests. The former alleged that, as in the tariff, so also in the financial proposals, they were being sacrificed, because of the political power of the landowning classes and their refusal to take a due share of the new burden of taxation—a share which, as the result of the high protection accorded by the German tariff, they were alleged to be fully able to bear. The resentment of the "industrials" found its expression in the formation of the so-called "Hanseatic League," to guard the interests of the manufacturers and merchants. But the general economic progress of the following years made this rivalry gradually less acute, and up to 1914 there was no strong reason for supposing that the broad lines of Germany's commercial and tariff policy would have been appreciably modified.

The depression which began in the latter part of 1907, though marked, was not acute nor very prolonged; by 1910 recovery had come, and from that year onward Germany shared to the full in the remarkable development of the world's industry and commerce, which continued until the outbreak of the general European War in 1914. In the period from 1906 to 1912 (both years included) the total imports for home consumption increased in value from 350 million £ to 526 million £, and the total exports of domestic produce and manufactures increased from 313 million £ to 440 million £. The most striking advances in the export trade were shown by iron and steel, and manufactures thereof (of which the export value rose from about 35 million £ in 1906 to nearly 60 million £ in 1912), and machinery of all kinds (from about 17 million £ to approximately 34 million £). Chemicals, drugs, and dyes increased from 29 million £ to over 40 million £, and in many other branches of production (cement; copper and brass goods; cotton and woollen yarns; dressed skins and furs; raw hides and skins; dressed leather and leather wares; paper of all kinds; fine wooden wares; toys) there were substantial increases in values. On the other hand, little progress was made in the value of cotton, silk, and woollen manufactures exported, though in the two first-mentioned classes of goods there were substantial increases in quantities. The exports of coal and coke rose from 16 million £ in 1906 to 28 million £ in 1912; grain, flour, and meal showed a large increase, though there was also a marked advance in imports; the quantities of sugar exported showed a very marked downward tendency.

The table on the following page shows the movement of certain of the more important indices of German trade for quinquennial periods from 1890 to 1909, and the three years 1910–1912.[1] To the data given in that table some further facts as to Germany's economic position may be added:

1. Of the total output of iron-ore in Germany and Luxemburg in 1912, amounting to 32·7 millions tons, 19·5 million tons were produced in Lorraine. The output of pig-iron in that province was, however, comparatively small—probably only about one-fifth of the total German make, and the production of coal was relatively insignificant. Alsace played a very important part in the cotton industry of Germany, spinning higher counts than any other German centre of the trade, and carrying on bleaching, dyeing and especially calico-printing. In 1909—the latest year for which detailed statistics are available—Alsace had 1·6 million spindles out of 10·2 millions in the whole of Germany, and 42,000 out of 260,000 looms. In Alsace also there are very large deposits of potash salts, not so developed as those of the Stassfurt area, but certainly as of equally great importance.

2. In certain of the non-ferrous metal industries

[1] The figures given in the table are based on those in *British and Foreign Trade and Industry*, 1909, and the *Statistical Abstract for the Principal and Other Foreign Countries* (No. 39), 1914.

	Annual Average.						
	1890-1894.	1894-1899.	1900-1904.	1905-1909.	1910.	1911.	1912.
	Million £.	Million £.	Million £.	Million £.	Million £.	Million £.	Million £.
Total imports for home consumption[1]	198·9	232·8	287·0	394·2	439·2	477·2	525·7
Imports of manufactured and partly manufactured goods for home consumption[2]	44·0	49·1	57·0	80·4	88·5	92·7	103·0
Total exports of German produce and manufactures	152·5	181·3	235·6	308·0	367·5	398·5	440·4
Exports of manufactured and partly manufactured goods[2]	98·6	116·9	154·2	213·9	244·8	274·6	295·4
	Million Metric Tons.	Million Metric Tons.	Million Metric Tons.	Million Metric Tons.	Million Metric Tons.	Million Metric Tons.	Million Metric Tons.
Output of coal[3]	72·0	89·3	110·7	139·6	152·8	160·7	174·9
Output of iron-ore[4]	11·5	15·2	19·4	25·5	28·7	29·8	32·7
Output of pig-iron[4]	4·8	6·7	8·9	12·1	14·8	15·6	17·6
Output of crude steel[4]	2·8	5·1	7·3	11·5	13·7	14·6	17·3
Output of potash salts (including kainit) ..	1·4	2·0	3·5	5·9	8·3	9·6	11·2
Imports of—	Metric Tons.	Metric Tons.	Metric Tons.	Metric Tons.	Metric Tons.	Metric Tons.	Metric Tons.
1. Raw cotton (for domestic consumption)	275,616	345,614	401,401	468,669	426,690	472,576	542,394
2. Raw sheep and lambs' wool (for domestic consumption)	148,445	174,218	155,138	180,252	197,944	197,559	218,278
3. Raw flax (for domestic consumption)	57,775	53,556	47,800	71,165	72,308	73,801	98,242
4. Palm kernels, etc. (for domestic consumption)	123,749	129,182	176,768	245,937	398,442	398,730	444,666

[1] The figures of imports and exports are not strictly comparable throughout, as after the 1st March, 1906, the returns included the free port areas of Germany—*i.e.*, they relate to the *Wirtschaftsgebiet* instead of the *Zollgebiet*, but this does not appreciably affect the validity of the impression given by the figures in this table.

[2] These figures are according to the classification adopted in the German trade accounts prior to 1906: the classification thereafter in force transferred a number of items from the "manufactured" to the "raw materials and semi-manufactured class."

[3] Exclusive of lignite (brown coal) of which the production increased from 19 million tons in 1890 to 81 million tons in 1912.

[4] Includes Luxemburg.

Germany had acquired a very strong position. In 1913 the world's production of spelter was estimated at 1,100,000 tons, of which Germany produced about 312,000 tons, being surpassed only by the United States. Her production of zinc ore had, from the early years of the last decade of the nineteenth century, ranged about 700,000 tons—in 1912 it was 644,000 tons with a zinc content of 240,000 tons; but Germany had obtained control of supplies of great importance from Australia. In 1912 the world's output of pig-lead was approximately 1,200,000 tons, the German Empire's share of this amounted to 177,000 tons (of which 78,000 tons from domestic ores), being surpassed only by the United States (about one-third of the total) and Spain. Of copper Germany's production was small, but her share of the world's consumption (about 1,000,000 tons in all) was approximately one-quarter. A group of German metal companies, by means of holdings in subsidiary companies in European and extra-European countries, had acquired an extremely strong position in the metal markets of the world, and controlled the European markets for spelter and lead by international conventions which they had forced upon the manufacturers of other countries, and directed.

3. Germany's foreign trade was essentially European. Taking values as a basis, in 1913 European countries supplied 55 per cent. of Germany's imports and took no less than 76 per cent. of her exports (special trade). America furnished 27·8 per cent. of her imports and took 15·3 per cent. of her exports. The United States were her largest supplier (15·9 per cent.), but took only a little over 7 per cent. of her exports. The United Kingdom was her best customer (14·2 per cent.), but supplied only 8 per cent. of her imports. Russia's shares were 13·2 per cent. of the imports and 8·7 per cent. of the exports, whilst Austria-Hungary's share were 7·7 per cent. and 10·9 per cent. respectively.[1]

This sketch of the history of German commercial

[1] Harms, *Deutschlands Anteil an Welthandel*, pp. 113 *seq.*

and tariff policy must of necessity conclude with the outbreak of the general European War of 1914. It would be inappropriate to enter here into any discussion of the extent to which the deliberate adoption by Germany of a policy of industrial and commercial expansion, at once subordinate to, yet instigating, political ambitions —the openly avowed pursuit of "Handels- und Machtpolitik"—contributed to the great catastrophe, and especially to the alienation of the sympathies of so many Powers throughout the world; but there can be no doubt that it did so contribute in large measure. And in view of the conditions created by her defeat—the loss of her world-prestige, the uncertainty as to her future political and social organization, and consequently as to the economic influences likely to be predominant, and the crippling terms imposed by the Treaty of Peace of 1919—it would be premature, and indeed impracticable, to attempt any forecast of the commercial policy which Germany is likely to pursue. During more than five years of war Germany's trade relations with a large part of Europe and ultimately with practically the whole of the extra-European world were suspended; her foreign trade was reduced to insignificant dimensions. After her defeat the cession of Alsace and Lorraine to France, and of the province of Posen to the Republic of Poland;[1] the application of the plebiscitary principle to Upper Silesia (an important industrial area, including large

[1] It may be noted that special provision is made in the Treaty of Peace (Art. 268) for the transitional commercial relations between Germany and the transferred territories. Thus, in the case of Alsace-Lorraine, natural and manufactured products originating in and exported directly into Germany from those provinces are to be exempt from German customs duties for five years (up to a maximum in each year of the average of 1911–1913), and for the same period the German Government is bound to allow the unrestricted exportation from Germany, and the subsequent reimportation, of yarns, tissues, and other textile materials sent to Alsace for finishing processes there. For three years Germany is bound to admit freely the produce and manufactures of the territories transferred to Poland (subject to the same maximum as in the case of Alsace and Lorraine); and the Allied and Associated Powers may require similar treatment for Luxemburg for a period of five years.

zinc mining and smelting works), to the southern portion of the province of East Prussia and the northern part of the province of Schleswig; the creation of the free state area of Danzig, under the protection of the League of Nations; the transfer to France of the unrestricted ownership and exploration of the coal mines of the Saar Valley, the control of that area by the League of Nations and the determination of its permanent status by a plebiscite after fifteen years; the exclusion of Luxemburg from the German Customs Union; the internationalisation of the navigable waters within Germany of the Elbe, Oder, Niemen, and Danube, and their subjection to the control of international commissions; the obligation imposed on Germany to give permanently to the "Allied and Associated Powers" "most favoured nation" treatment in all that relates to the importation, exportation, and transit of goods, and to navigation; the limitation, for a period of three years, of her power to increase customs duties; the loss of all her overseas possessions; the transfer to the Allies of her merchant fleet; and the heavy charges laid upon her by way of reparation—all those together impose upon German losses of resources and productive power, and restrictions of liberty of economic policy, such as no great nation has ever previously experienced in the history of the world.[1] The problem which she has to face is extraordinarily complex and of the utmost gravity, not only for herself but for the whole of Europe, for it is impossible to separate her future economic condition from that of the rest of continental Europe: and it may well be that she will be unable to solve it unaided, and that in some way or another the victors will have to come to her help and co-operate in the task of rebuilding the industrial and commercial organisation of Germany, and reviving its activities, with designs less ambitious than those which prevailed before the war, but with surer foundations.

[1] The English text of the Treaty of Peace of Versailles has been published as a Command Paper (Cmd. 1537, 1919).

A BRIEF BIBLIOGRAPHY

WEBER, W. *Der Deutsche Zollverein.* 1871.

BOWRING, J. *Report on the Prussian Commercial Union.* 1840.

ZIMMERMANN, A. *Geschichte der Preussisch-Deutschen Handelspolitik.* 1891. (I.)

ZIMMERMANN, A. *Die Handelspolitik des Deutschen Reiches, 1871–1900.* 1901. (II.)

GERLOFF, W. *Die Finanz- und Zollpolitik des Deutschen Reiches, von der Gründung des Norddeutschen Bundes bis zur Gegenwart.* 1913.

SCHIPPEL, MAX. *Grundzüge der Handelspolitik.* 1902.

LOTZ, W. *Die Ideen der Deutschen Handelspolitik,* 1860–91. 1892. (I.)

LOTZ, W. *Die Handelspolitik des Deutschen Reiches,* 1890–1900 (in *Beiträge zur Neuesten Handelspolitik Deutschlands,* vol. iii. 1901). (II.)

HARMS, BERNHARD. *Deutschlands Anteil an Welthandel und Weltwirthschaft.* 1916.

v. PHILIPPOVICH. *Ein Wirtschafts- und Zollverband zwischen Deutschland und Oesterreich-Ungarn.* 1915.

POSCHINGER, H. *Bismarck als Volkswirth.* 1889–90.

WUTTKE, R. "Der deutsch-oesterreich-ungarische Handelsvertrag vom 6 Dezember, 1891" (in *Verhandlungen des Vereins für Sozialpolitik,* 1902).

BLUM, H. *Das Deutsche Reiche zur Zeit Bismarcks.* 1893.

VON HALLE, E. *Volks- und See-Wirthschaft.* 1903.

DAWSON, W. H. *Bismarck and State Socialism.* 1891.

"VERITAS." *German Empire of To-day.* 1902.

ASHLEY, W. J. *The Progress of the German Working Classes.* 1904.

KUCZYNSKI, G. *Die Entwicklung der gewerblichen Löhne seit der Begründung des deutschen Reiches.* 1909.

British and Foreign Trade and Industry. (Board of Trade, Cd. 4954. 1909.)

Cost of Living in German Towns. (Board of Trade Report, Cd. 4032. 1908.)

Germany—New General Customs Tariff. (Board of Trade, Cd. 1479. 1903.)

New German Tariff as Modified by Treaties. (Board of Trade, Cd. 2414. 1905.)

Report on Tariff Wars. (Foreign Office, Cd. 1938. 1904.)

Statistisches Jahrbuch für das Deutsche Reich (annually).

Statistisches Handbuch für das Deutsche Reich. 2 vols. 1907.

Statistical Abstract for the Principal and Other Foreign Countries (annually).

HIRST, M. E. *The Life of Friedrich List.* 1909.

LIST, F. *System of National Economy* (trans. by Lloyd. 1885).

SCHMOLLER, G. *The Mercantile System* (trans. by W. J. Ashley. 1896).

SCHMOLLER, G. *Grundriss der Allgemeinen Volkswirtschaftslehre.* 2 vols. 1904.

SCHMOLLER, WAGNER, AND SERING (Editors). *Handels- und Machtpolitik.* 2 vols. 1900.

WAGNER, A. *Agrar- und Industriestaat.* 2nd edition. 1902.

POHLE, L. *Deutschland am Scheidewege.* 1902.

TROELTSCH, W. *Ueber die Neuesten Veränderungen im Deutschen Wirtschaftsleben.* 1899.

BRENTANO, L. *Das Freihandelsargument.* 1901.

BRENTANO, L. *Die Schrecken des überwiegenden Industriestaats.* 1901.

NAUMANN, F. *Mittel-Europa.* 1915.

DIETZEL, H. "The German Tariff Controversy" (*Quart. J. Econ.*, May, 1903).

GOTHEIN, G. *Die Wirkung der Handelsverträge* (in publications of the Berlin Volkswirthschaftliche Gesellschaft, 1895).

CONRAD, J. "Die Stellung der Landwirthschaftlichen Zölle" (*Verein für Sozialpolitik*, vol. xc.).

CONRAD, J. "Die Agrarzölle in der Zolltarifvorlage" (in *Jahrbücher für Nationalökonomie und Statistik*, February, 1902).

DADE, H. "Die Agrarzölle" (in *Beiträge zur Neuesten Handels-Politik Deutschlands*, vol. ii., 1901).

SCHACHT, H. "Inhalt und Kritik des Zolltarifentwurfs" (in Schmoller's *Jahrbuch*, 1902).

Verhandlungen des Vereins für Sozialpolitik, vol. xcviii.

PART II

THE UNITED STATES

CHAPTER I

THE ORIGINS OF AMERICAN COMMERCIAL POLICY

THE economic relations between the constituent states of the American Union at the end of the War of Independence resembled closely the condition of affairs in the Germanic Confederation after the Congress of Vienna. The separate colonies had been allowed by Great Britain to impose customs duties for revenue purposes, and had also been influenced somewhat by protectionist ideas;[1] and although after 1776 this latter motive seems to have lost its force, the customs duties continued to be levied by each state against all others, including even its fellow-members of the Union. Yet the feeling in favour of freedom of trade was sufficiently strong—partly as the result of reaction against the restrictive policy of Great Britain—to restrain the new Confederation from imposing any tariff laws between 1776 and 1781.[2] There were practically no manufactures to protect; the colonies were almost entirely engaged in agricultural pursuits or in the carrying trade; and although there was a certain amount of iron produced, yet "in the main, the colonies made only such manufactures as could not be imported."[3] When from 1782 onwards a change came over American policy, and tariff legislation began, the determining forces seem to have been chiefly political—the necessity of raising money for the purposes of government, and the desire to be able to meet and resist the commercial legislation of the European Powers, and par-

[1] Stanwood, i. p. 25, quotes from the preambles to the Revenue Acsts of various colonies. *Cf.* Hill, pp. 14–16.

[2] Hill, pp. 39–40.

[3] Taussig, p. 10.

ticularly the high tariff and Navigation Acts of Great Britain.[1] These considerations drove the States rapidly from political into commercial union; and after some years of uncertainty, owing to the unwillingness of some members of the Union to surrender their liberty of economic action, the Constitution of 1787 settled that " Congress shall have power to lay and collect taxes, duties, imposts, and excises, to pay the debts and provide for the common defence and general welfare of the United States; but all duties, imposts, and excises shall be uniform throughout the United States; . . . to regulate commerce with foreign nations, and among the several States, and with the Indian tribes; . . . to make all laws which shall be necessary and proper for carrying into execution the foregoing powers."[2]

The first use made by Congress of the authority so conferred appeared in the Tariff Act of 1789. It was a combination of specific and *ad valorem* duties, and was to continue in force for seven years. Specific duties—a fixed tax on a given amount of each commodity—were imposed on thirty-six articles, the chief being spirits (8–10 cents per gallon), tea (6–20 cents per lb.), sugar, salt, molasses, cordage, steel (56 cents per cwt.), and nails; and there were *ad valorem* duties of 15 per cent. on carriages, 10 per cent. on glass, china, earthenware, lace, and some other commodities; 7½ per cent. on paper, gloves, leather, buttons, clothing, hats, and metal wares, and 5 per cent. on all other imports except seventeen raw materials (such as saltpetre, wool, cotton, hides, fur,

[1] " At first the rates were low and the articles taxed few, being generally luxuries or commodities the importation of which was thought harmful. In this category slaves, rum, spirits, and wine, tea, coffee, and sugar held important places. The Southern States did not go beyond these purely revenue measures. In all the Northern States rates were advanced and other articles were added to the list, until in 1785 and 1786 the tariff schedules were generally extensive and taxes were imposed for both revenue and protective purposes, or, to use a phrase of more recent times, for revenue with incidental protection. In some of the states, indeed, protection was the principal end sought " (Hill, p. 43).

[2] Art. i., sec. 8. See text in Bryce, *Amer. Commonwealth*, i. p. 700.

dye-stuffs), which were admitted free.[1] Drawbacks of the full duty less 1 per cent. were granted for all commodities re-exported within twelve months; and finally, to stimulate the American carrying trade, an abatement of 10 per cent. of the duty leviable was given on all goods imported in vessels owned entirely by American citizens. Though the duties thus imposed were, on the whole, quite moderate, it is by no means certain that the legislation was inspired solely by financial needs.[2] It is true that these were considerable, and in face of the widespread dislike of direct taxation and of excises they could only be satisfied by recourse to customs duties; but it is also clear that in the minds of many of its supporters the Act had a protective purpose, and for that very reason it called forth a good deal of opposition, particularly from the Southern States. It was a policy of Protection, chiefly for manufactures, modified partly by the inexperience of the legislators[3] and partly by regard to considerations of revenue.[4] In the very next year, after Hamilton, the Secretary of the Treasury, had failed to secure an Excise Act, the tariff was increased all round to meet the growing financial needs of the Union; the specific duty on steel was advanced from 56 to 75 cents

[1] Stanwood, i. pp. 58–60.

[2] "It has often been said that the first Tariff Act, that of 1789, was a protective measure, and that in the debate on it the protective policy appeared full grown. But such considerations had little to do with the Act; and the discussions on Protection by no means indicate what was the real centre of interest. . . . Its main object was to secure revenue" (Taussig, pp. 14–15).

[3] Channing, *United States*, p. 139.

[4] For the evidence that protective considerations did weigh with the promoters of the measure, see Hill, pp. 108 *seq.*, and the account of the debates given by Stanwood, i. pp. 39 *seq.* Mayo-Smith and Seligman, p. 6, agree with Taussig, and remark that "it is erroneous to speak of any protectionist movement at this period"; but this seems to be based on the idea that the authors of the tariff did not regard average duties of 8½ per cent. *ad valorem* as protective—a supposition which is not proved, and is in direct conflict with the preamble to the Act, which asserts that "it is necessary for the support of the Government, . . . and the encouragement and protection of manufactures, that duties be laid," etc. Dewey (p. 84) holds that the evidence as to the consciously protective character of the tariff is conclusive.

per cwt., and many articles previously in the 5 per cent. *ad valorem* list were now made subject to rates of 7½ per cent. and 10 per cent. In the following year an excise on spirits (somewhat lower than the customs duty) was established; but it was always unpopular and difficult to collect, and in 1802 was finally abandoned.

In 1790 Congress had directed the Secretary to the Treasury to prepare and report plans "for the encouragement and promotion of such manufactories as will tend to render the United States independent of other nations for essential, particularly for military, supplies." Hamilton replied in December, 1791, with a "Report on Manufactures," which remains still one of the most elaborate general arguments for Protection, and contains most of the ideas which multitudes of writers have since developed.[1] There is the argument from the desirability of national self-sufficiency. "Every nation . . . ought to endeavour to possess within itself all the essentials of national supply. These comprise the means of subsistence, habitation, clothing, and defence. The possession of these is necessary to the perfection of the body politic, to the safety as well as to the welfare of society. The want of either is the want of an important organ of political life and motion; and in the various crises which await a state it must severely feel the effects of any such deficiency." There is the advocacy of the home market, though primarily in the interests of the agricultural producers; the restrictive policy of European Powers, and the fluctuations of their crops, make the foreign market too unreliable for the American farmer; it is therefore desirable to create for his produce the largest possible demand at home, and this can best be done by promoting "manufacturing establishments." "This idea of an extensive domestic market for the surplus produce of the soil is of the first consequence. It is of all things that which most effectually conduces to a flourishing state

[1] Full text in Taussig, *State Papers and Speeches on the Tariff*.

of agriculture." But the firm establishment of the necessary manufactures in the face of foreign competition is a task of great difficulty, and so we naturally come to the famous "infant industries" argument. "Whatever room there may be for an expectation that the industry of a people, under the direction of private interest, will, upon equal terms, find out the most beneficial employment for itself, there is none for a reliance that it will struggle against the force of unequal terms, or will of itself surmount all the adventitious barriers to a successful competition which may have been erected either by the advantages naturally acquired from practice and previous possession of the ground, or by those which may have sprung from positive regulation and an artificial policy" —this last phrase a reference to the eighteenth-century policy of Great Britain. Finally, Hamilton argues that an increase of prices arising from Protection will soon be more than counterbalanced by the increase of production, and resulting cheapness, which it will call forth; and he urges the essential harmony of the industrial and agricultural interests, since the farmers may have to pay more for a time for manufactured goods, but will find the value of their farms enhanced by the growth of the demand for agricultural produce, both food and raw material.[1] As definite proposals he recommends the grant of bounties, the free admission of raw materials (or the payment of drawbacks), and general protection

[1] "Though it were true that the immediate and certain effect of regulations controlling the competition of foreign with domestic fabrics was an increase in price, it is universally true that the contrary is the ultimate effect with every successful manufacture. When a domestic manufacture has attained to perfection, and has engaged in the prosecution of it a competent number of persons, it invariably becomes cheaper. . . . The internal competition which takes place soon does away with everything like monopoly, and by degrees reduces the price of the article to the minimum of a reasonable profit on the capital employed. . . . In a national view, a temporary enhancement of price must always be compensated by a permanent reduction of it. . . . Indeed, all the duties imposed on imported articles, though with an exclusive view to revenue . . . except where they fall on raw materials, wear a beneficient aspect towards the manufactures of a country."

against all manufactured articles which can be produced in the country.[1]

From 1790 onwards there were constant alterations in the tariff—between 1792 and 1816 there were some twenty-five Tariff Acts passed, all modifying the customs duties in one way or another. But Hamilton's Report, and the ideas it embodied, do not seem to have exercised any special influence on the legislation of this period; the motives were always financial.[2] Up to 1808 there were increases of duties on various commodities; some specific duties were replaced by duties *ad valorem;* and some articles (chiefly those useful for military purposes) were added to the free list. Alone in the duty imposed in 1804 on window glass "was any concession made to the protective policy."[3] But whilst this was the policy of Congress, it is evident that the feeling in favour of Protection was growing in the country at large. It was held back by the general prosperity of American trade during the Napoleonic wars, until the United States became involved in the European complications after the year 1807; before that date the American export and carrying trade had reaped great benefit from British difficulties. The following table shows the movement of the foreign

[1] Hamilton enumerates, as articles the manufacture of which had attained a substantial development at the date at which he wrote: tanned leather, boots and shoes, harness and saddlery, portmanteaus and trunks, gloves; bar and sheet iron and steel, nail rods and nails, agricultural implements, stoves, household utensils, anchors, tools and arms; ships, cabinet wares, and joinery; cables, sailcloth, cordage and twine; bricks, tiles, and pottery; spirits; paper; hats; refined sugar; oils, soap and candles; copper and brass wares; tin wares; carriages; tobacco; starch; colours and gunpowder; and other articles. In addition to these, which "are carried on as regular trades and have attained to a considerable degree of maturity," there was also "a vast scene of household manufacturing"—*e.g.*, coarse cloths, coatings, serges and flannels, woollen and cotton hosiery, cotton and linen shirtings, sheetings, etc.

[2] "With two or three exceptions, they had no other motive than to adjust the revenue to the needs of the Treasury" (Stanwood, i. p. 111). *Cf.* Taussig, p. 16.

[3] Stanwood, i. p. 115. Hamilton had recommended in 1791 a bounty on the production of window-glass.

trade of the United States from 1791 to 1807 (in million dollars):[1]

Financial Years ending September 30.	Gross Imports.	Gross Exports.	Re-exports of Foreign Produce
1791	29·2	19·0	0·5
1792	31·5	20·7	1·7
1793	31·1	26·1	2·1
1794	34·6	33·0	6·5
1795	69·7	48·0	8·5
1796	81·4	67·0	26·3
1797	75·4	56·8	27·0
1798	68·5	61·5	33·0
1799	79·0	78·6	45·5
1800	91·2	71·0	39·1
1801	111·3	94·0	46·6
1802	76·3	72·0	35·7
1803	64·7	55·8	13·6
1804	85·0	77·7	36·2
1805	120·6	95·5	53·2
1806	129·4	101·5	60·3
1807	138·5	108·3	59·6

The most striking column here is that of re-exports, which represents the growth of the carrying trade of the United States, and the commercial importance of the war to that country is most markedly illustrated by a comparison of the figures for 1802 and 1803, the years of the Treaty of Amiens, with those which immediately precede and follow them.

But with 1808 a change came. In November, 1806, Napoleon had replied to the British blockade of the French coast by the Berlin Decree, which declared the British islands blockaded, and forbade all trade in British goods. Great Britain answered by proclaiming the continental coasting trade—at least for ports under French control—closed to neutrals, and at the end of 1807 ordered " the condemnation of any American vessel seized while on a voyage to any European port closed to British vessels, unless such vessel had first touched at a British port. Napoleon, on his part, in the Milan Decree (December 17th, 1807) declared that any ship which had obeyed the above order was good prize if seized in any port under his control. At this time, Napoleon was the

[1] Taussig, p. 12.

virtual master of all the continental ports except those of Sweden, Norway, and Turkey, and the British were supreme on the ocean. These orders and decrees, therefore, provided for the speedy annihilation of American shipping, and this seems to have been the object of the last British Order in Council, if one may judge from a perusal of Mr. Perceval's correspondence on the subject. The official reason as stated was a desire to compel the United States to retaliate upon the French Government."[1] But it was not to be expected that the United States would quietly submit to this treatment. On December 23rd, 1807, Congress passed the Embargo Act, which prohibited American vessels from leaving for foreign ports, and foreign vessels from taking any cargo except that already on board. The vigorous enforcement of these orders on both sides—for although in March, 1809, the Embargo Act was repealed, it was replaced by the establishment of Non-Intercourse with France, Great Britain, their allies and colonies—was one of the chief causes of the Anglo-American War of 1812.

With the political effects of these various regulations we are not concerned; but they were of great importance in relation to the economic development of the United States. The following table shows the movement of American foreign trade (in million dollars) from the issue of the Embargo at the beginning of 1808 to the end of the war.[2] It should be noted that at the commencement of the war of 1812 the United States import duties were doubled.

Year.	Gross Imports.	Gross Exports.	Re-exports of Foreign Produce.
1807	138·5	108·3	59·6
1808	57·0	20·4	13·0
1809	59·4	52·2	20·8
1810	85·4	66·7	24·4
1811	53·4	61·3	16·0
1812	77·0	38·5	8·5
1813	22·0	27·9	2·8
1814	13·0	6·9	0·1

[1] Channing, *United States*, pp. 177–8. [2] Taussig, p. 12.

So by 1814 American foreign trade had practically ceased to exist. The war was equivalent in its effects to a policy of Protection amounting to prohibition, and American manufactures, left in secure possession of the home market, entered upon a course of rapid expansion. Especially was that the case with the production of woollen goods, which increased in value from four million dollars in 1810 to nineteen millions in 1815;[1] and with cotton spinning, which it is estimated employed 4,500 spindles in 1805, 87,000 in 1810, and 130,000 in 1815.[2] There were the beginnings of the manufacture of cotton textiles on a large scale, and a marked development of manufacture of iron, glass, and pottery.[3] It was during these years that the factory system began (but only began) to replace domestic industry in the United States: "the manufacture of cotton and wool passed rapidly from the household to the mill; but the methods of domestic and neighbourhood industry continued to predominate, even in those industries, down to and including the decade between 1820 and 1830."[4]

Just at the close of 1814 a treaty of peace was signed by Great Britain and the United States, and this was followed in 1815 by a commercial agreement, intended at first for four years, but prolonged in 1818 for another ten years; by it the contracting parties bound themselves not to impose discriminating duties on each other's products.[5] The first result of the cessation of hostilities was a swift rise of imports; from $13,000,000 in 1814 they rose to $113,000,000 in 1815 (with only six months of peace), and $147,000,000 in 1816. This last was the highest figure yet recorded, and moreover, as re-exports were comparatively small, "the value of net imports

[1] "A loose, though significant guess" (Taussig, p. 40 n.).

[2] Taussig, p. 28, from Woodbury's Report of 1836.

[3] "See what has been, only by the short operation of the Embargo and Non-Intercourse Act, done in America! . . . We have here before us the seeds of a great event—nothing less than the complete and absolute independence of America upon English manufactures" (William Cobbett, quoted in Bolles, ii. p. 289)

[4] *Twelfth Census of the United States*, vii. p. liii.

[5] Channing, *United States*, p. 198.

was almost double that of any year preceding the war."[1] The phenomena of Continental Europe at this time were repeated in the United States; the barriers erected during the long war were removed, and both continents found themselves exposed to a sweeping invasion by British manufactured goods, which severely threatened the very existence of some at least of the industries which had grown up under the shelter of the system of prohibition. In the United States the manufacturers of cottons, woollens and chemicals thought themselves particularly imperilled, and in 1815 President Madison called Congress to their help. "Under circumstances giving a powerful impulse to manufacturing industry," he wrote,[2] "it has made among us a progress and exhibited an efficiency which justify a belief that with a protection not more than is due to the enterprising citizens whose interests are now at stake, it will become at an early day not only safe against occasional competitions from abroad, but a source of domestic wealth and even of external commerce. In selecting the branches more especially entitled to the public patronage, a preference is obviously claimed by such as will relieve the United States from a dependence on foreign supplies, ever subject to casual failures, for articles necessary for the public defence or connected with the primary wants of individuals. It will be an additional recommendation of particular manufactures where the materials for them are extensively drawn from our agriculture, and consequently impart and insure to that great fund of national prosperity and independence an encouragement which cannot fail to be rewarded."

The result was the tariff of 1816, which commenced a series of enactments which for about twenty years became more and more protectionist. But the first steps were quite moderate. The original scheme was to reduce the war duties 29 per cent.—that is, to leave the permanent duties 42 per cent. higher than before the war of 1812; but the proposals were considerably modified in their

[1] Stanwood, i. p. 131.
[2] *Seventh Annual Message*, 1815.

passage through Congress owing to the opposition of the shipping interest and the rivalry of the various groups of States which sought protection for their industries.[1] So the proposed duty of $1·25 per cwt. on bar-iron was reduced by the House of Representatives to 45 cents; the proposed duty on sugar was cut down considerably; instead of the desired rate of 33⅓ per cent. *ad valorem* cotton manufacturers obtained only 25 per cent. for three years and 20 per cent. after the expiration of that term.[2] That protectionist motives exercised a strong influence over the tariff discussions there can be no doubt, but they had not yet obtained a complete control over the mind of the legislators.[3] The new tariff was a combination of specific and *ad valorem* duties.

The new customs laws seem to have had little effect, so far at least as the iron and cotton industries were concerned. The imports of bar-iron rose from 12,293 tons in 1816 to 21,160 tons in 1817, and, after a temporary decline, to 22,459 tons in 1820, whilst the home production fell rapidly—in part doubtless because of the technical defects in the manufacturing processes in vogue.

[1] "The difficulty is illustrated most clearly by the objections of Northern members to a protecting duty on sugar, and of Southern members to giving protection to cotton manufactures. On the question of protection to iron, the North and the South united against the Middle States" (Stanwood, i. p. 157).

[2] In connection with cottons the system of the "minimum valuation" was adopted; *i.e.*, it was directed that all cotton cloths, etc., "the original cost of which at the place imported shall be less than 25 cents per square yard, shall be taken and deemed to have cost 25 cents per square yard, and shall be charged with duty accordingly." Taussig writes (p. 30): "After 1818 the use of the power-loom, and the fall in the price of raw cotton, combined greatly to reduce the prices of cotton goods. The price of coarse cottons fell to 19 cents in 1819, 13 cents in 1826, and 8½ cents in 1829. The minimum duty became proportionately heavier as the price decreased, and in a few years after its enactment had become prohibitive of the importation of the coarser kinds of cotton cloths."

[3] Taussig (pp. 18–19) seems to think that the new duties (averaging 20 per cent.) were the outcome chiefly of financial needs. Dewey (p. 162) holds that "Protection was adopted as a fundamental basis of the fiscal system, and revenue was subordinated to industrial needs." He adds, however, that there was little opposition, because the country was confronted by a real crisis.

Similarly in the cotton manufacture "the tariff of 1816 was not protective so far as those establishments were concerned which had not the most efficient machinery. This is almost equivalent to saying that it was protective in relation to but one factory in the country."[1] The help given to the makers of woollens by the duties was also only slight; and the three industries soon began to invoke again the aid of Congress. In 1818 they secured an increase in the duty on bar-iron, and a prolongation of the 25 per cent. on cottons until 1826; but apart from these increases, the protectionist movement for some time met with little success. This was due in part to the attitude of the Southern States, where agriculture was prosperous owing to the world-wide demand for their cotton and tobacco; they believed that protection for manufactures, which were supposed to be practically impossible under the climatic conditions of the South and with slave labour, would be inimical to their interests. Moreover, in politics it was the "era of good feeling"—there were no organised political parties to seek an electoral advantage in the advocacy of Protection. But in 1818–19 there came an economic crisis; the prices of the agricultural staples of the United States, hitherto high, fell rapidly, thus imitating the prices of manufactured goods, which had declined sharply when the conclusion of the war had removed the restrictions on imports. This fall in agricultural prices to some extent benefited the manufacturers, but did not moderate their demand for protection; and the agriculturists, especially in the North, became more favourable to it in their desire—in view of European legislation—to develop the home market.[2] Thus one important effect of the crisis was to revive and strengthen the agitation in favour of more protection, just as the crisis of 1873 and the following years in Germany prepared the way for Bismarck's tariff legislation. In 1819 the Congressional Committee on Manu-

[1] Stanwood, i. p. 173. *Cf.* for the effect of the various duties, Taussig, pp. 34–5, 40–1, 50–1.

[2] Taussig, pp. 19–24.

factures, under the stimulus of the commercial troubles of that year,[1] brought forward proposals for a complete revision of all the tariff rates, with large increases all round, partly to provide revenue to meet a growing deficit in the national accounts, and partly to extend the protection already given to manufactured goods. There was a prolonged conflict, and in April the revision Bill was carried through the House of Representatives only to be summarily rejected by a majority of one vote in the Senate.

From 1820 to 1824 there was some agitation throughout the Union in favour of tariff changes, but practically no attempt was made to give expression to it in the legislature until the new Congress, to meet at the end of 1823, had been elected. The effect of the census of 1820, which determined the apportionment of seats in the House of Representatives,[2] had been to increase the representation of the Middle States—New York, Pennsylvania, Ohio, Kentucky, Tennessee—which were strongly protectionist. President Monroe invited the new Congress to " a review of the tariff for the purpose of affording such additional protection to those articles which we are prepared to manufacture, or which are more immediately connected with the defence and independence of the country." The response to this appeal was the Tariff Act of 1824, of which " it may be said without reservation that the sole object was the protection of manufactures ";[3] the financial position of the Govern-

[1] " Its causes were complex: in part the inability of the manufacturing industries to recover a stable footing after the abnormal growth occasioned by the embargo and the war, and in part a spirit of speculation developed by several years of rapid commercial expansion and bad banking " (Dewey, p. 166).

[2] " Representatives and direct taxes shall be apportioned among the several States which may be included within this Union, according to their respective numbers. . . . The actual enumeration shall be made within three years after the first meeting of the Congress of the United States, and within every subsequent term of ten years. . . . The number of Representatives shall not exceed one for every thirty thousand " (Original form of art. i., sec. 2 of the Constitution, given in Bryce, *Amer. Comm.*, i. p. 697).

[3] Stanwood, i. p. 202.

ment made it unnecessary to consider revenue.[1] It increased the duties on iron,[2] lead, wool, hemp—though not so much as those interested had desired; on cotton and woollen goods the *ad valorem* duties were raised from 25 to 33⅓ per cent., but the additional protection to woollens was discounted by the doubling of the duty on raw wool. Strong opposition came from the commercial classes of New England to the tariff as a whole; from the shipbuilders to the increases on hemp (for cordage), flax and iron; from the manufacturers there to the increases on molasses (for rum) and raw wool. But New England was not solid in its resistance to the new tariff for it had itself growing manufactures of cotton and woollen goods; and hence its vote was divided.[3]

[1] In the course of the debates Henry Clay, the most conspicuous of the legislative advocates of increased Protection, drew a most gloomy picture of the state of the country, with general distress, diminished exports and home trade, depression of shipping, financial stringency, unemployment, reduced wages, depreciation of the value of property, and other ills (*Speech* of March 30–31, 1824). Daniel Webster, who as a representative of New England occupied a difficult position, in the same debate, whilst admitting that there had been a considerable depression of prices and curtailment of profits, and that there existed in some parts of the country "a great degree of pecuniary embarrassment," asserted that "with these qualifications the general state of the country may be said to be prosperous, and they are not sufficient to give to the whole face of affairs any appearance of general distress."

[2] The estimated annual consumption of iron was from 48,000 to 50,000 tons, and the home production amounted to only about 17,000 tons (Webster, *Speech* of April, 1824).

[3] In the division on the Bill of 1819, 19 New England representatives voted for it, 18 against; New York, New Jersey, Pennsylvania, and Delaware gave 55 votes for, 1 against; the South, 8 for, 63 against; Ohio, Illinois, and Indiana, 8 for, none against (Stanwood, i. pp. 192–3). In 1824 the South voted against the proposed tariff, the Middle and Western States for; of the New England States, Rhode Island and Connecticut for, the rest against (Taussig, pp. 74–5). Daniel Webster's position (*Speech* of April, 1824) illustrates the difference of opinion which prevailed in New England. As a Massachusetts representative, he favoured a higher duty on woollen manufactures, but was opposed to the duties on wool to be imposed in the interests of agriculture; he thought the lower grades of cotton goods had sufficient protection, but favoured higher rates of duty in respect of cotton manufactures of a higher grade; and in the interests of shipping opposed the increases proposed in respect of iron, hemp, and copper.

The South was united; it exported cotton largely, and feared retaliation, particularly from Great Britain. The Middle and Western States, whose interests were chiefly agricultural, threw their whole weight on the side of the new proposals, partly in their desire for the development of the home market, and partly to obtain protection for their hemp, wool and flax.[1] The combination of these States and the manufacturers of New England carried the Act of 1824, but only by a small majority. In the course of the debates the doctrine of so-called "American policy," as already adumbrated in the Report of Alexander Hamilton in 1791, and Monroe's Message of 1815, made its appearance as a political force,[2] and from that time onward the tariff question bulks largely in the party politics of the United States.

Two other points about the proposals of that year are noticeable. A clause providing for the imposition of a surtax equivalent in amount to the bounty paid by a foreign country on any goods imported into the United States was rejected, on the ground that it would be a breach of the Commercial Treaty of 1815 with Great Britain, which guaranteed that no unfavourably discriminating duties should be imposed by the United States on commodities coming from that country. And

[1] Taussig, pp. 70–5.

[2] It found its expression in the great speech of Henry Clay, who followed to a large extent the lines laid down by Hamilton: "It is most desirable that there should be both a home and a foreign market. But with respect to their relative superiority, I cannot entertain a doubt. The home market is first in order and paramount in importance. The object of the Bill under consideration is to create this home market, and to lay the foundations of a genuine American policy. It is opposed; and it is incumbent upon the partisans of the foreign policy (terms which I shall use without any invidious intent) to demonstrate that the foreign market is an adequate one for the surplus product of our labour." He proceeds to argue that it cannot and will not be so partly because the growth of American producing capacity is outpacing, and will continue to outpace, the growth of the consuming power of foreign countries—an extraordinary doctrine; and partly because the policy of all Europe is adverse to the reception of competing agricultural products from the United States.

much more important than this was the question whether the levying of import duties for protective purposes was constitutionally within the power of Congress or not; the matter was raised only tentatively, and was not much discussed, but it was subsequently to form the subject of very considerable controversy.[1]

[1] Stanwood, pp. 220–5.

CHAPTER II

THE GROWTH OF PROTECTION, AND THE COMPROMISE OF 1833

FOR a short time after the passing of the Tariff Act of 1824 the manufacturers seem to have been satisfied; but in the latter part of 1826 a demand for a greater amount of protection made its appearance amongst the producers of woollen goods. Their complaint was to the effect that the British duties on raw wool had been reduced, that wages in Great Britain were lower, and that consequently they were unable to compete effectively with the British manufacturers, and were in a very depressed state.[1] They did not ask for a reduction of the duty on raw wool—probably believing that the agricultural states would not listen to such a proposal—but for an increase in the duties on cloth. The "Woollens Bill" of 1827, introduced in response to their demands, adopted the system of minimum values. All woollen manufactures, except worsted stuffs and blankets, costing less than 40 cents per square yard were to be rated, for the assessment of duty, at 40 cents; all costing between 40 cents and \$2·50 were to be rated at the latter figure; and all costing between \$2·50 and \$4 were to be rated at \$4. Unmanufactured wool was to be subject to a duty of 35 per cent. *ad valorem* for one year, and 40 per cent. subsequently, and for this purpose wool costing between 10 and 40 cents a pound was to be rated at the maximum figure. The Bill was passed by the House of Representatives, but was wrecked in the Senate, mainly owing to the cross-currents of party

[1] Stanwood, i. pp. 253–4, 277.

politics. But it had revived the whole protectionist movement, and a widespread campaign commenced in which the advocates of Protection found skilful and influential exponents of their views in Matthew Carey, an energetic pamphleteer, and Niles, whose *Weekly Register* became their storehouse of facts and arguments. After the Woollens Bill had been introduced, the Free Trade party had also realised the necessity of vigorous action, and they now began a counter-campaign. But unlike previous controversies on the tariff question, the economic discussion was now to become inextricably involved with party politics; and American tariff legislation entered upon a new stage. The "era of good feeling" was at an end; political parties were at last taking shape again, and round Andrew Jackson there was being formed a party which represented a break with all the traditions of the past.[1]

The outcome of the protectionist agitation was the Tariff Act of 1828, under which "the experiment of protecting was now to be carried to the highest point it ever reached."[2] That Act, destined to be known as the "Act of Abominations," was passed at a time when men's thoughts were concentrated on the approaching presidential campaign, and the determination of the Jackson party to secure the election of their chief. The supporters of the retiring President, Adams, whose leader was Henry Clay, were definitely in favour of Protection; the Jackson party was divided—the Southern members, who were united in their support of Jackson, being in favour of a considerable reduction of duties, whilst the Middle States, whose votes would turn the election, were almost as strongly protectionist. The outcome of this peculiar position was an extraordinary series of party complications and political manœuvres, in which Jackson's supporters were led with astonishing skill by Martin van Buren. A Tariff Bill was framed, greatly increasing duties on manufactured goods and raw materials alike; and ultimately it was passed by a curious

[1] Wilson, pp. 12–21.

[2] Bolles, ii. p. 407.

combination. The South voted solidly against it, as did two-thirds of the New England members; the vote of the Western and Middle States, combined with the protectionist vote from New England, carried it.[1] But the votes of the members were determined in the main by party considerations; many excessively high duties had been inserted in the Bill by the votes of Southern members desirous of making it so unpopular that it could not pass; yet though they voted against it at the last it was carried largely by the votes of people with whom they were politically allied, who were not anxious for Protection, but meant to capture the vote of the Middle States for their presidential candidate.[2] In this they were successful; at the election of November, 1828, Jackson was returned by an overwhelming majority.

The increases made by the new tariff in the customs duties were very considerable. The duties on hemp were raised from \$35 to \$45 a ton, though good hemp could scarcely be grown in the country; on molasses from 5 to 7½ cents a gallon, whilst drawbacks to the manufacturers of rum were refused; on pig-iron from 56 to 62½ cents per cwt.; on hammered bar-iron from 90 to 112 cents per cwt., and on rolled bar-iron from \$30 to \$37 a ton.[3] But the chief developments had regard to wool and woollen manufactures. It is admitted that the difficulties of the American manufacturers of woollen goods in meeting British competition were due in large measure to their technical deficiencies and the preference of the American consumers for the better quality goods from Great Britain;[4] but they secured in 1828 increased specific duties on woollen goods, though to nothing like the extent which they had desired. On the other hand, the old *ad valorem* duty on raw wool was replaced by a specific duty of 4 cents a pound, with the addition of an *ad valorem* rate which ultimately was to reach the height of 50 per cent. This particular clause seems to have

[1] Taussig, p. 98.

[2] The complicated story of these manœuvres can be read in Stanwood, i. chap. viii.

[3] Taussig, pp. 88–9, 93.

[4] Stanwood, i. p. 280.

been designed to secure the support of the agricultural states, and at the same time to damage the Tariff Act by making it unpopular with the manufacturers.

The passage of the Tariff Act of 1828 led immediately to one of the most fateful political conflicts in the history of the United States. We have seen that the Southern States were strongly opposed to Protection, and they were offended also by the appropriation of federal surplus revenues to the construction of public works, particularly roads and canals, almost entirely in the North, which with its growing manufactures was in urgent need of the development of its means of communication.[1] At the time when the new tariff proposals were being discussed in 1827, the inhabitants of South Carolina (always the leader of the South in action) had protested against the protective duties on the ground that "the duties laid by Congress, of whatever description, are levied in great part on articles purchased by Southern industry and consumed by the South; but these duties are expended almost exclusively for the benefit of other sections of the Union. . . . All that is taken from us is disposed of elsewhere. We are benefited in the South by those expenditures in no way that we can perceive and feel. All that we pay is accumulated in defending and improving distant sections of the Union, and the prosperity of the North is built upon the impoverishment of the South."[2] The Southern States had every claim for special consideration; in 1829 out of a total export valued at about $56,000,000, $34,000,000 represented the cotton, rice, and tobacco exported from the South.[3] The exports of raw cotton were valued at $26,575,000, as against $1,258,000 worth of cotton goods; South Carolina was fourth amongst the exporting states of the Union. In the tariff of 1828 protection for manu-

[1] Jackson was opposed to this policy, but was overruled by Congress (Wilson, p. 39).

[2] Quoted in Stanwood, i. p. 261.

[3] Wilson, p. 50. "The contribution of the South appears still more striking if it be compared with the total value of agricultural exports, which was a little under $44,000,000."

factures had reached a very high level; but the scheme then adopted was so thoroughly bad that all were agreed on the necessity of some changes; and for some time therefore, though its leaders were preparing their plans, the South did not think it necessary to take decisive action.

The first changes were made in 1830. The duties were reduced on tea by 50 per cent., on coffee by 60 per cent. (and after 1831 by 80 per cent.), and on cocoa by 50 per cent., whilst the duty on molasses was put back to the old level, and the system of drawbacks renewed. But these were not all the changes required; the agitation of the Free Trade party continued, though it is important to notice that they did not ask for a complete abolition of duties—in fact, they were willing on financial grounds to retain somewhat heavy rates. In the Petition to the Senate, from the Free Trade Convention at Philadelphia in 1831, it is stated that "the people prefer, in time of peace, duties raised on the importation of foreign merchandise to any internal tax, direct or indirect. Whether for good or for evil, that system affords an encouragement to domestic manufactures not less efficient for being incidental. *Duties on imports, amounting on an average to about 20 per cent. of the value, appear necessary to the support of Government.*"[1] The petitioners condemn the high duties of 1828, even after the changes of 1830, because without giving real help to the protected trades they hamper all the others. They point out that in the existing conditions of American industry manufacturers must have recourse to foreign supplies—they give as an instance iron goods, with growing imports in spite of increased duties[2]—and they complain that the duties

[1] Text in Taussig, *State Papers.* The Petition, which is an elaborate statement of the practical argument for Free Trade, was written by Albert Gallatin.

[2] The Petition gives the following figures of imports:

Period.	Rolled Iron.	Hammered Iron.	Manufactures of Iron.
1817–1820	2,237 tons	16,887 tons	Not ascertained
1821–1824	4,212 ,,	23,162 ,,	$2,600,000
1825–1827	5,400 ,,	22,650 ,,	$3,630,000
1828–1830	6,450 ,,	31,000 ,,	$3,660,000

greatly increase the cost of materials to manufacturers, especially the shipbuilders. The same petition also presents what is probably the best short statement of the Southern objections to the protective legislation: "The Southern States have always confined themselves almost exclusively to the cultivation of the rich products of their climate. This is the only advantage they enjoy, and they owe it to nature. As they make but few, they consume a much greater proportion of manufactured articles imported from other states or other countries. That system, therefore, that enhances beyond measure the price of those objects of necessary consumption operates most unequally and unjustly upon them. They are forbidden to supply themselves on the cheapest terms consistent with the revenue necessary for the exigencies of Government. As the greatest consumers, they must not only pay a greater share of the duties requisite to defray the necessary national expenditure, but they are compelled to pay the enhanced price occasioned by the protecting system. That system cannot be extended to them. They find in it no indemnity, no compensation for the injury which it inflicts upon them. They have not, they cannot, in self-defence erect manufacturing establishments. The nature of their population forbids it."[1]

[1] Readers of De Tocqueville's *La Démocratie en Amérique* will remember his description (17th ed., vol. ii. chap. x. pp. 320–5) of the contrast presented to the traveller down the Ohio River by the two banks, and his prophecy of a great conflict as the inevitable outcome of the difference between the economic and social organisation of North and South. With the opinion of the petitioners, quoted above, may be contrasted the belief of Hamilton, in his Report on Manufactures (Taussig, *State Papers*, p. 59), that "ideas of a contrariety of interests between the northern and southern regions of the Union are in the main as unfounded as they are mischievous. The diversity of circumstances on which such contrariety is usually predicated authorises a directly contrary conclusion." Forty years later De Tocqueville agreed with this: "Je vois bien dans les différentes parties de l'Union des intérêts differents, mais je n'en découvre pas qui soient contraires les uns aux autres" (*loc. cit.*, p. 369). But he anticipated conflict owing to the dissatisfaction of the South at seeing itself outpaced in prosperity and political power by the North, and the difference of temperament arising from the difference of economic conditions.

Moderate men in the Northern States were anxious to make some concession to the South, and the feeling in favour of a reduction of duties was strengthened by the condition of the public finances. The customs receipts had been sufficiently large to allow of the paying-off of the National Debt with great rapidity. Between January 1st, 1828, and Janaury 1st, 1832, the amount was reduced from $67,475,000 to $24,322,000, and the interest payable had fallen by one-half. Meanwhile the receipts from customs were rising; consequently, with the Congress which met in December, 1831, there began a revision of the tariff, and the new Act was adopted in June, 1832.[1] The duty on unmanufactured hemp was reduced by one-third; that on raw flax was abolished. The rates of duty on pig and bar iron were reduced, as were those on manufactured silk and a number of other articles. But the chief changes were in the case of wool and woollens; the cheaper kinds of raw wool were admitted free, on the others the duties were considerably reduced; on cheap woollen goods the *ad valorem* duty was reduced to 5 per cent., on worsted goods from 25 to 10 per cent.; on other qualities they were nominally increased but practically reduced, owing to the abolition of the system of minimums.[2] The number of absolutely free articles was increased from 49 to 180; tea and coffee imported in American vessels were to be free. "In fact, the protective system was put back, in the main, to where it had been in 1824. The result was to clear the tariff of the excrescences which had grown on it in 1828, and to put it in a form in which the protectionists could advocate its permanent retention."[3] But this very

[1] A Report of the Congressional Committee which prepared the scheme contains an elaborate discussion of the relative merits of specific and *ad valorem* duties, and declares in favour of the latter on the grounds that they affect all qualities of a commodity equally, as specific duties do not unless very elaborately detailed; and that they enable the proportion of taxation intended by the legislature to be maintained in spite of fluctuations of values. These advantages outweigh the disadvantage of the encouragement given to false declarations of value (Bolles, ii. pp. 415–16). For a fuller discussion of this question, see pp. 210-12.

[2] Stanwood, i. p. 384.

[3] Taussig, p. 105.

fact drove the Southern States into open revolt; so long as there was a chance, by ordinary legislative means, of overthrowing Protection, they were disinclined to have recourse to other weapons, but they interpreted the action of Congress in 1832 as meaning the permanent incorporation of Protection in the fiscal policy of the Union.

The line which the leaders of the South, especially Calhoun and Hayne, would take, had already been revealed; it was the adoption of a particular view as to the manner in which the Constitution should be interpreted. There were two possibilities: the Federal Government might be comparatively weak, and confined to the exercise of powers based on a strict and narrow interpretation of the actual terms of the Constitution, whilst the separate states enjoyed extensive rights and powers—that is to say, there could be a league of states, not a Union; or the Federal Government might continually increase in authority, and the terms of the Constitution might be liberally interpreted at the cost of a constant diminution of the powers of the various members of the Union. Economic and political considerations alike determined the Southern States to adopt the former view. Under their climatic conditions, and with slave labour, it was believed that there could be no considerable growth of manufactures, and it was quite certain that the South would be far outpaced in population and wealth by the North-Eastern, and still more by the Middle States. That would mean the political predominance of the North, and it seemed that the result would be the maintenance of the protective policy to which the South was so strenuously opposed—it might also mean the overthrow of slavery. The leaders of the South argued in the tariff controversies from 1827 to 1832, as we have seen, that the policy of Protection benefited one portion of the Union at the expense of another; and as they could not prevent the passage of the Tariff Acts, they maintained that the Acts themselves were unconstitutional, whatever the courts of justice might say. They argued that customs duties for protective purposes were not within the terms of that clause of the Constitution which authorised Congress "to lay and collect taxes, duties, imposts, and excises, to pay the debts and provide for the general defence and welfare of the United States"; or that even if they were so included, or could be by an application of the doctrine of "implied powers," the duties actually levied violated the rule that "all duties, imposts, and excises shall be uniform throughout the United States," since they bore more heavily upon the South than upon the North. But if the obnoxious tariff laws were passed, and maintained by the courts, what was to be done? In a famous debate in regard to public land, in 1830, Hayne, of South Carolina, had argued that "the Constitution of the Union was a compact between the states; that to make the Federal Government the sole judge, through its judiciary, of the extent of its own powers, was to leave the states utterly without guarantee of the rights reserved to them, and might result in destroying the federal character of the Government altogether; and that if the states could not defend themselves in cases where the unconstitutionality of acts of the Federal Government seemed to them deliberate and palpable, the government might be consolidated to a point of intolerable tyranny."[1]

Authority for the action now taken in 1833 was found in the resolutions passed by Virginia and Kentucky at the time of their entry into the Union, to the effect that "in case of a deliberate, palpable, and dangerous exercise of other powers, not granted by the said compact, the states, who are members thereof, have the right, and are in duty bound, to interpose, for arresting the progress of the evil, and for maintaining within their respective limits the authorities, rights, and liberties appertaining to them."[2] The practical application of this doctrine was the method of "nullification." On November 24th,

[1] Wilson, pp. 43–4.

[2] *Ibid.*, p. 45.

1832, a State Convention in South Carolina declared the Tariff Acts of 1828 and 1832 null and void within that state, and announced that, in the event of the Federal Government attempting to enforce the law, South Carolina would deem it necessary to withdraw from the Union. Jackson, originally elected with Southern support, had now been re-elected by an overwhelming majority, and whatever his personal views on the tariff question itself may have been,[1] he would have nothing to do with nullification, which he declared to be "incompatible with the existence of the Union, contradicted expressly by the letter of the Constitution, unauthorised by its spirit, inconsistent with every principle on which it was founded, and destructive of the great object for which it was formed."[2] In January, 1833, a Bill was introduced into Congress, known as the Force Bill,

[1] "That manufactures adequate to the supply of our domestic consumption would in the abstract be beneficial to our country there is no reason to doubt, and to effect their establishment there is perhaps no American citizen who would not for a while be willing to pay a higher price for them. But for this purpose it is presumed that a tariff of high duties, designed for perpetual protection, has entered into the minds of but few of our statesmen. The most they have anticipated is a temporary and, generally, incidental protection which they maintain has the effect to reduce the price by domestic competition below that of the foreign article. Experience, however, our best guide on this as on other subjects, makes it doubtful whether the advantages of this system are not counterbalanced by many evils, and whether it does not tend to beget in the minds of a large portion of our countrymen a spirit of discontent and jealousy dangerous to the stability of the Union.

"What, then, shall be done? Large interests have grown up under the implied pledge of our national legislation, which it would seem a violation of public faith suddenly to abandon. Nothing could justify it but the public safety, which is the supreme law. But those who have vested their capital in manufacturing establishments cannot expect that the people will continue to pay high taxes for their benefit, when the money is not required for any legitimate purpose in the administration of government. . . . Those who take an enlarged view of the condition of our country must be satisfied that the policy of protection must be ultimately limited to those articles of domestic manufacture which are indispensable to our safety in time of war" (Jackson, *Presidential Message of* 1832).

[2] Wilson, p. 61.

authorising the President to use the Federal military and naval forces to enforce the tariff, wherever the collectors might encounter obstacles. But neither side was anxious to push the matter to extremes. Not all the Southern States were prepared to follow South Carolina, and the Free Traders of the North cared more for the maintenance of the Constitution than for the overthrow of the tariff. On the other hand, the political leaders of the Protectionists recognised the necessity of yielding to some extent. In February Clay introduced his Compromise Bill. By it all duties in excess of 20 per cent. *ad valorem* were to be reduced by one-tenth of the excess in each alternate year up to 1839, and after that by a greater amount, so that the whole excess should be abolished by 1842; a number of duties were to be entirely abolished in 1833, and many more in 1842.[1] The result would be that by 1842 the free list would be much enlarged, and duties brought to a uniform level of 20 per cent. *ad valorem*. This amounted to "giving manufacturers ten years' notice to prepare for the final abandonment of the principle of Protection";[2] but it is more than probable that Clay and his friends did not anticipate any such event—they hoped that something would happen to enable the notice to be cancelled. The compromise was readily accepted by Calhoun on behalf of the South, and became law on March 2nd, 1833. On March 11th, South Carolina repealed the nullification ordinance, but also declared the Force Bill void.

As a temporary political expedient, Clay's compromise was successful in that it put an end to the crisis, but it did not settle the real question at issue. The Federal Government had asserted its right to enforce the Federal law even against the will of the individual states; but South Carolina still adhered to its doctrine of nullification. Practically, the South was victorious; it had compelled the North to repeal the obnoxious tariff, though the Force Bill remained on the statute book as

[1] Stanwood, i. pp. 307–8. [2] Bolles, ii. p. 425.

a statement of the powers of the Federal Government. The problem was put aside for a time, but it was to return a generation later to be solved only by war.[1]

[1] For the details of the conflict and the constitutional argument, see Wilson, pp. 23–65; Stanwood, i. chaps. ix. and x.; Johnston, *History of American Politics*, chaps. xi. to xiv.; and *cf.* Bryce, *American Commonwealth*, chaps. xxxi. to xxxv.

CHAPTER III

COMPROMISE, PROTECTION, AND REACTION—ECONOMIC DEVELOPMENT OF THE UNITED STATES TO 1860

FOR eight years the Customs Tariff established by the Compromise Act of 1833 remained untouched, and consequently during all that period the United States were moving steadily in the direction of the removal of restrictions upon foreign trade. The first four years, from the passage of the Act till towards the end of 1836, were a time of general prosperity, but, unfortunately, they were also coincident with the beginnings of financial disorder, resulting not from economic causes, but from the extraordinary policy of the Government.[1] The chief example of the reckless financial methods of the administration of President Jackson (1829–37) was the attack upon the United States Bank. That institution had been originally established in 1791 with a charter for twenty years, but from the first there had been considerable doubts as to the constitutional validity of the proceeding. The result was that the charter was allowed to lapse in 1811; but the bank had proved so useful that it was renewed in 1816. The Treasury had subscribed one-fifth of the bank's capital, and the President nominated one-fifth of its directors; it was the depository of the Federal revenues, its notes were legal tender for all payments to the United States Government, and it was bound to redeem its notes in specie on demand. From the first, the new Democratic party were hostile

[1] The year 1833 " marks the change, for some time impending, from rational and conservative, to reckless and destructive, finance, and from comparative prudence on the part of the business community to wild speculation " (Stanwood, ii. p. 1).

to the bank, partly because, with their theory as to the interpretation of the Constitution, they held the bank charter to be unconstitutional, in spite of a decision of the Supreme Court to the contrary effect in 1819; partly because they thought that its privileges constituted an "un-American monopoly"; and partly because they supposed it to exercise great political influence in the interest of their opponents. There seems to have been little basis for their charges in regard to this last matter, or for the further charges of mismanagement, but Jackson resolved to overthrow the bank, and when Congress passed an Act renewing the charter it encountered a Presidential veto, which the majority was not strong enough to override. Clay endeavoured to make the bank question the principal issue at the Presidential election in November, 1832, with disastrous results; the triumphant second election of Jackson only strengthened his determination to destroy the bank. In September, 1833, having at last secured a Secretary of the Treasury who was ready to help him, Jackson proceeded to withdraw the Government deposits from the bank, and not to replace them. The Federal revenues were henceforth to be deposited in certain selected state banks (*i.e.*, banks under state charters), which were not chosen always for their financial soundness, but in some cases at least for their usefulness for party purposes.[1]

In the years 1835 and 1836 there was a great increase in imports,[2] but in spite of this the reduction of duties

[1] Wilson, p. 88. Dewey (p. 209) apparently thinks that the charges against Jackson for favouritism in this matter are exaggerated; "the interests of the Government were well safeguarded."

[2] The following table shows the movements of imports and exports for the years 1831 to 1836 (in million £ sterling):

Years ending September 30.	Total Imports.	Total Exports.
	Million £.	Million £.
1831	20·0	15·0
1832	19·8	16·8
1833	21·0	17·8
1834	22·6	21·3
1835	28·5	24·0
1836	36·8	25·9

resulted in a diminished customs revenue. However, the sales of public land in these years were so great as to give the Treasury a huge surplus, and in 1836 the National Debt was extinguished.[1] If the sales of public land were to go on, a continued surplus might be expected. The obvious course would have been to reduce taxation, but no one was willing to touch the Compromise of 1833, which had already come to possess an almost sacred character. Consequently, it was decided, on the proposal of Calhoun, that on and after January 31st, 1837, all the surplus funds remaining in the Treasury above $5,000,000 should be distributed between the various states, with the proviso, however, that money so distributed could be recalled by the Federal Government if necessary—a course never adopted, and in fact impossible. Three such distributions were made in 1837, amounting to $37,000,000; after that there was no longer a surplus, but a deficit.

In the same period there was an extraordinary increase in the number of banks of issue (from 329 in 1829 to 788 in 1837),[2] stimulated by the new deposit system of the Federal Government, the growth of speculation, particularly in land, and the development of industry. The states exercised no control over the new banks, and allowed them, even when they possessed scarcely any capital, to issue notes freely. The country was flooded with paper money in all stages of depreciation, and prices rose rapidly. To protect itself as much as possible, the Treasury in July, 1836, issued a circular requiring all payments for public lands to be made in cash. This increased the difficulties of the money market, already very great and complicated by the calling-in of loans by English creditors;[3] and by the beginning of 1837 commercial credit was badly shaken. Food prices rose rapidly,[4] and then a sudden fall in the price of cotton,

[1] Stanwood, i. p. 284.

[2] Dewey, p. 225.

[3] *Ibid.*, p. 230.

[4] Between 1834 and 1837 flour rose from $5 to $11 a barrel, and corn from 53 cents to $1·15 a bushel; early in 1837 there were bread riots in New York (Wilson, p. 93).

following on the over-production resulting from the rapid rise in prices between 1833 and 1835, brought a general crash. All the banks in the country ceased payments in specie.[1] There was a sharp decline in the foreign trade of the United States, particularly in respect of imports.[2]

Little, if any, connection can be shown between the economic crisis thus brought about—a crisis the origin of which was purely financial—and the tariff legislation of 1833, for the reductions of duties under the Act of that year were to be very gradual, and would not become marked until about 1840.[3] The financial distress was due simply to the confusion into which the policy of the Jackson Administration and the growth of speculation, stimulated by the great sales of public lands and excessive credit to purchasers, had thrown the credit system of the country; consequently there seems to have been no proposal made in any quarter for an alteration of the tariff or a return to a greater measure of protection. After the crisis there was the inevitable period of stagnation—commercial recovery was very slow; and the general depression may have been, and probably was, increased by the knowledge of the manufacturers that under the Act of 1833 the pace of the reduction of duties was now to quicken. But, nevertheless, the efforts towards a change in the Tariff Act were very slight, and met with little support. Two financial reforms only

[1] Stanwood, ii. p. 8.

[2] The value of the total imports of merchandise was, for the year ending September 30, 1836, 36·8 million £; for 1837, 27·2 millions; and for 1838 only 20 millions. In the corresponding years the total exports of merchandise were 25·9 million £, 23·2 millions, and 21·9 millions respectively.

[3] Even Stanwood, who is strongly protectionist in sympathy, writes: "No candid student of history will hold that the Tariff Act of 1833 had even a slight direct influence, by an injurious effect upon domestic manufacture, in bringing on the crisis. The evidence is necessarily of a negative character, but it is conclusive. The fact that manufacturers were flourishing up to the time when the financial storm burst, as all authorities deemed that they were, is all-sufficing" (Stanwood, ii. p. 8). The connection of this and the following crisis with the tariff appears to have been a later invention of Henry Carey.

were made. In 1838 the State of New York began the policy of permitting the establishment of any bank without the need for a special charter, on condition of its promoters depositing with the State Treasury securities to the amount represented by its issue of notes. In 1840, further, the Independent Treasury Act was passed by Congress; under its terms the Treasury was itself to keep all the proceeds of the public revenue in its own hands (not making use of the banks), and to make and receive payments only in specie.[1]

By the time of the election of November, 1840, the Democrats were utterly discredited, in spite of some diplomatic successes of Van Buren, who had succeeded Jackson as President in 1837. The main defects of his administration had been his steadfast adherence to the financial policy of his predecessor, and his failure to devise any satisfactory measures for dealing with the commercial situation. The new political parties had now been definitely formed; on the one side were the Democrats, led by the President himself and Benton, with their advocacy of a conservative interpretation of the Constitution and their consequent opposition to the expenditure of Federal moneys on internal improvements, to Protection, and to the National Bank; and on the other side were the Whigs, as the Republican party of Clay and ex-President Adams was called since 1834, representing many diverse elements, but agreed upon a wide interpretation of the Constitution and protective legislation. Already there were signs of the difficulties to be caused later by the anti-slavery party—a more serious menace to the Democrats than to the Whigs, since the former were dependent for much of their political strength on the South.[2] The Whigs, not so much because of their new policy as because of the discredit into which the Democrats had fallen, were able to carry the election of Harrison, a successful soldier, as President

[1] Dewey, pp. 235–7.

[2] Wilson, pp. 112–14. *Cf.* Johnston, *American Politics*, chaps. xiii. and xiv.

in November, 1840, and immediately upon his taking office they prepared to enter upon a course of financial legislation. They proposed to repeal the Independent Treasury Act, to re-establish the National Bank, to amend the tariff in order to meet the large Treasury deficit, and also to distribute amongst the states the proceeds of the sales of public lands, so that these would not henceforth be reckoned as a source of Federal revenue. But scarcely had these proposals been put forward when the President died, and was succeeded by Vice-President Tyler. The new President was not a Whig at all, but a discontented Democrat, who had been adopted by the Whigs as one of their candidates only in order to detach a certain number of votes from their opponents and to attempt to secure doubtful states. He was by no means in sympathy with their proposals and immediately vetoed a Bill establishing a new National Bank. The Distribution Bill was carried only after some difficulties with the President and subject to the proviso (which in fact reduced it to impotence) that the distribution should be suspended if at any time it appeared necessary for revenue purposes to levy customs duties of more than 20 per cent. *ad valorem.* As a hasty expedient to provide money a temporary Tariff Act was passed in September, 1841, laying a duty of 20 per cent. on all merchandise previously paying less, or free; there were, however, certain exceptions to this general rule, and the proposal to tax tea and coffee was rejected.[1]

By the end of 1841, the financial situation was worse than ever. In spite of large issues of Treasury notes, there was a heavy deficit, and there seemed every likelihood that the final remissions of duty, now about to take place under the Act of 1833, would still further increase the difficulties of the Treasury. This fact, coupled with the general uncertainty, probably seriously

[1] One of the earliest acts of the new Whig administration was the repeal of the Independent Treasury Act in 1841. The Act was restored in 1846, and has remained in force since (Dewey, pp. 239, 252–5).

hampered the manufacturers and merchants; and the commercial troubles had again become acute. In 1841 fifty-five banks had stopped payment; in January, 1842, six states, including Pennsylvania and Maryland, were unable to meet their obligations; and by the end of April the operations of twenty-six more banks were suspended.[1] It was absolutely necessary for some action to be taken, and the only remedy which occurred to the statesmen of the United States was a revision of the tariff; after another temporary measure had been passed in June, 1842, to prolong certain duties, Congress adopted in August of that year a new Tariff Act, which was carried only after much difficulty, and by means of complicated parliamentary manœuvres. It was the work of the Whigs, and was therefore on the whole decidedly protectionist;[2] and it was much more elaborately detailed than any of its predecessors. It was based on the Tariff Act of 1832, and in comparison with that it increased the duties on cotton manufactures, on glass, and on the cheapest wools, whilst it reduced the duties on woollens, wool, leather, and some other commodities. But in contrast to the level of the duties in 1841, which under the Compromise Act were drawing close to an all-round rate of 20 per cent., the Act of 1842 marks a distinct return towards Protection. The average duty was to be about 30 per cent., though on manufactured goods it was decidedly higher. There can, on the whole, be little doubt that the new Act had a distinctly beneficent effect,[3] mainly because it gave the manufacturers certainty

[1] Stanwood, ii. p. 18.

[2] "It marks the last triumph of the protectionist policy before the Civil War" (Mayo-Smith and Seligman, p. 9.)

[3] Stanwood becomes enthusiastic on the point. "The final plunge to the 20 per cent. maximum rate of the compromise tariff was bringing the industries dependent upon protection to a standstill; and all business suffered in the stagnation of employment, in the cessation of the movement of money and goods, which are as the circulation of the blood in the body of commerce. The adoption of any improved tariff would have removed one cause of the existing evil—the uncertainty as to the future. The enactment of a tariff which promised prosperity and health to the starved manufacturers removed all causes, and actually restored

as to the conditions under which their industries were to be carried on, and helped to improve matters in the iron and cotton industries, which contributed an impetus to all the rest. It is at any rate certain that in 1842 there began a revival of trade and commerce, and although such a revival must assuredly have taken place in any case, it is probable that it was quickened by the increased protection afforded by the new tariff. And from the point of view of revenue the new rates of customs duties were quite satisfactory; in the year ending June 30th, 1844, and onwards,[1] the Treasury found itself again in possession of a surplus.

But the tariff was not destined to remain long untouched. The Presidential election of November, 1844, resulted in the triumph of the Democrats, represented by Polk.[2] The new President was opposed to the whole protectionist system, though his colleague in the campaign, the Democratic candidate for the Vice-Presidency, was a Protectionist, and so was able to secure Pennsylvania for his party. In his first message to Congress, President Polk urged that the power of that body to levy customs duties should be exercised solely for revenue purposes; and in December, 1845, his Secretary of the Treasury, Walker, presented to Congress a lengthy report on the tariff, which was simply an elaborate argument for Free Trade.[3] After expressing doubts as to the constitutional validity of protective duties, the Secretary proceeds to argue against them on economic grounds;

---

the prosperity which it promised. There is no other enactment affecting the duties on imports, the effect of which is so clear, so indisputable, as there was never another which worked so instantaneously" (ii. pp. 36–7).

Taussig is more moderate, but agrees that, in the manner indicated above, the tariff did have a decidedly good effect on the commercial and industrial situation.

[1] Since 1844 the United States fiscal year has ended on June 30; prior to that date it ended on September 30.

[2] The defeat of the Whigs was due in part at least to the abstention of the anti-slavery party, who threw away their votes on an independent candidate of their own.

[3] Full text in Taussig, *State Papers*.

and some passages from the Report may be quoted as illustrating his general line of argument. He wrote:—

"At least two-thirds of the taxes imposed by the present tariff are paid, not into the Treasury, but to the protected classes. The revenue from imports last year exceeded twenty-seven millions of dollars. This in itself is a heavy tax; but the whole tax imposed upon the people by the present tariff is not less than eighty-one millions of dollars—of which twenty-seven millions are paid to the Government upon the imports and fifty-four millions to the protected classes in enhanced prices of similar domestic articles.

"The occasional fall in prices of some articles after a tariff is no proof that this was the effect of the tariff; because from improved machinery, diminished prices of the raw material, or other causes, prices may fall even after a tariff, but they would in such cases have fallen even more but for the tariff. The truest comparison is between the present price of the same article at home and abroad; and to the extent that the price is lower in the foreign market than in our own, the duty, if equal to the difference, must to that extent enhance the price, and in the same ratio with the lower duty.

"An appeal has been made to the poor by the friends of Protection, on the ground that it augments the wages of labour. In reply it is contended that the wages of labour have not augmented since the tariff of 1842, and that in some cases they have diminished.[1] . . . A protective tariff is a question regarding the enhancement of the profits of capital. That is its object, and not to augment the wages of labour, which would reduce those profits. It is a question of percentage, and is to decide whether money vested in our manufactures shall by special legislation yield a profit of 10, 20, or 30 per cent., or whether it shall remain satisfied with a dividend equal to that accruing from the same capital invested in agriculture, commerce, or navigation.

[1] There seems to be no adequate evidence for this statement of the Secretary.

"The tariff is thus a double benefit to the manufacturer and a double loss to the farmer and planter—a benefit to the former in nearly a monopoly of the home market and in enhanced prices of his fabrics; and a loss to the latter in the payment of those high prices and a total or partial exclusion from the foreign market. The true question is whether the farmer and planter shall to a great extent supply our people with cheap manufactures purchased abroad with their agricultural products, or whether this exchange shall be forbidden by high duties on such manufactures, and their supply thrown as a monopoly, at large prices, by high tariffs, into the hands of our own manufacturers.

"Let our commerce be as free as our political institutions. Let us, with revenue duties only, open our ports to all the world, and nation after nation will soon follow our example. If we reduce our tariff, the party opposed to the Corn Laws of England would soon prevail and admit all our agricultural products at all times freely into her ports in exchange for her exports. And if England would now repeal her duties upon our wheat, flour, Indian corn, and other agricultural products, our own restrictive system would certainly be doomed to overthrow."[1]

Proceeding from these principles, the Secretary advocated duties for revenue purposes only, with the imposition of maximum rates on luxuries, the abolition of all minimums and of all specific duties, and the substitution of *ad valorem* rates.

The result of this policy of the President and his advisers was the Tariff Act of 1846, adopted after only a short, though at times exciting, parliamentary struggle. All minimums and specific duties were abolished, and commodities were divided into a number of classes with

[1] Bolles (ii. pp. 449–50) speaks of the British manufacturers "having zealously laboured for Polk's election, and contributed munificently to that end." He alleges that large sums of money were subscribed in England and expended on behalf of Polk's candidature in the United States. Elsewhere (p. 452) he speaks of the tariff of 1846 as "sponsored by the English nation." No satisfactory evidence for these statements is offered.

duties ranging from 5 per cent. to 40 per cent., and in the one case of brandy and spirits to 100 per cent. There was also a class of free articles, the chief being tea, coffee, and iron and copper ore. Manufactures of iron and other metals, wool and woollens paid 30 per cent., as did manufactures of leather and glass; cotton goods paid 25 per cent. On the whole, the duties were considerably lower than under the Act of 1842.

The new tariff remained in force for eleven years with practically no alterations; during that period the United States experienced a very rapid economic development, and it will be convenient to bring together in this place some evidences of the progress made in the two decades from 1840 to 1860. The total population (white and coloured) of the United States was 17,069,000 in 1840, and had increased to 31,443,000 twenty years later.[1] By 1850 the factory system was firmly established,[2] but the population was still overwhelmingly agricultural; in 1850, when the first really reliable census of the United States was taken, only 12·5 per cent. of the population, and in 1860 only 16·1 per cent., were living in urban areas with more than 8,000 inhabitants.[3] The quantity of wheat produced was 85,000,000 bushels in 1840, and had risen to more than double that amount (173,000,000) in 1860; during the same period the production of corn (maize) rose from 377,500,000 bushels to 839,000,000—in both cases the supply was almost entirely for the home market.[4] In 1840 the amount of

[1] In the first of these years negroes and Indians numbered 2,874,000, and in 1860 4,442,000. Allowance must be made for increases of territory (*e.g.*, in Texas and Mexico) between these dates. Between 1846 and 1857 the United States received more than three million immigrants (Stanwood, ii. p. 87). In each of the five years after 1849 the annual number was over 350,000.

[2] "It was not until about 1840 that the factory method of manufacture extended itself widely to miscellaneous industries, and began rapidly to force from the markets the hand-made products with which every community had hitherto chiefly supplied itself. It seems probable that until about the year 1850, the bulk of general manufacturing done in the United States was carried on in the shop and the household, by the labour of the family or individual proprietors, with apprentice assistance" (*Twelfth Census*, vii. p. liii.).

[3] As against 33·1 in 1900.

[4] *Statistical Abstract of the United States*, 1908, pp. 689–90.

cotton grown was 1,348,000 bales,[1] and ten years later it had reached 2,137,000 bales; subsequently, it underwent considerable fluctuations, but reached 4,310,000 bales in 1859, and 4,491,000 bales in 1861—the latter figure not being reached again until 1877.[2] The output of cane sugar was 248,000,000 pounds in 1840; subsequently, the fluctuations were more marked than even in the case of cotton, the maximum production being 525,000,000 pounds in 1854 and the minimum 87,000,000 pounds in 1857.[3]

The total value of the manufactured products of the United States was estimated in 1850 at 1,019 million dollars, and in 1860 at 1,886 million dollars.[4] A great stimulus had been given to industry by the discovery of a number of new processes, which came into general use from about 1845 onward. The year 1838 had witnessed the invention of Nasmyth's steam-hammer, and about 1840 anthracite coal began to be used for the production of iron; in 1841 the power-loom for carpet-weaving was invented, and some years earlier the knitting-frame had been first worked by machinery. The output of coal was in 1840, 1,848,000 tons; ten years later it was 6,266,000 tons, and in 1860, 13,045,000 tons (it had once exceeded this amount by nearly 1,000,000 tons, in 1859[5]). The production of pig-iron amounted to 287,000 tons in 1840, and by 1860 had reached 821,000 tons.[6] The quantity of steel rails manufactured in the United States was estimated at 24,000 tons in 1849, and 205,000 tons in 1860.[7] The number of cotton spindles employed in the United States was reckoned at 2,285,000 in 1840; it rose to 3,998,000 in 1850 and to 5,236,000 in 1860.[8] In the last-mentioned year more than two-thirds of the total number were in New England.[9] The exports of cotton goods were comparatively small

[1] Of 500 lb. gross weight.
[2] *Statistical Abstract*, p. 690.
[3] *Ibid.*, p. 690.
[4] *Twelfth Census*, vol. vii., p. xlvii.
[5] *Statistical Abstract*, p. 691.
[6] *Ibid.*, p. 693.
[7] Taussig, p. 134, quoting from *Report of the Iron and Steel Association for* 1876.
[8] *Statistical Abstract*, p. 696.
[9] Taussig, p. 141 n.

and variable, and the rapid increase of production failed to keep pace with the demand, with the result that imports also showed a marked expansion.[1] The woollen manufacturers were hampered by the duty of 30 per cent. *ad valorem* on raw wool, and there was little advance in the production of woollens of the best quality; but in regard to the coarser goods there was distinct progress, and the census returns gave the value of the products of the woollen manufacturers as 20 million dollars in 1840, 48·6 millions in 1850, and 73·5 millions in 1860.[2]

The foreign trade of the United States also underwent a great expansion. The following table gives the figures of the total imports and exports, of merchandise only, from 1847 to 1857, when another alteration in the tariff was made:[3]

Year.	Total Imports.	Total Exports.
	Million £.	Million £.
1847 ..	25·5	32·7
1848 ..	30·5	28·8
1849 ..	29·4	29·2
1850 ..	36·1	30·1
1851 ..	43·9	39·4
1852 ..	43·2	34·8
1853 ..	54·9	42·4
1854 ..	62·0	49·4
1855 ..	53·7	45·6
1856 ..	64·7	58·6
1857 ..	72·6	61·2

[1] The following table gives some representative figures:

Year.	Value of	
	Domestic Production of Cotton Goods.	Imports of Cotton Goods.
	Million $.	Million $.
1840 ..	46	6·5
1850 ..	62	20·8
1860 ..	116	33·2

[2] *Statistical Abstract*, p. 697. Against this must be set Stanwood's assertion (ii. p. 92) that "the new tariff practically ruined the woollen industry, which had revived and become fairly flourishing under the protection it received under the Act of 1842." Bolles (ii. pp. 456–7) shares this view, but both writers admit that one of the chief difficulties of the woollen manufacturers was the high duties imposed on raw wool.

[3] *Foreign Commerce and Navigation of the United States*, 1908, pp. 40–1.

It will be observed that from 1850 onwards there was thus, as regards ordinary merchandise, a relatively large preponderance of imports over exports, but this was counterbalanced by the great export of gold after the discovery of the Californian mines. In 1848 the gold produced in the United States was valued at about $10,000,000; it rose to $40,000,000 in the following year, and then steadily to $64,000,000 in 1853. It may be remarked that manufactured goods ready for consumption constituted 55 per cent. of the total imports in 1850, and 56·5 per cent. in 1860; they formed, on the other hand, only 12·7 per cent. of the exports in the former year, and 11·3 per cent. in the latter year. In spite of the lower rates of duty the customs revenue, which under the tariff of 1842 had reached the sum of $27,500,000, now increased by 1856 to $64,000,000.

Contemporary with this great economic development —at once a cause and a consequence of it—there was a rapid growth of means of transport. In 1840 there were 2,818 miles of railway in the United States; in 1850, 9,021 miles; and in 1860, 30,635 miles. The net tonnage of the shipping registered in the United States in each of these years is shown in the following table:[1]

Year	Net Tonnage of United States Shipping.		
	Engaged in Foreign Trade.	Engaged in Coastwise Trade.	Engaged in Commerce of Great Lakes.
1840	899,765	1,280,999	198,266
1850	1,585,711	1,949,743	211,145
1860	2,546,237	2,807,631	467,744

It is extremely difficult to form anything approaching an estimate of the influence of the tariff of 1846 upon the economic development thus briefly outlined; the opinions of American authorities on the subject differ with the

[1] *Statistical Abstract*, 1908, p. 702. Vessels engaged in the whale fisheries are classed with those in foreign trade; vessels engaged in the cod and mackerel fisheries with those in the coastwise trade.

general attitude of the writers towards the whole question of Protection and Free Trade. The critics of the tariff legislation of 1846 cannot profess that it did more than slightly retard the industrial progress of the United States; whilst its warmest supporters do not pretend that it did much to hasten the development. In fact, its effect in either direction was probably only small; the United States were just beginning to exploit their great and varied resources, and the movement of economic development as a whole was sufficiently strong (whatever might be the case with isolated industries) to be practically unaffected by tariff enactments.[1]

[1] "The wonderful revolution which was taking place in commerce and in history makes it impossible to generalize from this experience as to the effect of import duties upon economic development; very likely prosperity would have followed under any system of revenue laws" (Dewey, p. 257). *Cf.* Taussig, pp. 116–22.

CHAPTER IV

WAR TAXATION AND ITS RETENTION FOR PROTECTIVE PURPOSES

At intervals during a period of eleven years after the passage of the Tariff Act of 1846, suggestions were made from time to time, first by the Whig Presidents, Taylor and Fillmore (1849–1853), for a revision of the tariff in order to increase the protection given to manufacturers; but their recommendations remained unheeded, and when a change was at last made it was in the opposite direction. The Democratic successor of Fillmore, Pierce (1853–1857), repeatedly urged the reduction of the tariff duties on the ground that the Treasury was in possession of a surplus. But partly because of the party confusion caused by the break-up of the Democrats and the formation of the new Republican party, composed of the old Whigs and some of the Democrats, and partly because of the growing concentration of public interest on the slavery question, nothing was done until 1857. In that year an Act was passed, providing for a reduction of 20 or 25 per cent. all round on the rates of duty levied by the Act of 1846; the highest protective duty henceforward was to be 24 per cent. *ad valorem* (except for a few special cases, such as wines and spirits), and the general level was lower than in any period since 1816.[1]

[1] Mayo-Smith and Seligman, p. 10. The two highest rates were reduced from 100 per cent. (spirits) and 40 per cent. (wines) to 30 per cent. *ad valorem* each; the 30 per cent. duties (on such articles as manufactures of copper, brass, lead, iron and steel, glass and leather, and some cotton and woollen goods) to 24 per cent.; the 25 per cent. duties (on certain manufactures of cotton and silk) to 19 per cent.; the 20 per cent. duties (on such articles as barley, blankets, candles, linen, certain woollen and cotton manufactures, and window glass) to 15 per cent.; and so on.

The free list was extended, mainly for raw materials and including particularly the cheaper kinds of wool. The Act appears to have attracted very little public attention; no one was specially hostile to it, and the woollen manufacturers were anxious to secure the cheapening of their raw materials.[1] But it was somewhat unfortunate for the supporters of Free Trade that the passage of the Act, which reduced the duties to the lowest point they had reached for almost half a century, should have been followed almost immediately by a considerable financial crisis. There is no evidence that this was connected in any way with the tariff legislation, though some politicians subsequently alleged that the effect of the reductions of 1846 was now first felt, because had the old protective policy been maintained the crisis of 1857 would have been greatly mitigated.[2] The disasters of 1857 were, in fact, of a familiar kind; they were the result of the over-confidence arising from a long period of prosperity, from the consequent growth of speculation, the undue development of railways followed by a decline in the value of railway stocks, and from excessive importations; and they were intensified by an unsatisfactory banking system and the exaggerated issue of unsecured paper money. The crisis came suddenly; it affected the merchants and bankers rather than the manufacturers; and there is nothing to show that it seriously hindered, even for a time, the industrial progress of the country. There was an abrupt fall in the imports for home consumption, from a value of 69·5 million pounds in 1856–7 to 50·6 million pounds in 1857–8;

[1] Speaking of the woollen manufactures, Stanwood (ii. p. 109) has a curious phrase: "The situation previously existing was intolerable. . . . In the prevailing state of public opinion—made up of active hostility to Protection in the southern half of the country, and of indifference in the northern half, where the slavery question absorbed popular interest and left room for the consideration of no other business questions—they were hopeless of obtaining even a hearing upon the merits of the tariff controversy. They therefore asked for and ultimately secured *such a measure of protection as was afforded by cheaper raw material.*"

[2] So J. G. Blaine, quoted by Dewey, p. 264.

and the customs revenue declined consequently by one-third. The result was that the Treasury found itself again faced with a deficit, which continued for some time, and which it could not entirely meet even by means of loans.

The financial needs of the Government revived the protectionist movement, but action was delayed for a time by the complications of party politics. At the election of November, 1856, the Democratic candidate, Buchanan, had been elected to the Presidency, and the Democratic party was openly opposed to Protection. The new Republican party was for a time uncertain; it contained a number of ex-Democrats, and it was unsafe at first to alienate these by a strenuous advocacy of Protection; whilst, on the other hand, only such definite advocacy could secure the support of the great state of Pennsylvania and some other Middle States, whose action would probably be decisive at the next election. But by 1860 the advocates of the extension of the slave power had become so identified with the Free Traders, and the Republican party was so well united, that its leaders thought it safe to avow that "while providing revenue for the support of the general Government by duties upon imports, sound policy requires such an adjustment of these imposts as to encourage the development of the industrial interests of the whole country; and we commend that policy of national exchanges which secures to the working men liberal wages, to agriculture remunerating prices, to mechanics and manufacturers an adequate reward for their skill, labour, and enterprise, and to the nation commercial prosperity and independence." The Republicans controlled the House of Representatives which met in December, 1859, and therefore Morrill introduced in March of the following year the Tariff Act, which has since been known by his name. In theory it was an Act for revenue purposes only, and was to provide a remedy for the growing deficits, which amounted altogether to more than 10 million pounds for the years 1858–60; and it professed to restore duties to the rates of 1846. It encountered considerable difficulties, particularly in the Senate, where there was a Democratic majority, and the way only became clear for it when at the end of 1860 the secession of the Southern States, which followed closely on the election of Lincoln to the Presidency, had withdrawn a number of Democratic Senators, and given the control of that House also to the Republicans.

The new tariff, which came into force in March, 1861, was characterised chiefly by the increased protection which it gave to the manufacturers of iron and steel and of woollen goods, and to the growers of wool; these industries being especially favoured in an attempt to capture the votes of Pennsylvania and the west for the Republican party. The rates of duty on iron and steel goods had been reduced to 24 per cent. *ad valorem* by the Act of 1857; they were now changed into varying specific duties, ranging from $6 a ton in the case of pig-iron, to $15 to $20 a ton for iron rails, and to a combined specific and *ad valorem* rate (1½ to 2½ cents *plus* 15 per cent. *ad valorem* per lb.) in the case of steel—changes which involved a considerable increase. As regards wool and manufactures thereof, a complicated system was introduced; wool costing less than 18 cents a lb. was to pay a duty of 5 per cent. *ad valorem;* when costing 18 to 24 cents it was to pay 3 cents a lb., and when above that value 9 cents a lb. Woollen yarns and other manufactures in their turn were given *ad valorem* rates of 15 to 25 and 25 per cent. respectively, with an additional "compensating" duty in each case of 12 cents a lb. In the case of a number of other commodities specific rates were substituted for the *ad valorem* rates hitherto in force, and the general effect of the changes was to raise the rates above the level of 1846.[1] But in spite of the increased protection which it afforded,

[1] Comparative summary tables of this and other tariffs are given by Mayo-Smith and Seligman, pp. 66–72.

the general body of manufacturers cared little for the new tariff.[1]

That tariff was short-lived; the Civil War commenced, and Congress found itself compelled to enter on a course of extraordinary financial legislation in order to meet the tremendous expenditure which the struggle involved. In August and December, 1861, duties were imposed on many articles hitherto free, and the rates on a number of commodities, such as tea, coffee, sugar, hemp, hides, rubber, silk, spices, and a few others, were largely increased. In the following year financial needs compelled Congress to have recourse to internal taxation, and the imposition of specific duties on some home manufactures, such as iron and steel, paper and leather, and *ad valorem* duties on most others; a general income tax was also established. Partly in order to raise further supplies of money, and partly to compensate the manufacturers for the burdens which the new internal taxes imposed upon them, the Customs Act of July, 1862, again increased duties generally, raising them to an average of 37 per cent.[2] The free list established by the Morrill Tariff of 1861 was cut down by nearly one-half. But this was not the end; after some small additions, the culmination was reached in the Act of June, 1864, which was accompanied by an Internal Revenue Act, creating twenty-two new kinds of taxes—" a system of taxation more comprehensive, more burdensome and more confused than it has ever been the lot of any other civilised community to bear "[3]—and the issue of a huge loan. The Customs Act raised the average duty to 47 per cent., and enumerated 1,450 separate articles; it

[1] Mr. Morrill is reported to have said later that the tariff of 1861 " was not asked for, and but coldly welcomed, by manufacturers, who always and justly fear instability " (Taussig, p. 160).

[2] Mayo-Smith and Seligman, p. 12. " If we bleed manufacturers we must see to it that the proper tonic is administered at the same time " (Morrill, quoted by Taussig, p. 162). The duties on imports were required to be paid in specie, whilst internal taxes were paid in the rapidly depreciating paper currency of the United States (Bolles, iii. p. 186).

[3] Mayo-Smith and Seligman, p. 13.

increased the customs revenue from about 22 million pounds in 1863–4 to nearly double that amount in 1864–5.[1] The difficulties arising from the heavy burden of taxation were increased enormously by the rapid rise of prices, due in part to the depreciation of the inconvertible paper currency, which reached its lowest point in the last six months of 1864, when the average gold price of 100 dollars in currency was only about 43 dollars. Average prices rose 117 per cent. between 1860 and 1865, and money wages rose only 43 per cent.[2]

Unfortunately the manufacturers desirous of protection found their opportunity in the difficulties of the Government. It is true that they could reasonably claim some compensation for the heavy burdens laid upon them by the system of internal taxation which had been adopted, but they went much further than this.[3] They secured an almost unlimited protection, and their action and the general effect of the war tariff on the United States are thus described by two of the ablest economists of that country: "The tariff of 1864 is the real war tariff, and the basis of the present tariff. While the main reasons of its passage were without doubt the need of increased revenue for the Government and the desire to compensate the various interests for the burdens imposed on them by the internal revenue, it is undeniable

[1] The following table shows the movement of imports for domestic consumption and exports of United States produce from 1861 to 1866. The Civil War began in April, 1861, and ended with the surrender of General Lee at Appomattox in April, 1865:

Years ending June 30.	Imports for Domestic Consumption.	Exports of United States Produce.
	Million £.	Million £.
1861	57·2	42·7
1862	37·2	37·4
1863	47·0	38·8
1864	62·7	29·9
1865	43·7	28·5
1866	88·2	27·6

—*British and Foreign Trade and Industry*, 1909, p. 64.

[2] Dewey, pp. 293–4.

[3] "The Bill (of 1864) is full of examples of their prowess" (Stanwood, ii. p. 129).

that its final shape was largely owing to the endeavours of the protected manufacturers to gain each for himself the greatest possible advantage irrespective of the other's interests. Above all, the habits engendered during this period of comprehensive protection to everything led to a crystallisation of the sentiment in favour of national exclusion and isolation. The commercial policy of the United States for many decades was moulded by the feelings and habits generated during this period of the Civil War. Henceforth the movement in favour of high protection, which still in great part dominates the American people, was to become the leading feature in the commercial and political life of the country. What was in its origin a mere temporary expedient called forth by the exigencies of a great military struggle was to become a permanent institution."[1]

For a number of years after the close of the Civil War the tariff policy of the United States remained absolutely unchanged in its general character. The effects of the war had been bad enough in the North, but they were far worse in the South. In the states which had remained loyal to the Federal Government there had been indeed a terribly heavy burden of taxation, but to some extent compensation had been found for this in the growth of manufactures, which had resulted from the vast demand for military supplies and had been fostered by the high protective duties imposed by the war tariffs. But, on the contrary, the Southern states, dependent on the sale of their produce in foreign markets, had found their export trade destroyed by the rigorous blockading of their ports by the Federal Navy, and had practically no manufactures capable of development; moreover, as they had relatively but a small population[2] and were compelled to maintain very large armies, there had been little labour left available for agriculture or industry.

[1] Mayo-Smith and Seligman, pp. 13–14.

[2] The total population, white and black, of the Confederate States was about 9 millions (two-thirds being whites); the population of the Federal States was over 22 millions, less than 1 million being negroes.

This, coupled with a system of taxation even more oppressive than that employed in the North, had brought the South almost to complete economic ruin. Now, after the war was ended, the newly confirmed Union found itself confronted with an extremely heavy debt for that period in the world's history (nearly 600 million pounds), and a greatly depreciated currency (owing to the large amounts of inconvertible paper money issued by both sides during the conflict); the great ravages caused by military operations, particularly in the South, had to be made good; and the old slave states had the difficult problem of replacing slave by free labour, at the time when they were financially least able to do so.

The most urgent task was financial reorganisation, but it was undertaken only gradually, and in a one-sided manner; the tariff remained for some years untouched in most respects. For the delay, three reasons may be assigned.[1] There was first the concentration of the attention of Congress on the problem of political reconstruction. The President, Andrew Johnson, was inclined to follow in the treatment of the Southern states the liberal policy of his predecessor, Lincoln. But he possessed neither the power nor the judgment of Lincoln; and, moreover, he was a Southerner, and though a strenuous supporter of the Union, inclined to hold the doctrine of state rights. The triumphant Republican party of the North would have nothing to do with the President's conciliatory policy; it meant to use its power to the utmost, and adopted the theory that it could do what it liked in the reconstruction of the Southern states, and could, so far as they were concerned, suspend the Federal Constitution indefinitely. With the policy and methods actually adopted by Congress we are not concerned here; it is necessary only to point out that it was not until the beginning of 1871 that all the states of the Union were once more represented in Congress, and that during the four years of Johnson's Presidency (1865–9) there was an incessant conflict between the

[1] Mayo-Smith and Seligman, pp. 14–15.

President and the Legislature, which absorbed the energies of both parties.[1] The second reason was the desire to get rid as quickly as possible of the internal taxes, always peculiarly repugnant to Americans, and especially the income-tax. These constituted burdens which were severely felt by everyone, and felt directly, and they undoubtedly hampered industry in every conceivable way. It was therefore decided to remove them as quickly as possible, and by a series of Acts between 1867 and 1872 all were swept away except the excise on beer and spirits, and duties on matches, patent medicines and a few other commodities. The heavy import duties had been imposed, professedly at least, in part to compensate the manufacturers for the burden of the internal taxes, and theoretically, therefore, either the war surtaxes on imports should have been abolished at the same time as the internal war taxes, or, if financial considerations made that impossible, there should have been a simultaneous partial reduction of both classes. But the desire to get rid of the internal taxes was too strong; it therefore became necessary to maintain the import duties at a high level in order to meet the heavy cost of government, to prepare the way for the resumption of specie payments, and to reduce the debt as rapidly as possible. This retention of duties at the high existing level coincided with the desires of the manufacturers, who flourished (or thought they flourished) as the result of the protection afforded them, and could urge with some justice that there were a number of industries which had been called into existence only by the high tariff and the war, and must collapse if protection were withdrawn. This was the third and not least potent reason; the country seems to have made up its mind without much difficulty that for a time at least the extreme protective system must be maintained, and even in some cases increased.[2]

[1] See Wilson, pp. 254–72.

[2] "The whole industry of the country gradually adapted itself to the existence of the high tariff, and the people soon became convinced of the advantages of a policy of commercial stability. . . . Just as the country had accommodated itself to the so-called

In 1867 a Bill was introduced, prepared by a newly appointed Special Commissioner of the Revenue, and supported by the Secretary of the Treasury, which proposed to reduce substantially the rates of duty on raw material—lumber, dyes, coal, flax and others—and to reduce slightly the rates in respect of manufactured goods. The Bill secured a majority in both Houses of the Legislature, but it did not pass, owing to the failure to obtain the two-thirds majority in the House of Representatives necessary to overcome certain technical difficulties. The attempt to reduce the rates of duties thus failed, and no further effort was made until 1870; whilst, on the contrary, two Acts were passed with the opposite effect. The first of these was the Woollens Act of 1867. During the war there had been a considerable development of the manufacture of woollen goods, owing partly to the practical cessation of the manufacture of cottons, and partly to the great demand for clothing for the Federal troops. With the return of peace, these abnormal conditions passed away, and the woollen manufacturers found themselves in face of a crisis. They began, therefore, as early as 1865, to bring pressure upon the Government, and they were skilful enough to make it appear that the growers of wool were in agreement with them. They succeeded in obtaining in the new Woollens Act an extension of the so-called "compensation system," which had been adopted for the first time in the Morrill Tariff of 1861.[1] The plan which had then been adopted was simply this: there was a specific duty imposed on wool, and it was therefore thought necessary to give the manufacturers, in addition

---

Free Trade policy of the period 1846–57, so now again the tendency seemed to be averse to any sudden change" (Mayo-Smith and Seligman, p. 15). "The country at large, and especially those parts of it in which the protected industries were concentrated, began to look on the existing stage of things as permanent. The extreme protective system, which had been at first a temporary expedient for aiding in the struggle for the Union, adopted hastily and without any thought of deliberation, gradually became accepted as a permanent institution" (Taussig, p. 174).

[1] Taussig, pp. 195 *seq.*

to the *ad valorem* duty which was intended to afford them protection, a specific duty to compensate them for the duty on raw wool, and the consequent increase in price of their raw material.[1] The duties so imposed under the Morrill Act had, like all others, been increased during the war, and the manufacturers now asked for and obtained a still further advance of nearly 100 per cent. in the actual amount of the duties, though this was to some extent concealed by an elaborate reclassification. The manufacturers got more than the amount of compensation which they might perhaps have justly claimed; they benefited by the Woollens Act more than the growers of wool, yet it did not yield them anything like the results which they expected. "The Wool and Woollens Act of 1867 was designed expressly to make possible the production at a profit of goods from the wool fibre. It did not effect that object, nor did it accomplish that which was equally its object—the growing of wool at a profit. On the contrary, wool declined in price, and the manufacture of wool was greatly depressed. . . . It is not possible to doubt that the price of woollen and worsted goods must be enhanced so long as a duty is laid upon wools which are not produced in this country and which are yet necessary for mixing with the domestic wool. This is but to state a fact, and not to pronounce a judgment upon the expediency of the system. It is a consequence of the enhanced price that the consumption of woollen goods has never had, and cannot have, an expansion like that which has taken place in cotton, in sugar, in iron, and in many other articles. Wool and woollens are always the strongest arguments of the Free Trader, and the most difficult to answer."[2]

[1] Thus the duty on the cheaper wool was 3 cents per lb., and it was estimated that four lbs. of wool were required for each lb. of cloth; therefore the compensating duty imposed on each lb. of cloth imported was 12 cents (the theory being that this put the manufacturer in the same position over against foreign competition as if he received the wool duty free), and 25 per cent. *ad valorem* for actual protection.

[2] Stanwood, ii. p. 169.

Similar advances were made by the Copper Act of 1869. The duty on copper ore before the war had been only 5 per cent. *ad valorem,* and on copper bars and ingots only 2½ cents per lb.; but in the late sixties the copper mines of the Lake Superior district were producing so largely that the price of copper fell rapidly, and the mine-owners began an agitation for the increase of the import duties. Early in 1869 the duty on copper ore was made specific, and increased to something between 25 per cent. and 30 per cent. *ad valorem,* whilst the duty on copper bars was doubled. The Bill was vetoed by the President, but was passed in spite of him, and incidentally had the effect of closing a number of smelting-works at Boston and Baltimore, which had been engaged in the smelting of imported ores. At the same time, the price of home-produced copper in the United States was raised.[1] Some other increases of duty were the substitution of specific for *ad valorem* duties on steel rails in 1870—a change which made the duty heavier, as prices fell after about 1873; on marble also by the Act of 1870; on nickel, for which the rates were doubled in the same year; and even on such an important raw material as flax.

Yet gradually the necessity for some changes in the opposite direction was making itself felt, and the feeling in favour of reform was strengthened by the persistent advocacy of the Commissioner of Revenue, Mr. Wells. In 1870 the first step was taken, but the reductions then made were confined almost entirely to the non-protected commodities. That is to say, the duties on such revenue articles as tea, coffee, cocoa, sugar, spices, and wines were lowered; there was also an addition to the free list of 130 articles, chiefly raw materials and foodstuffs.[2] The only really protective duty reduced was that on pig-iron, by about 22 per cent., and, as we have seen, some duties on flax, marble, nickel, and steel rails were increased. The net effect was a partial mitigation of the tariff, but an increase of the financial dependence of the

[1] Taussig, pp. 220–1. [2] Stanwood, ii. p. 173.

Federal Government on the strictly protective duties as a source of revenue. The feeling in favour of tariff reduction steadily increased, especially amongst the farmers, who were dissatisfied with the manner in which Congress seemed to regard only the interests of the manufacturers, and were forming in the West the political association of the "Patrons of Husbandry," or "Grangers." The movement was aided by the condition of the finances; the Exchequer revenue from customs rose from about 41 million pounds in 1869–70 to over 45 millions in 1871–2 and the surplus revenue exceeded the amount required for the Sinking Fund. The Protectionists in Congress came to the conclusion that it was desirable to give way to some extent, and they resolved to continue the policy of 1870. They accepted a Bill introduced in the Senate in 1872, which made a reduction of 10 per cent. on cotton, wool, woollens, metals, paper, glass, and leather manufactures,[1] and also lowered the duties on coal and steel. But they added to this a reduction of the customs and excises on whisky and tobacco, and the abolition of the duties on tea and coffee.[2] Whilst apparently a concession to Free Trade, the new Act really strengthened the position of Protection; its authors had gratified the general desire for a reduction of taxation, but they had done this particularly in regard to internal duties and what may be called "breakfast-table taxes"; and consequently, as in 1870, they had made the country still more dependent for Federal revenue upon the purely protective duties. They believed quite correctly that should it become necessary to raise more revenue, it would be easier for them to increase the protective duties than for the Free Traders to re-establish revenue taxes.[3]

[1] A method known as the "horizontal" reduction of duties.

[2] Mayo-Smith and Seligman, p. 19. *Cf.* Taussig, pp. 184–9.

[3] "The removal of the tea and coffee duties in 1872 served to fix for a long time the character of our legislation on the revenue articles of which they are the type. Step by step, in the various Tariff Acts passed since the war, all the non-protective duties have been swept away. By far the most important recent legislation in this direction was the removal of the duties on sugar in the Act of 1890, a change which, like the removal of the tea and coffee

The accuracy of their calculations was soon to be proved. In 1873 there were grave commercial difficulties in the United States—part of the almost universal crisis of that year.[1] Imports, which had risen rapidly from 1870 onwards, fell quickly, and so did the customs revenue in consequence. The following table gives the figures of United States foreign trade from 1870 to 1875.[2] It must be remembered that in 1872 and 1873 prices were much inflated.

IMPORTS AND EXPORTS OF MERCHANDISE, 1870-6.

Years ended June 30.	Imports for Home Consumption.		Exports of United States Produce.	
	Total.	Manufactured and Partly Manufactured Goods.	Total.	Manufactured and Partly Manufactured Goods.
	Million £.	Million £.	Million £.	Million £.
1870	88·8	47·4	78·5	14·6
1871	104·2	57·4	89·3	18·6
1872	116·8	67·8	89·3	18·0
1873	138·2	68·5	105·2	21·0
1874	118·2	55·1	118·6	22·3
1875	109·6	50·3	104·2	21·2

The fall in the customs revenue gave the Republicans their opportunity,[3] and their action was hastened by

duties in 1872, emphasised the determination of the Protectionists to give up the simplest and surest sources of revenue rather than yield an abatement of the protective duties" (Taussig, pp. 188–9).

1 "In the United States the phenomena antecedent to the crisis were enumerated at the time to be, 'a rise of prices, great prosperity, large profits, high wages, and strikes for higher; large importations, a railway mania, expanded credit, over-trading, over-building, and high living.' The crisis began on the 17th of September, 1873, by the failure of a comparatively unimportant railway company. By the 29th twenty banking houses failed" (Wells, *Recent Industrial Changes*, p. 5).

2 *British and Foreign Trade and Industry*, 1909, p. 64. It was not until 1868 that the American returns of foreign trade were put on a really satisfactory basis, as a result of the efforts of Mr. Wells and General Walker, the well-known American economist. See Worthington Ford's article on "Financial Tariff Comparisons" in the *Political Science Quarterly*, vol. xiii. No. 2.

3 They could point to the fact that the customs revenue, as a result of the legislation of 1872, had fallen from 45 million pounds in 1871–2, to 34 millions in 1872–3, in spite of the increased value of imports in the latter year, and that the subsequent decline in imports had accentuated the loss of revenue.

the fact that their long tenure of absolute power was coming to an end. The country had been growing more and more dissatisfied with the unsatisfactory results of General Grant's second Presidency, and the Republicans were discredited by a number of legislative and administrative scandals.[1] It was clear that the new Congress would have a strong Democratic majority in the House of Representatives, and the Republicans resolved to make the most of the short time left to them. In February, 1875, they carried an Act which repealed the "horizontal" reduction made in 1872, and increased the duty on molasses, sugar, tobacco, and spirits. The Act passed without very great difficulty, though the President and his Secretary of the Treasury were both in favour of the re-establishment of the revenue duties on tea and coffee. The result, then, was simply a return to the high war rates with such additions as had been made in 1867, 1869, and 1870. In criticism of the proceeding it is only necessary to quote the judgment of the most recent historian, himself a strong advocate of the principle of Protection. Of the Republicans he writes: "When they were forced to give up the control of the lower House of Congress, and thus to surrender the power to initiate revenue legislation, they signalised their last day of unlimited authority by restoring the duties levied for purposes of protection to the giddy height they had attained when war's terrible greed of money insured a favourable response to every request manufacturers might make for higher rates. . . . As a political move the passage of the Act seems ill-judged. . . . It divided men into two parties of extremists, at a time when moderate counsels would have produced a reasonable tariff system that might have stood unchanged for several years. At almost every succeeding period of Congressional or Presidential election until 1896 the tariff was an issue in the canvass, to the great disturbance and distress of business, and during the short period of fourteen years, from 1883 to 1897, there were four com-

[1] Wilson, pp. 281–3.

plete revisions of the tariff. It would not be fair to lay all the uncertainty and anxiety which the agitation produced to the charge of the Republicans in the forty-second Congress. But it is certain that they had more regard for the interests of the moment than a statesman-like foresight of the consequences of their eager grasp at a vanishing opportunity."[1]

[1] Stanwood, ii. p. 191.

CHAPTER V

POLITICAL PARTIES AND THE TARIFF—ECONOMIC PROGRESS OF THE UNITED STATES TO 1890

THE Act of 1875 was followed by a lull in tariff legislation which lasted, in spite of one or two attempts at renewed activity, for eight years. Towards the end of that period the country had recovered from the acute commercial depression which had followed the disasters of 1873; the Government found itself able to resume specie payments in 1879; the Southern states were rapidly adjusting themselves to their new economic conditions; manufactures had greatly increased, if not so rapidly as during the war period, yet to an extent altogether satisfactory when the retarding effect of the commercial disorders is taken into account.[1] After some years of quietude, there was a marked revival of foreign trade; there was a great advance of exports in 1880 and 1881 (the advance being chiefly in agricultural produce, partly as a result of the extension of the trans-continental railway system of the United States); whilst imports made a great upward bound in the same years and in 1882. The increase of customs revenue gave the Treasury

[1] The census estimates of the value of the manufactured products of the United States are: 1860, 1,885 million dollars; 1870, 4,332 million dollars; 1880, 5,369 million dollars. It should be noted, however, that the increase between 1860 and 1870 was somewhat less, and the increase between 1870 and 1880 somewhat more, than appears from these figures; since the valuation was based in 1860 and 1880 on a gold currency, and in 1870 on a very unsatisfactory paper currency. The estimates themselves are by no means complete, but they are fairly indicative of the progress made.

a surplus in 1881. The movement is shown in the following table:[1]

Years ended June 30.	Imports for Home Consumption.		Exports of United States Produce.		
	Total.	Manufactured and Partly Manufactured Goods.	Total.	Agricultural Produce.	Manufactured and Partly Manufactured Goods.
	Million £.	Million £.	Million £.	Million £.	Million £.
1876 ..	96·8	41·0	109·5	95·0	22·1
1877 ..	91·6	36·3	122·8	95·8	30·0
1878 ..	91·3	35·7	141·8	111·7	29·0
1879 ..	91·5	37·5	145·5	113·8	27·8
1880 ..	130·7	64·0	171·7	142·9	25·4
1881 ..	135·5	60·7	184·2	152·2	28·2
1882 ..	149·2	70·3	152·8	115·0	33·7

The Democratic party had persistently advocated a reduction of the customs duties, and the establishment of a tariff for revenue purposes only; and now that in 1880 and 1881, with the rise of the customs revenue from about 45 million pounds in 1878–9 to over 80 millions in 1879–80, the Treasury found itself again in possession of a surplus,[2] it seemed to the Republicans, who still retained power, but saw signs of their approaching fall,[3] desirable to make some concessions to the popular feeling in favour of a reduction of Federal revenue and a mitigation of the high protective duties. Accordingly, in 1882 a commission was appointed "to take into consideration and to thoroughly investigate all the various questions relating to the agricultural, commercial, mercantile, manufacturing, mining, and industrial interests of the United States, so far as the same may be necessary to

[1] *British and Foreign Trade and Industry*, 1909, pp. 64–5, and Mayo-Smith and Seligman, p. 48. There is some small amount of duplication in the fifth and sixth columns of the table.

[2] The debt was reduced from 2,046 million dollars in 1870 to 1,723 millions in 1880; in the two years 1878–80 the reduction was 100 millions.

[3] They had lost at Congressional elections, and they had very nearly lost the Presidential election of 1876. In 1880 they had done better, but it now seemed likely that they would lose their hold on the Executive Government.

the establishment of a judicious tariff, or a revision of the existing tariff, upon a scale of justice to all interests."[1] The composition of the commission did not encourage any hope of appreciable reform in the direction of Free Trade;[2] its members, or some of them at least, seem to have interpreted their instructions to mean simply that they were to make such modifications of the existing duties as would be likely to remove some part of the public hostility without in fact affecting the protective character of the tariff. The commission, nevertheless, admitted in its report "that a substantial reduction of tariff duties was demanded, not by a mere indiscriminate popular clamour, but by the best conservative opinion of the country, including that which has in former times been most strenuous for the preservation of our national industrial defences."[3] By the end of the year the committee felt itself able to report, and legislation was commenced on the lines which it indicated. The new Tariff Act became law in March, 1883, after the House of Representatives, with its strong protectionist majority (including a number of Democrats), had made considerable alterations in the Bill as passed by the Senate, where it was first introduced.[4] It was therefore not approved by all the Republicans, but those who disapproved would not vote against it.

In a number of instances the rates of duty were reduced. In the case of raw wool, hitherto subject to a combined specific and *ad valorem* duty, the *ad valorem* portion was remitted—the effects being a real reduction on carpet wools, which were not produced in the United

[1] Quoted in Stanwood, ii. p. 203.

[2] "Four of the commissioners were themselves personally or officially interested in industries classed as protected. All the commissioners, without exception, were favourable to the principle of Protection" (Stanwood, ii. p. 204). The chairman was the Secretary of the most energetic protectionist association in the country, the National Association of Wool Manufacturers.

[3] Quoted in Dewey, p. 421.

[4] The passage of the Bill was accompanied, and promoted, by the usual complicated parliamentary manœuvres and manipulation of rules (Stanwood, ii. pp. 207–18).

States at all; a small reduction of little importance on the better kinds of ordinary wools; and the maintenance of a practically prohibitive rate on the inferior grades. As a consequence of this reduction of duty on the imported raw material, the "compensating" specific part of the duty on woollen goods was likewise diminished—somewhat more than proportionately; but in the case of the finer qualities of goods this remission was counterbalanced by an increase of the *ad valorem* rates. On the cheap kinds of cotton goods the decrease of duty was 50 per cent., but these were hardly imported into the United States at all, and were actually exported on a considerable scale; silks were largely imported, so the *ad valorem* rate was lowered only some 16 per cent. On pig-iron the rate was lowered very slightly, from $7 to $6·72 a ton; on steel rails, on the other hand, the reduction was 40 per cent. (from $28 to $17 a ton), though a fall of prices between 1881 and 1887 deprived this change of much of its force. Other reductions of varying (but generally slight) degrees of importance were on marble, nickel, and copper;[1] a reduction was made for barley at the request of the brewers.

None of these changes were of sufficient value to secure a favourable reception of the new tariff by the advocates of freer trade, whilst other alterations were of a nature to arouse their hostility. There were a number of distinct advances in the customs rates, and, as was perhaps to be expected, the chief advantage was reaped by the woollen manufacturers. Thus the rate of duty on dress goods, which have never been manufactured in any large proportion in the United States, was increased, in spite of the fact that the tax on imported wool was at the same time lowered; the *ad valorem* duty on the higher-valued kinds of fine cloths was also raised. On the best grades of cotton goods, such as embroideries and hosiery, there was a rise of about 14 per cent. The rates of duty on various steel manufactures (chiefly machinery parts, such as rods and shafts) were also

[1] Taussig, pp. 239-49.

increased, as were those on quicksilver, and a number of manufactures of brass, pewter, tin, and lead. The rate of duty on iron-ore was advanced from 20 per cent. *ad valorem* to 75 cents a ton (equivalent to about 35 per cent.).[1]

The changes were then, on the whole, of no great effect in either direction.[2] The average duties collected were in 1882–3, 42·45 per cent. of the value of imported goods, and in 1883–4, 41·61 per cent. Practically nothing was changed, and so far the protectionist party might count the new tariff as yet another addition to their long list of victories. Some attempts were made in 1884 and 1886 to renew the tariff discussion, and reduce duties, but without success, partly owing to the fact that people were tiring of the constant changes, and partly because the Democratic party was by no means unanimous on the subject. A revolt of some of its members defeated the Morrison Bill of 1884, which proposed an average all-round reduction of 20 per cent., with the rates of duty of the Morrill Tariff of 1861 as the maximum. Consequently, in spite of the fact that the Democratic victory in the election of President Cleveland in November, 1884, gave that party for the first time since Buchanan left office, in 1861, the control of the Executive Government, nothing was done during its four years of power. But in December, 1887, the President, in his annual message to Congress, declared uncompromisingly in favour of a very considerable reduction of duties. After asserting that an increase in the cost to the home consumer of all commodities, wherever produced, was a result of Protection, the President continued: " It is not proposed to entirely relieve the country of this taxation.

[1] Taussig, pp. 233–8. " As a rule duties were advanced on protected articles of which importations continued in considerable volume. The advance was by no means universal . . . but it was made in so large a number of important cases as to give the Act a distinctly protectionist flavour."

[2] " Although the changes in the rates of customs duties were numerous, few of them were large enough to work a perceptible alteration in the conditions under which either commerce or manufacturing industry was prosecuted " (Stanwood, ii. p. 218).

It must be extensively continued as the source of the Government's income; and in a readjustment of our tariff the interests of American labour engaged in manufacture should be carefully considered, as well as the preservation of our manufactures. It may be called Protection, or by any other name, but relief from the hardships and dangers of our present tariff laws should be devised with especial precaution against imperilling the existence of our manufacturing interests. But this existence should not mean a condition which, without regard to the public welfare as a national exigency, must always insure the realisation of immense profits instead of moderately profitable returns. . . . We are in the midst of centennial celebrations, and with becoming pride we rejoice in American skill and ingenuity, in American energy and enterprise, and in the wonderful natural advantages and resources developed by a century's national growth. Yet when an attempt is made to justify a scheme which permits a tax to be laid upon every consumer in the land for the benefit of our manufacturers, quite beyond a reasonable demand for governmental regard, it suits the purposes of advocacy to call our manufactures infant industries, still needing the highest and greatest degree of favour and fostering care that can be wrung from Federal legislation." Even at this early stage of their development the President called attention to the industrial trusts, and their probable effect on home prices when foreign competition should be eliminated; and he ended by declaring that "it is a *condition* which confronts us, not a theory. . . . The simple and plain duty which we owe the people is to reduce taxation to the necessary expenses of an economical operation of the Government. . . . These things can and should be done with safety to all our industries, without danger to the opportunity for remunerative labour which our working men need, and with benefit to them and all our people, by cheapening their means of subsistence and increasing the measure of their comforts."[1]

[1] *Congressional Record*, vol. xix. part i. pp. 10–11.

The message established a distinct line of division between political parties; it committed the Democrats finally to Free Trade, and therefore identified the Republicans with Protection; and it provided a clear and definite issue for the Presidential election of November, 1888.[1] The two rival policies to be placed before the country were exemplified by two Bills—one (the "Mills Bill") introduced and passed in the House of Representatives by a substantial Democratic majority, and the other brought forward in the Senate by the Republicans. The former proposed to abolish the duties on a large number of raw or semi-manufactured materials of industry, such as wool, flax, hemp, jute, tin plates, and on other articles, as salt and soap; and to reduce the rates of duty on woollens, cotton goods, iron, earthenware, and sugar; it also substituted *ad valorem* for specific duties in many cases. It was estimated that the result would be a loss to the revenue of about fifty million dollars, nearly one-quarter of this arising from the proposed reduction of the rates in respect of woollens, and more than one-fifth from the reductions in regard to sugar and molasses.[2] On the other side, the Senate Bill made some reductions and readjustments, but in a large number of instances increased the duties. Neither Bill passed, or was expected to pass; but the country had a definite choice offered to it, and the elections of November, 1888, gave a narrow victory to the Republicans by the return of President Harrison; and in spite of some disturbing influences, they were entitled to consider this as a decision in their favour on the tariff question. In their election "platform" they had declared that they would "effect all needed reduction of the national revenue by repealing the taxes upon tobacco, which are an annoyance and burden to agri-

[1] "From that time on, the tariff question became the chief line of division between the two great political parties" (Mayo-Smith and Seligman, p. 23). It had the effect of "making this question more distinctly a party matter than it had been at any time since the Civil War" (Taussig, p. 253).

[2] Details in Mayo-Smith and Seligman, pp. 24–5.

culture, and the tax upon spirits used in the arts and for mechanical purposes, and by such revision of the tariff laws as will tend to check imports of such articles as are produced by our people, the production of which gives employment for labour; and release from import duties those articles of foreign production, except luxuries, the like of which cannot be produced at home. If there shall still remain a larger revenue than is requisite for the wants of the Government, we favour the entire repeal of internal taxes rather than the surrender of any part of our protective system, at the joint behest of the whisky trust and the agents of foreign manufacturers."[1] They now resolved to make full use of their new lease of power, and the result appeared in the McKinley Tariff of 1890.

It was not possible for them to argue that the country required more Protection—the proposed new tariff was the outcome rather of political events than of the economic condition of the United States. By 1890 industry and commerce had recovered from the depression and become free from the difficulties which had more or less hampered them since about 1873, and had grown acute for the last time in 1885–7; and the country was now making a rapid advance on the upward path. Population had increased from 38½ millions in 1870 to 62½ millions in 1890; and the development was particularly marked in the great agricultural states of the Middle and North-West. The total production of grain was estimated in 1870 at 761 million bushels (it had gone back somewhat during the Civil War period), in 1880 at 1,755 millions, and in 1890 at 2,122 millions.[2] Railways had advanced with extraordinary rapidity, particularly in the decade 1880–90; in 1870 there were 60,000 miles in the United States; in 1880, 93,000; and in 1890, 164,000. With this development there had come a marked cheapening of the cost of transport; the charge for the carriage of a bushel of wheat from Chicago to New York fell from 30½ cents in 1868 to 14½ cents (or rather less than one-

[1] Quoted in Stanwood, ii. p. 238.
[2] *Twelfth Census*, vol. vi. p. 23.

half) in 1888.[1] These changes had greatly stimulated agriculture, and rendered possible the growth of the export trade in agricultural products, which from 1875 to 1890 averaged about 75 per cent. of the total exports of the United States.[2] Next to grain, the most important product so exported was cotton; the output of that raw material fluctuates considerably, but it rose from an average of 3,325,000 bales in 1869–73 to an average of 6,553,000 bales in 1885–9, whilst the export advanced in about the same proportion—from 1,040 million pounds in the former to 2,015 millions in the latter period.[3] The manufacturing industries were increasing with equal or even greater rapidity; the value of their products was estimated at the census of 1870 at 4,232 million dollars, and in 1890 at 9,372 millions, and the increase was even greater than appears from these figures, since the former estimate was based on a depreciated paper currency, and the latter on the gold currency.[4] The development of industry in the United States during the twenty years from 1870 to 1889 is indicated in the following table:[5]

	Annual Average.			
	1870-1874.	**1875-1879.**	**1880-1884.**	**1885-1889.**
	Million Tons.	Million Tons.	Million Tons.	Million Tons.
Production of coal	43·10	52·2	88·7	115·3
Production of pig-iron	2·20	2·2	4·2	6·0
Production of crude steel	0·14	0·6	1·6	2·8
Number of cotton spindles employed	8,217,000	10,381,000	12,087,000	13,560,000
Consumption of raw cotton	Million Cwts. 5·0	Million Cwts. 6·2	Million Cwts. 8·3	Million Cwts. 10·0
Consumption of raw (sheep and lambs') wool	Million Lbs. 230·5	Million Lbs. 240·5	Million Lbs. 343·1	Million Lbs. 391·6
Shipping built and added to register	Tons. 218,273	Tons. 190,453	Tons. 206,811	Tons. 154,118

[1] Conner, p. 47. [2] Mayo-Smith and Seligman, p. 48.

[3] Mayo-Smith and Seligman, p. 5.

[4] *Twelfth Census*, vii. pp. xlvii *seq.*

[5] The figures are taken from *British and Foreign Trade and Industry*, 1909, pp. 120–1 and 157–171.

Industrial progress was no longer confined to the Northern and Middle States; the South also was beginning to have its share, especially in the production of cotton goods. The one unsatisfactory feature was the condition of American shipping and shipbuilding; between 1870 and 1890 the tonnage registered for over-sea trade declined from 1,517,000 to 947,000 tons,[1] though there was an increase in coasting, river and lake shipping from 2,678,000 tons in 1870 to 3,478,000 in 1890. In spite of various Navigation Acts, and partial remissions of duty on goods borne in American vessels, the percentage of the United States foreign trade carried in native vessels had fallen from 35·6 in 1870 to 12·3 in 1890 (in 1860 it had been as much as 66·5 per cent.).[2]

The statistics of the foreign trade of the United States up to 1882 have already been given; the following table carries them up to the year 1890:[3]

Years ended June 30.	Imports for Home Consumption.		Exports.	
	Total.	Manufactured and Partly Manufactured Goods.	Total.	Manufactured and Partly Manufactured Goods.
	Million £.	Million £.	Million £.	Million £.
1883	146·0	71·2	167·5	33·4
1884	139·1	63·0	151·0	32·5
1885	120·7	54·3	151·4	31·3
1886	130·3	59·7	138·7	30·3
1887	142·4	67·3	146·5	31·1
1888	148·4	69·3	142·5	32·1
1889	154·5	68·2	152·1	34·6
1890	161·8	71·6	176·1	37·3

[1] It reached 1,629,000 tons in 1878.
[2] Mayo-Smith and Seligman, p. 57.
[3] *British and Foreign Trade and Industry*, 1909, pp. 64–5.

CHAPTER VI

THE NEW THEORY OF PROTECTION AND THE McKINLEY TARIFF

It was clearly difficult for the advocates of Protection to urge the "infant industries" doctrine any longer (save in some few special cases). Perfectly valid as this argument may have been in the early days of the industrial history of the United States, it could not now serve the Republicans as their avowed principle of action, and they found it necessary to provide themselves with another and more defensible theoretical basis for the practice of Protection. They therefore turned to the ideas of the home market and national self-sufficiency; their policy had, indeed, from the first been in that direction, but was now to become so more definitely. "The world's progress is now dependent upon the development of internal resources, and not of external trade. We need a systematic development of all those opportunities for labour with which each country has been endowed by nature. We must make a better use of all our natural resources if the world is to advance to a higher industrial state. Progress must come from the development of large continental states, rich in natural resources."[1] Protection is to be no more temporary expedient; it becomes "a consistent endeavour to keep society dynamic and progressive. Protection also ceases to be an isolated exception to the general passive policy which it has been popular to advocate, and becomes a

[1] Patten, *Economic Basis of Protection* (first published in 1890), 2nd ed., p. 15. A sympathetic exposition of the theories of the less scientific Protectionists in the United States will be found in Maurice Low, *Protection in the United States*. For a criticism of Patten, see Rabbeno, *The American Commercial Policy* (Essay III.).

part of a fixed national policy to increase the value of labour with the increase of productive power, and to aid in the spread of knowledge and skill and in the adjustment of a people to its environment."[1] This by itself was somewhat too subtle an argument (at least in such a form) for popular use, but it was interpreted by the Republicans at the election of 1888 as implying the necessity for the protection of the highly-paid American workman against the competition of the ill-paid European labour. This was to be done, not by the exclusion of European commodities, but by the imposition of duties which would counterbalance the disadvantage of the greater cost of production in America, and also give a moderate protection. It would thus protect labour, for it "cut off the privilege of the foreigner to come in with cheaper wares and to gain a foothold in the market, if perchance he had gone forward at a little more rapid pace than the American in adapting his manufacture to new conditions. It relieved the home manufacturer from the necessity of cutting down wages, supposing that he could have reduced them; and in this respect the tariff was a boon to the working man."[2] This wages

[1] Patten, pp. 7–8.

[2] Stanwood, ii. p. 256. The following extracts (quoted by Low, p. 54) illustrate the attitude and reasoning of Mr. McKinley: "The revenue tariff accomplishes but a single purpose—that of raising revenue; it has no other mission, while a protective tariff accomplishes this and more—it brings revenue to the American Treasury, and discriminates in favour of the American citizen. . . . The protective tariff invites the [products of] foreign labour and foreign capital which are necessary to the wants of the people, and which we cannot produce in the United States, to occupy our markets and go untaxed to the people, but insists that every foreign product, the like of which is produced at home, or can be produced successfully in quantities capable of supplying the domestic consumption, shall, whenever necessary to maintain suitable rewards to our labour, bear a duty which shall not be so high as to prohibit importations, but at such a rate as will produce the necessary revenues, and at the same time not destroy, but encourage, American production" (*Protection and Reciprocity Illustrated*, 1892). "The chief obstruction in the way of a revenue tariff is the wages paid American workmen, and any return to that policy involves a reduction of the cost of labour. We cannot afford to have cheap labour in the United States" (Speech at Atlanta, 1888).

argument was not new—it had first made its appearance in the thirties, and had been discussed slightly in the debates on the tariff proposals of 1842 and 1846; but it appears not to have become prominent until the eighties. Even the Democrats felt it necessary to take somewhat the same line. In 1884 they had been careful in their "platform," whilst asserting that reform was urgently required, to add that "the necessary reduction in taxation can and must be effected without depriving American labour of the ability to compete successfully with foreign labour, and without imposing lower rates of duty than will be ample to cover any increased cost of production which may exist in consequence of the higher rate of wages prevailing in this country."[1] And in 1888, when their advocacy of greater freedom of trade was much more vigorous, they retained the proviso that the revision of duties must be "with due allowance for the difference between the wages of American and foreign labour." But their attitude was not satisfactory to the electors; the Republicans pushed the argument for all, and more than all, that it was worth—without any regard to the problem of the relative efficiency in the long run of well-paid and ill-paid labour, or to the relation of wages to the cost of living—and "the campaign of 1888 was won on the 'pauper labour' argument."[2]

The new Tariff Bill of the Republicans was introduced in April, 1890, by Mr. McKinley, the Chairman of the Committee on Ways and Means; it received the Presidential approval on October 1st, and came into force five days later. Its most novel feature was the extension of Protection to agriculture—a policy which was inspired largely by the desire on the part of the Republicans to allay the dissatisfaction of the farmers, who believed that they were being exploited in the interests of the manufacturers, and to detach them, if possible, from the

[1] Quoted in Stanwood, ii. p. 222. It is noteworthy that in 1884 the Democrats, like the Free Traders of fifty years before, asserted openly that "taxes collected at the custom house" must continue to be the chief source of Federal revenue.

[2] Mayo-Smith and Seligman, p. 23.

Democratic and Free Trade party. Its economic defence was found in the increase of the imports of agricultural produce, the value of which amounted to over 53 million pounds, out of total imports valued at about 155 million pounds in the year ending June 30, 1889, and the growing competition of Canada. So the duty on barley was increased from 10 cents to 30 cents a bushel; on oats from 10 to 15 cents; on wheat from 20 to 25 cents; on potatoes from 15 to 25 cents; on hay from $2 to $4 a ton; whilst eggs and apples, hitherto free, were subjected to duties of 5 cents a dozen and 25 per cent. *ad valorem* respectively.

The duty on tobacco suitable for cigar wrappers, which could be grown in the United States only in Connecticut and was largely imported from Sumatra, was increased from 75 cents to $2 a pound, with the additional important proviso that if any portion, no matter how small, of any bale of tobacco imported should be suitable for wrapping, the whole should pay the rate of $2 a pound.[1] Other increases were on flax and hemp, neither of which were grown in good qualities in the United States.[2] And finally, the duties on wool were raised considerably; the rate on clothing wool was indeed advanced only from 10 to 11 cents a pound, and on combing wool only from 10 to 12 cents, but on carpet wool the change was much greater. This is wool of a coarse kind which was not grown in the United States; it was now made subject to a higher duty because it was believed that better qualities were imported as carpet wool, and therefore paid a smaller duty than they would otherwise do—though no satisfactory evidence of this was produced; an *ad valorem* rate, varying from 32 per cent. to 50 per cent., was now imposed on carpet wool instead of the former specific rate, and represented in fact a substantial increase.[3]

[1] Mayo-Smith and Seligman, p. 32.

[2] "It may be said without qualification that the purpose of the increase of duties on agricultural products was political, and that the object was accomplished. The farmers were taken into the Protection partnership" (Stanwood, ii. p. 266).

[3] Taussig, pp. 256–9.

Naturally, the manufacturers of woollen goods of all kinds strongly resisted the concessions made by the growers of wool, and could be pacified only by more consideration for themselves; and, in fact, the woollens schedules showed the most vigorous application of the protective policy. It is true that in the case of the cheapest kinds of woollen goods there was little, if any, increase, because whilst the *ad valorem* part of the duty was slightly raised, the specific "compensating" part was commonly reduced; but on the better qualities the increase was large, and at the same time the rates were greatly complicated by new classifications and further applications of the principle of the sliding-scale.[1] To take only a few instances of an increase—the rates of duty on ready-made clothing were raised from 40 cents a pound + 35 per cent. *ad valorem* to 49½ cents + 60 per cent., and on Brussels carpets from 30 cents the square yard + 30 per cent. *ad valorem* to 44 cents + 40 per cent., whilst in the case of dress goods the advance made them subject to a rate amounting to nearly 100 per cent.[2] The same policy was pursued with other textiles; there were remissions of duties on the cheaper qualities of

[1] The following table gives a simple illustration of this in the case of woollen cloths (Taussig, p. 260):

1883.	1890.
(1) If worth 80 cents or less per lb., 35 cents per lb. + 35 per cent.	(1) If worth 30 cents or less per lb., 33 cents per lb + 40 per cent.
(2) If worth more than 80 cents per lb., 35 cents per lb. + 40 per cent.	(2) If worth between 30 cents and 40 cents per lb., 38½ cents per lb. + 40 per cent.
	(3) If worth more than 40 cents per lb., 44 cents per lb. + 50 per cent.

[2] Yet in spite of these high duties, the tariff on wool has greatly hampered the industry in the United States. "The effect of this duty is perceptible, not only upon the price of home-grown wool, which is enhanced by some considerable part of the duty, but also in its curtailment of importations of the most desirable varieties of Australian and South American fleeces. For this reason, among others—and there are several others of importance—there has thus far been no serious attempts to develop an American export trade in woollen goods. The one possible exception to this rule is in the case of carpets" (S. N. D. North, in *Annals of the American Academy*, vol. xxiii. No. 1, January, 1904).

cotton, linen, and silk goods, and radical increases on all the better kinds. Some other advances, not on textiles, may also be conveniently noted here—on fine plate-glass from 40–45 per cent. to 60 per cent. *ad valorem*, and on cigars (to compensate the manufacturers for the change in the tobacco duties) from \$2·50 a pound + 25 per cent. to \$4·50 + 25 per cent.

In the case of iron and steel goods, which had once furnished the friends of Protection with their most effective arguments, the situation was altogether different. The production of pig-iron and crude steel in the United States exceeded that in the United Kingdom in 1890 for the first time, and the United States output of coal had reached nearly to the British figure (it first exceeded it in 1891).[1] The American manufacturers were in control of the home market; they no longer feared foreign competition, and were quite willing to allow some reductions which probably would benefit only those consumers on the Eastern coast to whom transport by water from Europe was as cheap as, or cheaper than, transport by rail from distant parts of the United States. The duty on steel rails was lowered to \$13·44 a ton,[2] and there were decreases on the inferior qualities of boiler iron and steel ingots. But, on the other hand, the manufacturers in the East, especially near the coast, could secure no remissions on pig-iron or iron ore, which they obtained largely from Cuba and Spain. On a number of other metal manufactures (brass, copper, lead) there were reductions. A concession was made to the shipping industry by extensive grants of drawbacks on all materials "which may be necessary for the construction and equipment of vessels built in the United States for foreign account and ownership, or for the purpose of being employed in the foreign trade, including the trade between the Atlantic and Pacific ports of the United States."[3]

[1] *British and Foreign Trade and Industry*, 1909, pp. 169, 171, 172.

[2] "It left the duty still at a prohibitory rate" (Taussig, p. 272).

[3] Section 8.

The one great change was in the case of tin plates, which were scarcely manufactured at all in the United States, but were imported in enormous quantities (with an average value of 4¼ million pounds in the fiscal years 1887–8 to 1889–90), owing in part to the growth of the canning industry. Since 1873 attempts had been made to develop the manufacture in America, but without success, for the competition from South Wales was too strong. A determined effort was now made by increasing the rate of duty from 1 cent to 2⅕ cents a pound (about 70 per cent. *ad valorem*) with the proviso that after October, 1897, tin plates should be admitted free unless in any one year the production of tin plates in the United States should equal "one-third the amount of such plates imported and entered for consumption during any fiscal year after the passage of this Act." The idea seems to have been that unless there was evident indication, by the end of six years, that the new industry which it was proposed to try to create had really established itself, the attempt should be given up; the proviso was a concession to the consumers of tin plates, who were strongly opposed to the proposed increase of duty, and anticipated serious difficulties for the various canning industries; they were also met to some extent by the grant of a drawback, equivalent to 99 per cent. of the original duty, on tin-plate re-exported in the form of tinware utilised for canning purposes (this as part of a general system of drawbacks). There can be no question that the higher protection did enable the manufacture to get a start and obtain a firm footing; in the four years 1887–90 the average value of the imports of tin plates from Great Britain into the United States was £4,279,000, and the quantity manufactured there practically nil; in the four years 1898–1901 the average value of imports from Great Britain was only £807,000, and the average production in the United States was 347,000 tons.[1]

The most revolutionary change made by the new Act had reference to sugar, on which the duty hitherto in

[1] *British and Foreign Trade and Industry*, 1903, p. 132.

force varied from $1\frac{1}{5}$ cents to $3\frac{1}{2}$ cents per pound—a fairly high rate. The revenue from sugar was very large; in the five fiscal years 1885–6 to 1889–90 it averaged rather more than 11 million pounds a year. There had been a number of suggestions for the reduction of duty, and there was even a Bill introduced by the Republicans of the Senate, prior to the election of 1888, which proposed a remission of about 50 per cent. The McKinley Tariff abolished the duty on raw sugar altogether, but made refined sugar subject to a rate of $\frac{1}{2}$ cent per pound. But in order to help the producers of sugar in the United States, chiefly in Louisiana, the Federal Government undertook to pay a bounty amounting to 2 cents per pound on the best qualities for fourteen years, until the end of June, 1905. At the same time a small surtax was imposed on all bounty-fed sugar coming from other countries. From the Treasury's standpoint the effect of this change was to reduce the customs revenue from sugar from $11\frac{1}{4}$ million pounds in 1889–90 to about £16,000 in 1891–2, whilst at the same time the amount to be paid in bounties was over $1\frac{1}{2}$ million pounds in 1891–2, and over $2\frac{1}{2}$ million pounds in 1893–4.

One other characteristic feature of the McKinley Act should be noticed, and that is the increased elaborateness of the classification adopted and the use which was made of detailed sliding-scales with minimum values, instead of simple *ad valorem* duties. Illustrations of the system have already been given from time to time; its further application greatly complicated the Tariff, as the following example shows. The Act of 1883 contented itself with the simple statement that "penknives, pocket-knives of all kinds, and razors shall pay 50 per cent. *ad valorem*," but in the Act of 1890 that direction had grown into the following elaborate statement as to the duties to be levied:

"Penknives or pocket knives of all kinds, or parts thereof, and erasers, or parts thereof, wholly or partly manufactured, valued at not more than fifty cents per dozen, twelve cents per dozen; valued at more than fifty cents per dozen and not exceeding one dollar and fifty cents per dozen, fifty cents per dozen; valued at more than one dollar and fifty cents per dozen and not exceeding three dollars per dozen, one dollar per dozen; valued at more than three dollars per dozen, two dollars per dozen; and in addition thereto on all the above, fifty per centum *ad valorem*. Razors and razor blades, finished or unfinished, valued at less than four dollars per dozen, one dollar and seventy-five cents per dozen; and in addition thereto on all the above razors and razor blades, thirty per centum *ad valorem*."[1]

Not only does this method of levying duties greatly increase the difficulty of customs administration, but it offers a very strong temptation to under-valuation on the part of importers.

The complications of the tariff, and some defects in the existing organisation, rendered a rearrangement of the customs organisation desirable, and the task was accomplished by the Customs Administrative Act of June, 1890, which established the system still in force. Under that Act all goods imported must be accompanied by an invoice containing a declaration by the purchaser or manufacturer with "a full statement of the time when, the place where, and the person from whom the purchase was made, and the actual cost thereof and of all charges thereon"; and such declaration must have been produced to, and countersigned by, the United States Consul or commercial agent at the place where the goods were purchased or manufactured.[2] The invoice must

[1] The following table shows the effect of this change in the amount of the duty (Worthington Ford, in *Political Science Quarterly*, vol. xiii. No. 2, p. 283):

	Actual *ad valorem* Duty.	
	1883. Per Cent.	**1890.** Per Cent.
Penknives, etc., valued at not more than 50 cents per dozen	50	74·06
,, ,, valued over 50 cents and not exceeding $1·50 per dozen	50	96·17
,, ,, valued over $1·50 and not exceeding $3 per dozen	50	94·74
,, ,, valued over $3	50	86·95

[2] The value of the imports into the United States, as given in the official returns since August 1, 1890, is "the actual market value or wholesale price of such merchandise as bought and sold in usual wholesale quantities at the time of exportation to the United States in the principal markets of the country from whence im-

be sworn to by the importer; the goods are then valued by an "appraiser," and if the duty is *ad valorem* and the valuation by the appraiser exceeds the valuation on the invoice, double duty is levied on the difference. Appeal lies to a general appraiser, then to Boards of General Appraisers, and then to the Federal Courts.

This elaborate machinery is almost inseparable from any system of *ad valorem* duties, and consequently most nations have preferred the simpler method of specific duties. The main advantages of *ad valorem* duties are that the tax always bears the same relation to the value of the commodity on which it is imposed, and is perfectly intelligible even to the non-expert; the effect of specific duties, on the contrary, can only be determined by a trade specialist, and unless they are frequently changed they are apt to become much heavier or much lighter than was intended at the time of their imposition—a striking illustration of this from the early history of the German Zollverein has already been given.[1] To prevent such occurrences the tariff must be frequently readjusted, but this involves much labour and a certain amount of uncertainty to foreign traders.[2] Moreover, without extreme minuteness of tariff classification, it is impossible to keep the specific duties from weighing more heavily on the cheaper than on the better qualities of goods.[3] These considerations, as we have seen, induced an American Congressional committee in 1831-2 to declare strongly in favour of the *ad valorem* system, and after various changes, the United States for a long period seemed resolved to use *ad valorem* rates to the fullest

---

ported, and in the condition in which such merchandise is there bought for exportation to the United States or consigned to the United States for sale, including the value of all cartons, cases, crates, boxes, sacks, and coverings of any kind, and all other costs, charges, and expenses incident to placing the merchandise in condition ready for shipment to the United States" (Section 19 of *Customs Administrative Act*, 1890).

[1] See p. 5.

[2] Most foreign tariffs, however, are for long terms of years.

[3] An instance is the single British tax on tea, which is the same for all qualities.

possible extent. Yet the fact that most protective nations have not imitated the United States in this respect suggests that there are some very strong objections to this method of levying duties. The machinery for collection has to be much more elaborate than when specific rates are employed—at every port, however small, there must be a (more or less) competent appraiser. Secondly, it is not easy to secure that the valuations at the various ports are uniform; complaints on this point were frequent in the United States at one time, and other countries which use the *ad valorem* method seem to have the same experience. The system of standard values, determined from time to time by a central authority, overcomes this difficulty to a large extent, but not entirely. Appeals can as a rule be made from the local appraisers to some central tribunal, but these usually mean much trouble to the importers. Thirdly, the temptation to undervaluation is strong, and fraudulent declarations are encouraged; the elaborate precautions taken and penalties provided by the Customs Administrative Act in the United States only show how deep-seated this evil may become. On the whole the practice of European countries has tended generally towards the system of specific duties, but the example of the United States has been followed to a considerable extent by non-European Powers.[1]

[1] For an account of another most important part of the McKinley Tariff Act—the clauses relating to Reciprocity—see Chapter VIII.

CHAPTER VII

THE WILSON AND DINGLEY TARIFFS

THE passage of the McKinley Tariff Act was followed by an immediate and violent reaction. A month after it came into force the election for Congress took place, and resulted in a tremendous defeat for the Republican party. The reaction continued, and the Presidential campaign of November, 1892, ended in the return of the Democratic candidate, Cleveland, who represented the anti-protectionist policy. The Western states went almost solidly Democratic; and the new "farmer's party," the Populists, also detached many votes from the Republicans. The Democrats even secured a small majority in the Senate, and so for the first time since the period before the Civil War, they had complete control of the Federal Government. The causes of the change in public opinion are not very clear; the new tariff had not been sufficiently long in force for any definite opinion to be formed as to its effects; but no one could allege that the issue had not been clearly set before the country. The Democrats in their platform for the Presidential election had declared that it was a "fundamental principle of the Democratic party that the Federal Government has no power to impose and collect tariff duties, except for revenue purposes only," and denied that there had been any increase of prosperity under the McKinley Tariff. Their candidate himself was more moderate; in his letter of acceptance of the party nomination, Cleveland wrote: "Reform is still our purpose. Though we oppose the theory that tariff laws may be passed having for their object the granting of discriminating and unfair governmental aid to private ventures, we wage no exterminating war against any American interests. We believe a readjustment can be accomplished, in accordance with the principles we profess, without disaster or demolition. We believe that the advantages of freer raw material should be accorded to our manufacturers, and we contemplate a fair and careful distribution of necessary tariff burdens rather than the precipitation of Free Trade." The Republicans in their turn asserted that "the prosperous condition of our country is largely due to the wise revenue legislation of the Republican Congress," and claimed that the fall in the prices of manufactured commodities was in fact due to the tariff. The new President considered his large majority as a mandate for a reform of the customs tariff on the lines which he had indicated, but the hopes with which he undertook the task were doomed to disappointment. The problem was complicated by two circumstances; one being the small and uncertain Democratic majority in the Senate, and the other the silver question. The problem which the last presents lies outside our subject; it is necessary here only to state that the Republicans had yielded in 1890 to the demand for the freer coinage of silver, and that the excessive issues of silver currency under the Silver Purchase Act of that year had produced a rapid fall in prices, and a good deal of commercial confusion. President Cleveland and his advisers thought themselves compelled to propose the repeal of the Purchase Act; they carried it after a hard struggle, but in so doing they threw confusion into the ranks of their own party, which contained a strong section in favour of "free silver." These difficulties and others weakened the Government seriously, and though it encountered comparatively little opposition in carrying its scheme for tariff reform (subsequently named the Wilson Tariff, after the Chairman of the Committee of Ways and Means) in the lower House, it was not able to overrule the sweeping amendments made by the

Senate[1]—amendments which gravely modified the proposals, and in some cases made them of no effect.

Nevertheless the Wilson Tariff Act did make considerable changes. The additions of the duty-free list included a number of chemicals (including mineral oils), copper and certain manufactures thereof, lumber, flax, hemp, raw wool, hides (raw or uncured), coffee, fresh fish, various agricultural products, and a number of other commodities. Reductions exceeding 75 per cent. of the rate of duty imposed by the McKinley Tariff were made in respect of iron in bars and blooms, and the cheaper kinds of woollen yarns and cloths; there were reductions of from 50 to 75 per cent. of the rates previously in force in respect of numerous commodities, including various chemicals, lead, zinc in sheets, a number of manufactures of iron and steel, the better qualities of woollen yarns and cloths, blankets, carpets, knitted wearing apparel, flannels, some dress goods, and certain agricultural products (including barley and hay); and there was a very lengthy list of articles on which smaller reductions were made. The new or increased duties, on the other hand, were comparatively few in number—the most noticeable being those on molasses and sugar, malt and pearl-barley, rye, pineapples, dressed or undressed meat, iron and steel-wire rope, and tubes and pipes.[2]

One of the most important manifestations of the new policy was, as already indicated, the treatment of the tariff numbers relating to wool and woollen goods, which had played so conspicuous a part in previous tariff controversies. The duties on raw wool were abolished; on woollen and worsted yarns rates of 30 and 40 per cent. *ad valorem* were substituted for the McKinley rates of 27½ to 38½ cents a pound + 35 or 40 per cent. *ad valorem;* the rates of duty on blankets ranged from

[1] As sent back by the Senate to the House of Representatives, the Bill contained 684 amendments (Stanwood, ii. p. 340).

[2] *Return respecting the Customs Tariff of the United States* (C. 7579 of 1894, issued by the Board of Trade), pp. 70–79.

25 to 35 per cent. instead of 30 to 40 per cent. + a specific duty varying from 16½ to 38½ cents a pound; and simple rates of 40 and 50 per cent. *ad valorem* on dress goods took the place of the same *ad valorem* rates combined with specific rates varying from 7 to 44 cents per pound. In all these, as in the case of other woollen manufactures, the abolition of the specific portions of the duties followed naturally upon the abolition of the duties on raw wool, for which they were intended to be compensatory; the manufacturers were caused some trouble by the change, but it cannot be said that they were treated unfairly. As regards other textiles, there were large reductions in the case of the cheapest kinds of cotton goods, and smaller ones in respect of the finer qualities; and here again the tariff was greatly simplified by the abolition of the mixed specific and *ad valorem* rates. There were small reductions also on silks and linens.

The President had intended that all raw materials should be admitted free, and had carried the House of Representatives with him; the Senate, however, could not be induced to go so far. The chief illustrations of this were furnished by iron ore and coal. The House of Representatives had abolished the duty on both of these commodities; the Senate was content to reduce the duty in each case from 75 cents to 40 cents a ton. Other commodities which the House of Representatives had placed on the free list, but on which the Senate re-imposed duties, were nickel, mica and quicksilver, unmanufactured clays or earths, various chemicals (such as ammonia, borax, sulphur), molasses, raw or refined sugar, beef, mutton, pork, bacon, meats, dressed, undressed, or preserved, lard, apples, eggs, and coke.[1] The duty on pig-iron was lowered from \$6·72 to \$4 a ton, on steel rails from \$13·44 to \$7·84 a ton, and even on tin plates from 2⅖ cents to 1⅕ cents per pound.

One other serious change was in the case of sugar.

[1] *Return respecting the Customs Tariff of the United States*, pp. 68–9.

The clauses affecting that commodity in the McKinley Tariff had caused very considerable dissatisfaction: for one thing, the financial results had been somewhat unsatisfactory, and for another, it was widely believed that the duty on refined sugar and the bounties were largely in the interests of the Sugar Trust—one of the earliest of those organisations which now play so great a part in American industrial life. The Democrats now proposed to admit refined sugar as well as raw sugar free, and to abolish the bounty system, but the Senate made many amendments admittedly in the interest, and under the influence, of the Sugar Trust. An *ad valorem* duty of 40 per cent. was imposed on raw sugar; refined sugar was made subject to this rate with the addition of ⅛ cent per lb., and the surtax on bounty-fed sugar, imported into the United States, was retained. The House of Representatives was unable to overrule the Senate, and "on the whole, the refining monopoly, while it lost something, came out of the struggle victorious, and was left in little less secure control over the trade after the Act of 1894 than under the Act of 1890."[1]

Altogether the new tariff brought relatively little change; none of the high hopes which the Democrats had formed after the Presidential election were realised.[2] The President himself was grievously disappointed; in order to save something of his policy, he allowed the Act to pass, but he would not give it his signature; it became law merely because he took no action to the contrary in the time required by the Constitution. The weakness of the Democrats, the confusion in the party, the disruption caused by the silver question, the conflict between the President and the Senate, and the Treasury diffi-

[1] Taussig, pp. 313–14.

[2] On the basis of the imports in the year ending June 30, 1893, the yield of the duties under the McKinley Tariff was estimated at 49·6 per cent. of the total value of all dutiable imports; the yield of the duties under the Wilson Tariff (as finally enacted) was estimated at 38·7 per cent. The reduction was not sufficient to diminish appreciably the protective character of the tariff.

culties with which the Cleveland Administration failed to cope, brought about a reaction as sharp as that of 1890–2, and again placed the Protectionists in power. The Democrats had hoped to establish an income tax, to meet the deficiency resulting from the reduction of duties and to enable them to continue the removal of the customs restrictions, but the Supreme Court now reversed its decision of the Civil War period, and declared the income tax to be unconstitutional.

But at the election of 1896 the country was not concerned mainly with the question of Protection or Free Trade. The advocates of free silver had grown in force astonishingly, and had completely captured the Democratic party machine; in their election platform the Democrats declared for "the free and unlimited coinage of both silver and gold at the present legal ratio of 16 to 1, without waiting for the aid or consent of any other nation,"[1] and added that "until the money question is settled we are opposed to any agitation for further changes in our tariff laws, except such as are necessary to meet the deficit in revenue caused by the adverse decision of the Supreme Court on the income tax." To prevent all misconception as to their policy, the Democrats chose as their candidate the foremost platform representative of free silver, and the Populist party also gave him their support. The Republicans had intended to fight the election mainly on the tariff issue, and had therefore chosen McKinley as their representative. But they were compelled by force of circumstances to drop that question for the time, and to go to the electors chiefly as the opponents of the revolutionary monetary proposals of the Democrats. And there can be no question that this was the chief cause of their overwhelming victory; it is true that they had announced their intention to amend the tariff, but "the tariff gave way to the free coinage issue, and the election ultimately

[1] A reference to the argument that this would be practicable only as the result of an international agreement.

turned upon that almost exclusively."[1] The Democrats were broken up; large numbers of the party in the Eastern states either abstained from taking part in the election or voted for McKinley. The Republican candidate was elected by a very considerable majority, and the Republicans found themselves supreme in the House of Representatives, and masters of the Senate by a few votes. The new President could scarcely claim that the nation had given a definite judgment on the tariff problem, and, moreover, he owed his election in part to the votes of those Democrats who could not support the extreme views represented by his opponent. But nevertheless the President and his advisers made up their minds that they were justified in carrying out tariff changes immediately. The United States had passed through a period of marked commercial depression, originating in widespread financial difficulties there and elsewhere in 1893 and subsequent years, and the Treasury had to meet a large deficit. The facts that the crisis had commenced in 1893, while the McKinley Tariff was still in force, and that the deficit was largest in that year and had been growing smaller ever since,[2] had no weight with them; and the President now invited Congress to provide adequately for the wants of the Treasury, and suggested that the duties imposed for this purpose "should be so levied upon foreign products as to preserve the home market as far as possible to our own producers; to revive and increase manufactures; to relieve and encourage agriculture; to increase our domestic and foreign commerce; to aid and develop mining and building; and to render to labour in every field of useful occupation the liberal wages and adequate rewards to which skill and industry are justly entitled." The result was the so-called Dingley Act, which became law in July, 1897,

[1] Stanwood, ii. p. 376.

[2] In the financial year 1893–4, the deficit was 70 million dollars; in 1894–5, 43 millions; in 1895–6, 25 millions; in 1896–7, 18 millions.

after a rapid progress through both Houses of Congress. It imposed duties higher than under any preceding tariff.

The most important feature of the new tariff was the return to the duties on certain raw materials, especially wool. The import of that commodity had tripled between 1893 and 1896, and the supply of woollen manufactures from abroad had also doubled. It was therefore resolved to re-impose on clothing and combing wool the rates of the tariff of 1890, and on carpet wool graded duties higher than in any other period of United States tariff history. The manufacturers were strongly opposed to the change, but political considerations and the desire to do something to counteract the effect of the appeal made by the silver party to the farmers prevailed with the Executive. Largely for the same reason, a duty of 15 per cent. *ad valorem* was imposed on hides, which had been free since 1872; and the rates of 1890 on flax were also restored.

In regard to textiles, the restoration of the wool duty was followed inevitably by an increase of the protection given to woollen manufactures, and the old principle of a combination of specific compensating duties and *ad valorem* protective duties was again applied, with its great administrative complications and difficulties.[1] On the chief class of woollens imported the protective *ad valorem* rate was increased, so that it had advanced from 25 per cent. in 1875 to 55 per cent. in 1897. On cotton goods the rates of duty were somewhat lower than in 1890, but a good deal higher than in 1894, and here again the combined specific and *ad valorem* duties were adopted. The same complicated method was applied to silks and linens, with a marked increase in the amount of the duties. There were advances also in the case of china,

[1] For a comparative statement of the rates of duty on articles of each class, the quantity and value imported, and the customs yield under the Wilson and Dingley tariffs, see *Imports and Duties*, 1894–1907 (House of Representatives Document No. 1504, 60th Congress, 2nd Session).

earthenware, and glass, by a return to the rates of duty imposed in 1890. In the case of metals, there was little change so far as iron ore, pig-iron, steel rails, and copper were concerned; but the rates on certain manufactures of iron and steel, such as cutlery, and on lead and lead ore were restored to the levels of the McKinley Tariff. The duty on tin-plate was increased only slightly, from $1\frac{1}{5}$ cents to $1\frac{1}{2}$ cents. The duty on coal was raised from 40 cents to 67 cents a ton (which was 8 cents less than in 1890). In the sugar duties the *ad valorem* duty of 40 per cent. imposed by the Act of 1894 on raw sugar was now replaced by a specific duty of about double that amount; there was also an increase, in fact, on refined sugar, though the Sugar Trust did not secure anything like the advantage for which they had striven.

From the administrative point of view, the new tariff was even more complicated than its predecessors. The elaborate clause concerning knives, penknives, and razors in the McKinley Tariff has already been quoted;[1] the clause referring to the same commodities in the Act of 1897 will serve to show how the complication had increased:

> "Penknives or pocket knives, clasp knives, pruning knives, and budding knives of all kinds, or parts thereof, and erasers or manicure knives, or parts thereof, wholly or partly manufactured, valued at not more than forty cents per dozen, forty per centum *ad valorem;* valued at more than forty cents per dozen and not exceeding fifty cents per dozen, one cent per piece and forty per centum *ad valorem;* valued at more than fifty cents per dozen and not exceeding one dollar and twenty-five cents per dozen, five cents per piece and forty per centum *ad valorem;* valued at more than one dollar and twenty-five cents per dozen and not exceeding three dollars per dozen, ten cents per piece and forty per centum *ad valorem;* valued at more than three dollars per dozen, twenty cents per piece and forty per centum *ad valorem; Provided,* That blades, handles, or other parts of either or any of the foregoing articles, imported in any other manner than assembled in finished knives or erasers, shall be subject to no less rate of duty than herein provided for penknives, pocket knives, clasp knives, pruning knives, manicure knives,

[1] *Vide supra*, pp. 270–1.

and erasers valued at more than fifty cents and not more than one dollar and fifty cents per dozen. Razors and razor blades, finished or unfinished, valued at less than one dollar and fifty cents per dozen, fifty cents per dozen and fifteen per centum *ad valorem ;* valued at one dollar and fifty cents per dozen and less than three dollars per dozen, one dollar per dozen and fifteen per centum *ad valorem ;* valued at three dollars per dozen or more, one dollar and seventy-five cents per dozen and twenty per centum *ad valorem.* Scissors and shears, and blades for the same, finished or unfinished, valued at not more than fifty cents per dozen, fifteen cents per dozen and fifteen per centum *ad valorem ;* valued at more than fifty cents and not more than one dollar and seventy-five cents per dozen, fifty cents per dozen and fifteen per centum *ad valorem ;* valued at more than one dollar and seventy-five cents per dozen, seventy-five cents per dozen and twenty-five per centum *ad valorem.*"[1]

As another illustration, the duties on silk piece goods may be quoted. They are as follows:[2]

Silk piece goods:

	Per lb.
(1) Containing 20 per cent. or less in weight of silk, if in the gum	0·50
If dyed in the piece	0·60
(2) Containing 20 to 30 per cent. in weight of silk, if in the gum	0·65
If dyed in the piece	0·80
(3) Containing 30 to 45 per cent. in weight of silk, if in the gum	0·90
If dyed in the piece	1·10
(4) Containing 30 per cent. or less in weight of silk, if dyed in the thread or yarn, black	0·75
Other colour	0·90
(5) Containing 30 to 45 per cent. in weight of silk, if dyed in the thread or yarn, black	1·10
Other colour	1·30

The McKinley Tariff had inaugurated an elaborate policy of drawbacks, by a sweeping clause which provided that "where imported materials on which duties have been paid are used in the manufacture of articles manufactured or produced in the United States, there shall be allowed on the exportation of such articles a drawback equal in amount to the duties paid on the materials

[1] Quoted by Ford in *Political Science Quarterly*, vol. xiii., No. 2, pp. 284–5.

[2] Taussig, p. 339.

used, less 1 per cent. of such duties." The Dingley Tariff continued the system, but the conditions and regulations proved cumbersome and often difficult to comply with,[1] and the system admittedly hampered the manufacturers for export.

[1] S. N. D. North, in *Annals of the American Academy*, January, 1904, p. 7.

CHAPTER VIII

THE UNITED STATES AND RECIPROCITY—ECONOMIC PROGRESS OF THE UNITED STATES, 1890–1908

It will have been noticed that hitherto little has been said of the international commercial relations of the United States, and no reference has been made to any treaties similar to those which have played so important a part in the commercial history of continental Europe during the last half-century. The explanation of this fact is that until quite recently the United States have stood almost altogether aloof from such a treaty system, and the slight attempts made from time to time to enter it have been ill-fated. It is true that various agreements made by the United States have contained the "most favoured nation" clause, but the effect of that provision is much more limited than in the treaties ordinarily made by European States, for it has been construed by American legists to apply merely to privileges voluntarily granted by the United States to a third country, and not to anything given in return for reciprocal advantages. That is to say, that if the United States, in return for certain reductions of duty made by France in favour of American goods, should on their side lower the rates of duty on certain of their imports from France, they are not bound to extend the same reductions to the similar products of any third nation with whom they may have a treaty containing the "most favoured nation" clause.[1]

[1] "Up to the time of the American Revolution the 'most favoured nation' provision appeared in but one form; the pledge was not qualified; no limitations were laid down as to the circumstances under which concessions granted to other States should be

It is unnecessary to point out that this interpretation practically destroys the value of the clause in question, since the privileges granted by the United States without return are not likely to be numerous or important; but it simplifies the making of reciprocity treaties, since it enables the Federal Government to consider simply the effect of any treaty on the trade between the two contracting countries, and thus to escape the complications which are apt to arise under the European method.

The outcome of the earliest attempts at reciprocity was not very encouraging; the proposal for a treaty with the German Zollverein in 1844 was rejected by the Senate, and it was not until ten years later that a commercial agreement of any kind was actually made. That was with Great Britain acting on behalf of Canada, and was the outcome of negotiations extending over eight years; signed in 1854 it came into operation in March, 1855, and it remained in force for eleven years; it provided for the admission of a large number of agricultural products from either country into the other free of duty; it also gave certain fishing privileges to American seamen, and provided for mutual freedom of the transit trade. It seems to be generally agreed that on the whole Canada

---

extended as between the contracting parties. But in the first American treaty—that made by the American Confederation with France on February 6, 1778—the clause was given a new phraseology. In this treaty there appeared the usual pledge that advantages which either of the contracting parties had granted or might grant to a third State should be granted to the other, but there was attached a qualifying conditional provision, '. . . freely, if the concession (to the third State) was freely made, or on allowing the same compensation, if the concession was conditional. . . .' From the time when its representatives first subscribed to the conditional form of the clause, the United States, when pledging itself to 'favoured nation' treatment, has employed that form almost without exception. . . . The earliest American statesmen adopted the 'special bargain' principle, and the American Government has acted ever since in conformity with the conception that commercial concessions are to be given for specific compensation, and that 'most favoured nation' treatment implies and requires nothing more than the granting of opportunity to purchase, on the basis of reciprocal give and take, treatment identical with, or similar to, that accorded other States" (*Reciprocity and Commercial Treaties*, United States Tariff Commission, p. 18).

profited rather more than the United States,[1] at least in the latter part of the treaty period, and the United States had by 1866 become completely dissatisfied. One ground for this was certainly the fact that the Canadian provincial governments increased the duties on manufactured goods to make up for the financial losses sustained by them owing to the reductions on raw materials. In 1866, partly because of this, partly because of the need for higher customs duties in the United States as a source of revenue, and partly for political reasons (notably the sympathy which Canada had shown with the Confederate states), the United States denounced the treaty. Thereafter for some thirty years attempts were made from time to time to re-establish reciprocity between the two neighbouring states, but they were all abortive, and from 1896 to 1910 the issue was never raised. A number of other contemplated agreements with other countries failed of realisation.

Negotiations opened with Hawaii in 1855 were abandoned; treaties prepared by the Executive with Mexico in 1859 and 1883, with Hawaii in 1867, and with Canada in 1874 were rejected by the Senate, and arrangements made in 1884 with Spain, for Cuba and Porto Rico, and with San Domingo were abandoned by the Executive. One treaty alone was made—with Hawaii in 1875, but the adoption of that in the United States (it came into force in September, 1876) was determined rather by political than economic considerations; it was a step on the road to annexation.[2]

[1] "Whilst the treaty actually benefited some American producers and injured none save fishing, lumber, and possibly coal interests—and these in small degree—it was, on the whole, of greater benefit to the export trade of Canada than to that of the United States" (*Reciprocity and Commercial Treaties*, pp. 22–23).

[2] "The reciprocity treaty concluded between Hawaii and the United States in 1875, which was in operation for twenty-five years, was a product of political rather than of economic considerations. The location, resources and political weakness of Hawaii made the islands, from the early part of the nineteenth century, attractive to several strong Powers. Their strategical position made it inevitable that the United States should view with uneasiness and dissatisfaction their being brought under the control

The first definite and general provision for reciprocity was made by the McKinley Act of 1890, at the instigation of Blaine, the Secretary of State, who had been the moving spirit in the summoning of the Pan-American Congress which met at Washington in October, 1889. Eighteen countries, including the United States, were represented there, and considerable attention was given to the suggestions for an American Customs Union. It was agreed that a union for customs purposes on the lines of the German Zollverein was altogether impossible for many reasons—economic and political; and absolute free trade between the various countries was held to be, for the time, out of the question, since most of them were largely dependent on the customs duties for their State revenues. The committee which reported on the proposals could urge only the making of separate treaties with reciprocal reductions of duty. Even this report did not secure unanimous support; the representatives of four countries voted against it, and Chile and Argentina especially urged that so long as the United States insisted on the maintenance of their high protective duties reciprocity was impossible.

But Blaine was not altogether discouraged, and he thought that commercial agreements, which would extend the United States markets in South America, might be obtained in another way. He put forward his idea when the McKinley Tariff was under discussion,[1]

---

of any other Power. . . . In the treaty there were no political concessions other than the pledge that while the treaty remained in force Hawaii would not lease territory or grant special privileges to any other Power, or that any other Powers should obtain the same privileges which were assured by the treaty to the United States. The commercial provisions involved the admission by each country of a considerable number of products of the other free of duty" (*Reciprocity and Commercial Treaties*, pp. 24–5). The Hawaiian products which benefited were brown sugar, molasses, rice, fruit, and nuts, representing three-quarters of the islands' exports.

[1] "I do not doubt that in many respects the Tariff Bill pending in the Senate is a just measure, and that most of its provisions are in accordance with the wise policy of Protection. But there is

and a clause in that Act, inserted in the Senate, provided that the President should be authorised to impose certain duties on sugar, molasses, coffee, tea, and hides (which were duty free) coming from countries which levied on agricultural or other produce of the United States duties to an extent, in his judgment, "reciprocally unequal and unreasonable." Taussig has pointed out that this method offers decided economic advantages over that commonly pursued, namely, "the simple remission of duties to a favoured country, duties remaining on goods coming from countries not favoured. Such a remission is likely not to redound to the advantage of the domestic consumer. Unless the favoured country can easily supply the whole market, or other countries are quickly admitted to the lower duties, prices are not affected, and the foreign producer reaps the whole benefit of the remission."[1] Under this clause treaties were made with Brazil and a number of the Central American States—San Domingo, Salvador, Nicaragua, Honduras, Guatemala, with Spain for Cuba and Porto Rico, and with Great Britain for most of the West Indian Islands and British Guiana. In most of these cases the United States got a very considerable return for the mere promise to retain the enumerated articles on their free list. Thus Brazil admitted wheat, flour, pork, agricultural and mining machinery, coal, and railway material free, and reduced the duties on a number of other commodities. Cuba made thirty-nine classes of articles free, and gave a reduction of 50 per cent. on seventeen classes and 25 per cent. on fourteen classes.[2] The fact that Germany and Austria-Hungary were largely interested in the export of sugar enabled the American Government to make terms with those countries also. Germany abandoned the prohibition, which had been in force for some years, of the importation of American meat, and gave

---

not a section or line in the entire Bill that will open the market for another bushel of wheat or another barrel of pork" (Blaine, in letter quoted by Stanwood, ii. 278).

[1] Taussig, p. 279.

[2] Osborne, p. 64.

the United States the benefit of the conventional tariff on agricultural products; from Austria-Hungary they secured " most favoured nation " treatment.[1]

These later arrangements did not continue long enough to enable any definite opinion to be formed as to their effect on trade, since the reimposition of the customs duties on sugar by the Wilson Tariff of 1894 practically destroyed the system, which was dependent on the general freedom of that commodity, and after that year only the treaty with Hawaii remained in operation.

Fresh provision for reciprocity was made by two clauses in the Dingley Act of 1897, but not on the lines of 1890. Under section 3 of the new Act, the President was authorised, in return for concessions by other countries, to reduce by a definite amount the duties on certain articles specified in the clause. The list was a curious one; it included only argols, brandies, champagne, and other sparkling wines, still wines, and vermouth, pictures and statuary. Section 4 provided further that the President might make treaties (which, however, needed the approval of Congress) with reductions on duties up to 20 per cent. on any or every article; but such treaties must be made within two years after the passing of the Act. This latter clause proved practically inoperative; some eleven treaties were negotiated under it, mainly affecting Central or South American States[2] and the West Indies, but they all fell through owing to the impossibility of securing the approval of the Senate, in spite of the support of President McKinley and his successor, Roosevelt. A Manufacturers' Reciprocity Convention at the end of 1901 had declared for reciprocity only when it could be secured without injury to any of the domestic interests of manufacturing, commerce, or farming.

Action under section 3 could be taken merely by Presidential proclamation without any necessity for

[1] The penal duties provided for by the clause in the Act of 1890 were actually applied against Haiti, Venezuela and Colombia.

[2] Nicaragua, Dominican Republic, Ecuador, the Argentine.

Congressional sanction, and eight treaties were so made —with France in 1898 and 1908, with Germany,[1] Italy, and Portugal in 1900, and subsequently with Switzerland, Spain, Bulgaria and the Netherlands. In return for the very small concessions indicated above, the United States secured from France the minimum tariff rates on a large number of agricultural products, from Germany the full conventional tariff, from Italy low rates on machinery and some raw materials, and from Portugal "most favoured nation" treatment, with fixed rates for agricultural products and machinery generally. Similar concessions were obtained in the other cases. It is difficult, if not impossible, to estimate the results of these treaties—at best they were only small, and the very limited list of articles on which reductions might be made by Presidential proclamation was a considerable obstacle to any large extension of the system. Finally, it should be stated that in November, 1907, an agreement was made between the United Kingdom and the United States, whereby in return for certain customs house facilities granted by the former in respect of commercial travellers' samples coming from the United States, the latter country extended to British works of art the lower rate of duty authorised by Section 3 of the Dingley Tariff Act.

The Dingley Tariff remained in force and unaltered for twelve years, and its long continuance was due to a combination of political and economic factors. During the whole of the period the Republican party was in power; at the Presidential election of 1900 the Spanish War, and the new foreign policy of the American commonwealth which resulted therefrom, were the most conspicuous questions before the electors; and the Democrats, whose uncertain attitude towards this problem was a source of weakness, were still further handicapped by their adherence to the silver policy which had caused them disaster four years earlier. At the election of

[1] The German Treaty was renewed in 1907.

1904 they indeed shook themselves free of this incubus, or at least their candidate did so—it is doubtful how far in this respect he was fully representative of his party—but the personal popularity of Mr. Roosevelt, the general approval of his administration after the death in 1901 of Mr. McKinley, who had been re-elected the previous year, and the continued prosperity of the country, gave the Republicans an overwhelming victory. Though the tariff question played a comparatively small part in these elections, the Republicans always made the maintenance of the existing protection (subject to some possible modifications as a result of reciprocity treaties) a cardinal point of policy; whilst, on the other hand, there were not wanting in this regard signs of disintegration among the Democrats some of whom (particularly in the South, where industrial development was very marked) were becoming inclined to regard protection as a permanent system, and consequently to get what they could out of it for their own industrial interests.

On the economic side there was, after 1897, a natural reaction against the frequency of change which, by altering the whole tariff three times in eight years, had kept commerce and industry in a constant state of doubt and unrest. Moreover, by 1898 the effects of the general depression which had characterised the early years of the last decade of the nineteenth century had entirely passed away, and the United States had its full share of the world-wide commercial and industrial activity which characterised the last years of the old and the opening years of the new century. The expansion continued unchecked until the latter part of 1907, when, partly as the inevitable reaction after a period of almost violent activity, but mainly as the result of some financial disorders and a grave monetary crisis, there came a sudden and very acute depression. The table given on pp. 232, 233,[1] illustrates the economic development of the United

[1] Compiled from *British and Foreign Trade and Industry*, 1909, and the *Statistical Abstract of the United States*, 1918.

ECONOMIC PROGRESS OF THE UNITED STATES, 1890–1908.

	Annual Averages.			1905.	1906.	1907.	1908.
	1890-1894.	1895-1899.	1900-1904.				
	Millions.	Millions.	Millions.	Millions.	Millions.	Millions.	Millions.
Population	65·1	71·6	79·0	83·1	84·2	85·7	87·3
	Million Winchester Bus.	Million Winchester Bus.	Million Winchester Bus.	Million Winchester Bus.	Million Winchester Bus.	Million Winchester Bus.	Million Winchester Bus.
Agriculture:							
Production of wheat	476·7	529·5	626·2	693·0	735·3	634·1	664·6
Production of maize	1602·2	2068·0	2172·6	2708·0	2927·4	2592·3	2668·7
	Million Bales (500 lb. gross).	Million Bales (500 lb. gross).	Million Bales (500 lb. gross).	Million Bales (500 lb. gross).	Million Bales (500 lb. gross).	Million Bales (500 lb. gross).	Million Bales (500 lb. gross).
Production of cotton	8·3	9·5	10·9	10·6	13·3	11·1	13·3
	Million Lbs.	Million Lbs.	Million Lbs.	Million Lbs.	Million Lbs.	Million Lbs.	Million Lbs.
Production of sugar—							
(1) Cane	457·7	638·8	589·3	784·0	766·1	544·3	788·5
(2) Beet	19·3	71·6	324·6	484·3	625·8	967·2	927·3
Production of rice	152·5	147·6	421·5	378·0	496·0	520·5	608·0
	Million Tons.	Million Tons.	Million Tons.	Million Tons.	Million Tons.	Million Tons.	Million Tons.
Industry:							
Production of coal	153·3	189·1	281·0	350·8	369·8	428·9	371·3
Production of iron ore	14·1	18·7	30·9	42·5	47·7	51·7	36·0
Production of pig-iron	8·1	10·6	16·4	23·0	25·3	25·8	15·9
Production of crude steel	4·3	7·6	13·4	20·0	23·4	23·4	14·0
	Million Lbs.	Million Lbs.	Million Lbs.	Million Lbs.	Million Lbs.	Million Lbs.	Million Lbs.
Production of tin plates	66·9	545·8	930·3	1105·4	1293·7	1153·1	1203·1
	Tons.	Tons.	Tons.	Tons.	Tons.	Tons.	Tons.
Production of copper	140,400	216,960	301,632	402,637	409,735	387,945	420,791
	Short Tons.	Short Tons.	Short Tons.	Short Tons.	Short Tons.	Short Tons.	Short Tons.
Production of lead	164,400	200,500	282,200	308,000	336,200	352,400	311,700

Industry: Production of petroleum	Million Gals. 2,086	Million Gals. 2,408	Million Gals. 3,690	Million Gals. 5,658	Million Gals. 5,313	Million Gals. 6,976	Million Gals. 7,498
Cotton spindles employed ..	Millions. 15·2	Millions. 17·2	Millions. 21·4	Millions. 23·7	Millions. 25·3	Millions. 26·4	Millions. 27·5
Consumption of raw cotton ..	Million Cwts. 11·7	Million Cwts. 14·5	Million Cwts. 18·2	Million Cwts. 21·8	Million Cwts. 22·2	Million Cwts. 20·1	Million Cwts. 17·4
Consumption of raw (sheep and lambs') wool	Million Lbs. 409·4	Million Lbs. 466·5	Million Lbs. 448·4	Million Lbs. 542·1	Million Lbs. 495·0	Million Lbs. 498·7	Million Lbs. 431·3
Shipbuilding (vessels built and added to the Register)	Thousand Tons. 214·4	Thousand Tons. 173·6	Thousand Tons. 361·4	Thousand Tons. 277·1	Thousand Tons. 350·9	Thousand Tons. 390·3	Thousand Tons. 513·6
Transport: Railways	Miles in Operation. 175,497	Miles in Operation. 189,072	Miles in Operation. 208,408	Miles in Operation. 225,196	Miles in Operation. 230,761	Miles in Operation. 236,949	Miles in Operation. 240,846
Shipping— (1) Foreign trade	Gross Tons. 952,660	Gross Tons. 814,936	Gross Tons. 877,184	Gross Tons. 954,513	Gross Tons. 939,486	Gross Tons. 871,146	Gross Tons. 940,068
(2) Lake, river, and coasting trade	3,723,995	3,929,631	4,895,983	5,502,030	5,735,483	6,067,648	6,425,377
Foreign trade:[1] Imports for home consumption— (a) Total	Million £. 162·7	Million £. 145·5	Million £. 186·0	Million £. 227·2	Million £. 250·1	Million £. 293·2	Million £. 243·4
(b) Manufactured and partly manufactured articles ..	66·4	58·3	78·6	88·0	108·4	131·4	108·0
Exports of domestic produce— (a) Total	184·7	212·6	292·3	310·8	357·9	386·2	382·2
(b) Manufactured and partly manufactured articles ..	38·8	61·6	99·8	127·4	142·9	154·2	156·4

[1] The foreign trade statistics are for the twelve months ended on the 30th of June of the years given.

States from 1890 to 1908, and shows how sharp was the revulsion in the latter year.

But it was essentially a monetary crisis, and, though recovery is necessarily somewhat slow (it would appear to have been delayed in part by causes which were not primarily economic), there can be no doubt of its completeness.

One conspicuous feature of the industrial and commercial life of the United States must be mentioned here—the wide development of "trusts"—if only because the Democrats, where they had become inclined to avoid the direct issue in regard to the tariff, turned to attack those powerful combinations and thereby indirectly to assail the protective system which they claimed, by practically eliminating foreign competition renders it easier for such organisations to secure a monopoly in the home market, and to exploit the consumer.[1] The combinations in question are the almost inevitable outcome of modern industrial and commercial conditions, such as excessive competition and the economy of production on a large scale; they appear to a greater or less extent in all industrial countries;[2] but it is open to doubt whether, even when the peculiar conditions which prevail in the United States are taken into account, the trusts would have attained their present proportions in that country had it not been for the restrictive effect of a tariff which had for long been far higher than that of any other industrially developed country.[3] The

[1] *Cf.* Beardsley, "The Tariff and the Trusts," in *Quarterly Journal of Economics*, May, 1901, and Franklin Pierce, *The Tariff and the Trusts*, 1911.

[2] *Cf.*, for example, Macrosty's *Trust Movement in British Industry*, and the references give on p. 83 *supra* as to the development of industrial combination in Germany.

[3] There is a very extensive literature on Trusts in the United States. A large collection of facts is contained in Moody, *The Truth about the Trusts*, and detailed information about some of the better-known combinations in the *Reports of the Commissioner of Corporations on the Beef Industry*, 1905; *on the Petroleum Industry*, 1907; and *on the Tobacco Industry*, 1909; Tarbell, *History of the Standard Oil Trust;* and Berglund, *The United States Steel Industry*. A good discussion of the trust problem will be found in Ripley

political use of this anti-trust agitation has, however, been to some extent weakened by the fact that some of the Republicans, including Mr. Roosevelt and, in a lesser degree, his successor, Mr. Taft, shared this hostility to the trusts, though contending that their evil effects can be removed without tampering with the tariff. They claimed that much of the astonishingly rapid progress of the United States in the last few years in manufactures[1] was due to the steady adherence to Protection, and they argued that that system, even where it gives the domestic manufacturers a practical monopoly, does not necessarily tend to check improvements in the methods of production, but rather that it encourages them by offering the producers greater security and inviting them to the conquest of the home market.[2] It could be claimed with justice that American manu-

(ed.), *Trusts, Pools, and Combinations*. A very detailed information as to the attempts made to control the Trusts by legislation is contained in J. E. Davies, *Trust Laws and Unfair Competition*, issued by the U.S. Department of Commerce, 1916, and Harvey and Bradford, *Manual of the Federal Trade Commission*, 1916.

[1] The Census estimate of the value of the manufactured products of the United States was 9,372 million dollars in 1890 and 13,014 millions in 1900.

[2] "In fact, history shows that either result may ensue. It would seem, for instance, that in France, under the system of absolute prohibition against competing imports which prevailed throughout the first half of this century—in fact, up to the great commercial treaty of 1860—not a few manufacturers failed to make use of proved and familiar processes, and were inferior to British rivals. On the other hand, there were industries in France itself which had reached out into foreign markets, thus giving conclusive proof of not being behind the times. In the United States it would doubtless be possible to find examples of the former sort: a benumbing influence has sometimes been felt. But these are exceptions. As a rule, if American manufacturers have been unable to meet foreign competition, it has not been because of inert routine. . . . In the United States the Free Trader is shown by economic history to be in the wrong on this particular point: if protected industries have continued to need protection, as so often they have, the explanation is not to be found in the retention of antiquated processes. So far as the question of economic method is concerned, here again it is clear no abstract reasoning can suffice: the history of each people and the facts of each case must be investigated, and generalisation from *a priori* reasoning must be shunned" (Taussig, in "Iron Industry in the United States," in the *Quarterly Journal of Economics*, August, 1900, pp. 496–7).

facturers had shown few signs of any enervating influence exercised upon them by Protection; by the foundation of Schools of Commerce their Universities preceded the British Universities in their response to new national needs; in the conduct of business their manufacturers had shown extraordinary energy, ability and enterprise; and the policy of taking care of the home market and concentrating attention upon that, in the assurance that foreign trade would then take care of itself, seemed to be meeting with a large measure of success.[1]

[1] In recent years, however, much energy has been expended on the promotion of foreign trade, with the active assistance of the Government through a vigorous Consular Service and Special Inquiry Agents.

CHAPTER IX

THE TARIFF OF 1909

BY the time that the Presidential election of November, 1908, drew near, it was apparent that there was a growing dissatisfaction with the tariff of 1897. The causes of this dissatisfaction were of two different kinds: on the one hand there was the increasing feeling among those interested in the maintenance of high protection that, owing to its hasty construction, the changes in industrial conditions and the elaboration of foreign tariffs, the Dingley Tariff had become technically imperfect, and there was a desire to secure a better basis for reciprocity; and, on the other hand, there was a belief, steadily gaining ground, that the increased power of the large industrial combinations, the rise in prices and consequent advance of the cost of living, were to some appreciable extent connected with the tariff. The Government itself was actuated by the necessity of providing more revenue, though it was apparent that little of this could be obtained by a revision of the tariff.

Consequently the tariff question played a very important part at the elections. The Democrats, in adherence to their old policy, pronounced in favour of an effective and extensive reduction of the rates of duty, though it may be doubted if there was any section of the party which would have supported a measure tending at all strongly towards Free Trade; many of the members of the party (particularly in the Southern States) were inclined to regard Protection as an inevitable condition, and either to consider opposition thereto futile, or to go further and to try to secure some share in it for themselves. The Republicans were forced by the action of some of their leaders, notably Mr. Roosevelt and Mr. Taft, their candidate for the presidency, to declare for tariff revision, but though one section was favourable to a real reduction in the amount of protection afforded, another and more powerful section clearly intended from the first that the revision should be little more than "a revision of the tariff by its friends."[1]

Immediately after the election the task was commenced, and it is desirable to set out here the general principles which guided the leaders of the Republican party. It will be remembered that for a considerable number of years the ruling assumption had been that the relatively high rates of money wages current in the United States could not be maintained except by the imposition on imported articles of duties which should counterbalance the difference between the remuneration of American and foreign labour. So in his message to Congress in 1901 Mr. Roosevelt wrote: "Reciprocity must be treated as the handmaiden of Protection. Our first duty is to see that the protection granted by the tariff in every case where it is needed is maintained, and that reciprocity be sought for so far as it can be safely done without injury to our home industries. Just how far this is must be determined according to each individual case, remembering always that every application of our tariff policy to meet our shifting national needs must be conditioned upon the cardinal fact that the duties must never be reduced below the point that will cover the difference between the labour cost here and abroad. The

[1] On the tariff of 1909, in addition to the reports of the proceedings of the Committee of Ways and Means, and of the debates in the House of Representatives and the Senate, see Taussig, "The Tariff Debate of 1909, and the New Tariff Law," in the *Quarterly Journal of Economics*, November, 1909; H. Parker Willis, "The Tariff of 1909," in the *Journal of Political Economy*, November, 1909, and January, 1910; and Fisk, "The Payne-Aldrich Tariff," in the *Political Science Quarterly*, March, 1910. For the full text, and a comparison of the old and new rates of duty, see the *United States of America—New Customs Tariff* (published by the Board of Trade, Cd. 4856, 1910).

well-being of the wage-worker is a prime consideration of our entire policy of economic legislation." But gradually this doctrine had given way to, or become incorporated with, another, which made its first appearance in the Republican "platform" of 1904, when it was declared that "the measure of protection should always at least equal the difference in *cost of production* at home and abroad." Four years later this was elaborated into the principle, enunciated in the "platform" of 1908, that "in all protective legislation the true principle of protection is best maintained by the imposition of such duties as will equal the difference between the cost of production at home and abroad, together with a reasonable profit to American industries." In his Report on the draft tariff prepared by the Committee of Ways and Means, the Chairman, Mr. Payne, asserted that the Committee had throughout been guided by this consideration; but it is a clearly established fact that in spite of strenuous efforts the United States Government had failed to procure any considerable body of reliable evidence as to comparative costs,[1] and the test which the Committee applied was, as a rule, simply that of *profit*[2]—that is, their consideration was, in the main, given only to the question whether a particular business could, or could not, be carried on profitably under the existing amount of protection.

The Committee of Ways and Means of the House of Representatives, after collecting a great mass of material, held a number of public sittings for the taking of evidence; at these, and, in fact, throughout the whole discussion of the tariff, as was to be expected, the supporters of the existing tariff and the advocates of increased protection were well organised and represented, whilst the

[1] Taussig, *loc. cit.*, pp. 12–14.

[2] Mr. Taft had declared that "the measure of the tariff should be the cost of production of the article in this country, and such cost abroad; and, in the estimate of the cost of production abroad and in the estimate of the cost of production here, there should be included, among other elements, what is regarded in each place as a reasonable manufacturer's profit."

opponents were, as a rule, ineffective, partly because of lack of organisation, and partly because of indifference, since there was a widespread belief that no serious revision was intended.

After three months' deliberation the Committee, or rather the Republican members thereof (for the Democrat members took no part), produced what was known as the "Payne Bill," described in its title as "a Bill to provide revenue, equalise duties, and encourage the industries of the United States." It was proposed to increase the rates of duty, or impose new ones, on two groups of commodities: (*a*) on certain articles, such as tea and crude cocoa, which had hitherto been on the free list, solely in order to provide revenue; and (*b*) on a number of articles, such as mercerised fabrics, women's gloves, hosiery, plate-glass, zinc in ore, lemons, pine-apples, grapes and figs (these increases in respect of fruit being chiefly in the interest of California), "because the Committee found that there was not sufficient protection under the present law." On the other hand, it was proposed to abolish the duties on iron ore, hides, raw flax, and pulp-wood; to reduce the duties on lumber by one-half; to admit free coal and coke and agricultural implements from countries which should not impose duties on similar products coming from the United States—these provisions having in view the development of trade with Canada and (in the case of coal) some satisfaction to the New England States; and to reduce more or less substantially the rates of duty on numerous other articles, such as chemicals, iron and steel goods, refined sugar, carpet wool, shoddy and tops.

A fundamental change of policy was represented by the provision for *minimum* and *maximum* rates of duty. The former—the rates of the tariff schedules—were to apply to imports coming from all countries which should not in their tariffs discriminate in any way against the products of the United States; the maximum rates, which were to be as a rule 20 per cent. higher than the minimum rates, or 20 per cent. *ad valorem* in the case of articles on the free list, were to apply against all countries practising such discrimination.[1] As a consequence of this provision notice was to be given to terminate all existing reciprocity conventions, except that with Cuba.

Further, the Bill provided for reciprocal free trade between the United States and the Philippine Islands, subject, however, to a definite limitation of the amount of sugar, unmanufactured tobacco and cigars, which could be annually imported from the Islands into the United States free of duty.

The provisions in regard to reciprocity and free trade with the Philippines were generally acceptable, but the proposals made by the Committee in respect of rates of duty encountered considerable opposition. From the side of the consumers objection was taken to the proposed imposition of the tea duty, and the increase on refined sugar; to the higher duties on cotton goods, where the justifiable increases in respect of mercerised goods were accompanied by a reclassification and a rearrangement of the method of levying the duties which was alleged to have substantially increased them, though the manufacturers had admitted that the old rates were sufficient; and to the failure of the Committee to meet the widespread demand for a modification of the woollen duties —there was much complaint, for example, that the effect of the existing duty on raw wool had been to encourage the use of shoddy and to depreciate gravely the quality of the cheaper grades of woollen goods, the production of which for domestic consumption was entirely in the hands of United States manufacturers. On the side of the producers, the North-Western states and Maine were opposed to the reduction of the lumber

[1] The Committee inserted in the Bill during the discussion in the House of Representatives an amendment to the effect that " these provisions for additional duties shall not apply to the cases where the preferential duties to other countries are those which are given by and between a province, dependency, colony, or the mother-country only, or by and between a province, dependency, or colony of the same country." This was dropped later owing to the action of the Senate, *vide infra*, p. 243.

duties; the South and Middle West to free hides; and the Middle West to the reduction of the metal duties.

There was some amount of active opposition in the House of Representatives, but the opportunities of amendment there were limited, since by a small majority the House decided in favour of the fate of practically the whole Bill being determined by a single vote—that is to say, no voting was allowed on any amendments except those proposed on behalf of the Committee of Ways and Means and certain selected tariff numbers. As a result of serious defections in the Republican party, a few changes of importance were made; the proposed duty on tea was dropped, and that on cocoa reduced; petroleum was made duty free, and the curious scheme of imposing an import duty on coffee coming from any country which subjected it to an export duty (a proposal obviously aimed at Brazil) was abandoned. There was much discussion, but little effective criticism in the House of Representatives, partly because the Southern Democratic demands for increased protection for tropical fruits, raw cotton, some cotton manufactures, iron and steel and lumber rendered Southern members willing to compromise with the representatives of other interests; and partly because the opponents, as on previous occasions, now concentrated their attention on the Senate.

Meanwhile the Finance Committee of the Senate had been preparing a Bill of its own, which it substituted for the Payne Bill when that Bill, after reaching the Senate, was referred to the Committee. The differences between the Committee's Bill and the Payne Bill were numerous and important; iron ore and raw flax were replaced on the dutiable list; in response to the demands of representatives of the interests concerned, the duties on certain agricultural products and cotton hosiery reduced in the House of Representatives Bill were restored to the existing level; changes in respect of classification and definition had the effect of increasing the rates on iron and steel goods; the proposed duties on lead products were increased; cocoa was placed on the free list. More important in its effect on the new tariff law as ultimately enacted was the changed form of the proposals in regard to the maximum and minimum rates; the Senate Committee proposed that the maximum duties should consist of the minimum rates plus 25 per cent. *ad valorem,* and should apply as from April 1, 1910, to goods coming from all countries other than those admitted by Presidential proclamation to the benefit of the minimum tariff, as not discriminating against United States products. The only serious criticisms of these proposals made in the Senate was by the representatives of some of the Middle States (Wisconsin, Iowa, Minnesota, Indiana, Kansas, Nebraska and South Dakota), but they were practically powerless.

Then followed conferences between representatives of the two Houses; there were some points of difficulty, and President Taft, who is understood to have refrained from any direct intervention hitherto, is reported to have felt impelled to take action in certain cases—notably in respect of hides, iron ore, coal and lumber, and the maintenance of the rates of duty on hosiery and gloves at the Dingley tariff level (though he consented to some increases). The agreed Bill was signed on August 5, and the new minimum rates came into force immediately. The main features of the new tariff law were as follows:[1]

(*a*) The provision for minimum and maximum rates of duty, and the conditions under which they are to be imposed, were as proposed by the Senate Committee. The responsibility of determining whether a country was or was not discriminating by import duties against United States products, and was or was not by export bounties or prohibitions discriminating in respect of trade to the United States, rested solely with the President (*i.e.*, the *executive* authority); and, further, his decision in regard thereto might apply to the whole of any foreign country, or might be confined to or exclude

[1] The full text is given in the *United States of America—New Customs Tariff* (Board of Trade, Cd. 4856, 1909).

from its scope any dependency, colony, or political subdivision having authority to adopt separate tariff legislation.

(*b*) There was to be reciprocal free trade in all commodities except rice between the United States and the Philippine Islands (for which Congress subsequently enacted a new tariff law with increased rates of duty), subject, however, to a limitation of the amount of sugar, wrapper and filler tobacco and cigars, which might be imported annually from the Islands into the United States.

(*c*) There was a fairly extensive reclassification of commodities, and numerous alterations in the rates of duty. There were comparatively few changes, and those of only small importance, in the schedules relating to sugar and its products, wool and woollens (in spite of a widespread demand for reductions), tobacco, flax, hemp and jute and manufactures thereof, spirits and wines, and agricultural products and provisions. In the iron and steel schedule there were reductions in respect of iron ore, pig-iron, steel rails, bar-iron, and similar products, and corresponding reductions on certain classes of finished iron and steel goods; on the other hand, there were increases in respect of ferro-silicon, antimony ore, zinc ore, tungsten-bearing ore, some classes of cutlery and structural steel.[1] There were reductions in respect of numerous chemicals, window glass, firebricks, lumber, printing paper, leather goods, harness and saddlery, the lower qualities of carpets and rugs, oilcloth and linoleum, coal, fresh meat, and various other articles; raw hides, mechanically ground wood-pulp, and petroleum became free. Increases were made in the rates of duty on a number of chemicals, cement, some grades of glassware,

[1] "The vast majority of the reductions made in the metal schedule affected articles of which the imports had been comparatively trifling. In other words, a reduction in tariff rates was made in those cases in which the superiority of the United States had been demonstrated to be such as more than to offset the extremely moderate reduction—conditions of the industry being considered—which was made in rates" (Willis, p. 599).

the lower-priced silks (the silk schedule was entirely remodelled by the Senate, which substituted simple specific duties for the combined specific and *ad valorem* rates of the Dingley tariff); mercerised and other cotton goods (by the addition of a surtax in respect of mercerisation—a new process since the previous tariff—new provisions as to the basis of classification and some direct advances of rates of duty); undressed and dressed hemp, oats, hops, some Southern fruits and other products. The net result was that the revision of the tariff in a downward direction had been almost inappreciable: whilst some of the reductions or abolitions of duty, as in the case of coal, wood-pulp and printing paper, and some iron and steel products were likely to be advantageous, especially to the Eastern States, others, as in the case of fresh meat, hides, and petroleum, were clearly illusory, so far as foreign competition with the United States producers was concerned.[1]

(*d*) Provision was made, following the example of the Canadian tariff law, for the levying upon all bounty-fed imports of surtaxes equal to the net amount of the bounties, as determined by the Secretary of the Treasury after due inquiry.

(*e*) All materials of foreign production which might be necessary for the construction of vessels to be built in the United States for foreign account or ownership, or *for the purpose of being employed in the foreign trade (including the trade between the Atlantic and Pacific ports of the United States)*, for the machinery of such ships, and for their outfit and equipment, might be imported under bond, and no duty was payable if their use for these purposes was proved.

(*f*) When imported materials on which duties had

[1] According to the calculations of the Senate Committee on Finance, the yield of the old rates of duty, on the basis of the statistics for the latest year available, amounted to 23·25 per cent. of the value of the total entries for consumption (dutiable and free), whilst the yield of the new rates would have been 23·57 per cent. As regards *necessaries* (dutiable and free), however, the percentages were estimated at 15·35 and 14·95 respectively. *Cf.* Willis, p. 593.

been paid were used in the manufacture of articles produced or manufactured in the United States, there was to be allowed on the exportation of such articles a drawback equivalent to 99 per cent. of the duties paid on the materials used; this was the continuation of a system in force since the establishment of the McKinley tariff.

(*g*) An additional duty of 10 per cent. *ad valorem* was to be levied on all goods not imported in United States vessels, except in the case of goods imported in vessels of a country entitled by treaty or Act of Congress to national treatment in the United States in respect of matters relating to shipping and navigation.[1]

(*h*) The "Customs Administrative Act" of 1890 was revised and incorporated in the new tariff law; the most noticeable change was the provision for the establishment of a Court of Customs Appeal to deal with cases of disputed classification.

In accordance with the provisions of the Tariff Law, the United States Government gave the necessary notice to terminate the various reciprocity conventions with certain European States which had been made in pursuance of the powers granted to the executive authority by Section 3 of the Dingley Tariff Act, the latest date to which any of them were to continue being consequently August 7, 1910. The President appointed a Commission[2] to assist him in determining what countries could continue to receive the benefits of the minimum tariff after March 31, 1910 (the date at which the maximum tariff was to be applied to imports from all countries not specifically excepted by Presidential

[1] The United Kingdom is entitled to such national treatment under the Treaty of 1815.

[2] The section of the Customs Act which provided for maximum and minimum rates included a clause enabling the President, in order "to secure information to assist the President in the discharge of the duties imposed upon him by this section, and the officers of the Government in the administration of the customs laws" to employ such persons as might be required. Advantage was taken of this clause to appoint a Commission to advise on tariff questions generally.

proclamation).[1] By the end of March the Commission had fortunately been able to advise that all the countries of the world gave the United States such treatment as entitled them to receive the benefits of the minimum tariff.

In regard to three states only had any serious difficulty been anticipated. The first of these was Germany; in that country the United States did not enjoy the advantages of the minimum tariff in respect of all their products, whilst the importation of meat from the United States into Germany was particularly hampered by the inspection laws of that country. On the other hand, it was thought unlikely that Germany would be willing to grant the United States the full conventional tariff without an endeavour to secure some reductions on German goods entering the United States, and it was certain that she would be unwilling to relax the administration of her meat inspection laws. Both parties, however, were anxious to avoid a conflict, and accordingly, early in 1910, an agreement was reached, each according the other the benefit of its minimum tariff, and the question of the German meat inspection being shelved. When,

[1] "Fear had been expressed, both in Congress and in the Press, that the provision in Section 2 which authorised the President to apply the maximum duties to all countries which discriminated unduly against the United States would lead to tariff wars and, in application, to an increase of the import duties above the high level already fixed in the minimum schedule. In his message to Congress of December 7, 1909, President Taft made it clear that he would use caution in applying these rates and expressed the hope and belief that the United States would not be led into tariff wars as a result of the authority conferred upon him. He pointed out that the term 'unduly discriminatory' used in Section 2 allowed him wide discretion; before applying the maximum duties upon the imports from a country it was necessary that he should find not only that that country discriminated against the trade of the United States, but that the discriminations were 'undue'—that is, without good and fair reason. He expressed the belief that this authorisation had been conferred in the hope that there would never be occasion to apply the maximum duties, and in the expectation that the power to apply them would enable the President and the State Department through friendly negotiations to secure the elimination of whatever was unduly discriminatory against the United States from the laws and practices of foreign countries" (*Reciprocity and Commercial Treaties*, pp. 270–1).

however, in 1911 the United States granted to Canadian wood-pulp and paper lower rates than those imposed on similar products from Germany, that country in turn refused to extend to the United States the rates of duty established by the treaties between Germany and Japan and Sweden, which came into force late in 1911.

France regarded herself as especially aggrieved by some of the changes in the United States tariff, notably those relating to silk goods, and it is generally believed that some of the increases in her own new tariff, especially in the case of agricultural machinery, were intended as measures of retaliation. But here again both parties were unwilling to enter upon a tariff war, and a solution of the difficulty was found. France made some concessions (especially in respect of agricultural and other implements, tools and machinery) and was granted the United States minimum rates.

As regards the commercial relations between the United States and Canada, the position was more difficult. Not only did Canada give preferential treatment, in respect of the rates of duty on imports, to the United Kingdom, but under a convention with France numerous articles imported from the latter country paid rates of duty intermediate between those of the British preferential tariff and those of the general tariff, to which goods from the United States were subjected; the intermediate tariff had been established by the Canadian Tariff Act of 1897 for bargaining purposes. Whilst the President and his advisers were not inclined to regard the British preference as unfair discrimination against the United States, they could scarcely ignore the provisions of the Canadian-French Convention, though it is true that French imports into Canada were not to any large extent competitive with those of the United States. There were other questions at issue between Canada and the United States, such as the prohibition of the export of wood-pulp from the former country; but the importance of the Canadian market to the United States, and the reluctance of the latter country to become involved in a tariff war with its northern neighbour, rendered the United States Government willing to come to terms. On the other hand, Canada found her export trade to the United States threatened with the latter's maximum duties, and was anxious to avoid so disastrous an experience. Negotiations were opened early in 1910. In March an agreement was reached whereby Canada would extend the benefits of her intermediate tariff to thirteen commodities imported from the United States (especially soap, cotton-seed oil, leather, tableware and perfumery), and receive complete minimum tariff treatment in return. The agreement, however, aroused strong opposition in Canada, partly because it was regarded as a yielding to threats on the part of the United States, and partly because it was avowedly intended by its authors as the preliminary stage to a much more far-reaching reciprocity arrangement. Such an arrangement was in fact reached at the beginning of 1911. It did not take the form of a treaty, but was an undertaking by the two Governments to introduce concurrent legislation, the nature of which was duly set out in four schedules.[1] The first was a list of commodities to be admitted duty-free into both countries: it included most agricultural products (except wool), fish, timber in various forms, some minerals, coal and coke, and a few manufactured commodities (especially galvanised or tinned sheets, wire and wire-rods). The second schedule included articles to be reciprocally admitted at identical rates of duty; these were chiefly secondary products or manufactures of which the chief component materials were included in the first schedule; the rates of duty fixed were generally lower than those in force at the time in either country. The third schedule covered six commodities to be admitted by the United

[1] Details of the Schedules are given in *Canada—United States of America : Reciprocity Arrangement* (Board of Trade, Cd. 5537, 1911). A lengthy sketch of the negotiations, and a criticism of the proposals from an independent United States standpoint is contained in *Reciprocity and Commercial Treaties*, pp. 368–381. The main lines of opposition in Canada are summarised in a statement issued by a group of leading business men of Toronto (set out in *British Dominions*, ed. W. J. Ashley, pp. 257–9).

States at special rates (these were aluminium, laths, shingles, planed or finished lumber, iron ore and coal slack), and the fourth schedule comprised seven articles on which Canada was to make reductions (cement, bituminous coal, fruit trees, condensed milk, unsweetened biscuits, canned fruit, pea-nuts). The agreement offered substantial advantages to Canada as it would greatly facilitate her export of agricultural produce to the United States: the rates granted by her to the United States were as a rule those of the intermediate tariff, and fell below those rates only in a very few instances. Legislation to give effect to the arrangement was introduced simultaneously in the two countries. After considerable resistance from the interests affected the Bill was passed by the Congress of the United States by very substantial majorities in July, 1911. In Canada, however, very strong opposition developed; the country was enjoying a period of great prosperity, which appeared to make it less dependent than ever before on the goodwill of its neighbour; and the agreement was represented as a menace to Canada's agriculture and growing industries, to her trade with the United Kingdom, and her political position within the British Empire and over against the United States. Political considerations played a very large part in the debates and in the General Election to which the Government was forced to submit the issue; and that election resulted in the overthrow of the ministry. The reciprocity proposals were consequently abandoned; the United States enactment remained unrepealed, but the trade relations between the two countries were thenceforward governed by the agreement reached in 1910.

It was generally recognised that the duration of the new tariff was very doubtful. A considerable body of moderate Republicans was dissatisfied with the outcome of the latest revision, and convinced that another and more genuine revision, with a really appreciable reduction of duties, was desirable in the true interests of the nation. That movement of Republican opinion was supported by the widespread belief that the apparently arbitrary action of certain of the great industrial combinations was facilitated by the maintenance of high protection, and there was a strong tendency to ascribe to the same cause the rapid increase in the cost of living, though that was undoubtedly to a large extent due to economic developments on which changes in tariff policy have little influence.

CHAPTER X

REACTION AND THE TARIFF OF 1913

THE recovery of trade and industry from the depression which followed the financial crisis of the autumn of 1907 was only very gradual. The chief illustrative statistics are set out in the table on pp. 254-5,[1] and comparing them with the corresponding figures for previous years given on pp. 232-3 it will be observed that the value of the imports into the United States for domestic consumption was in 1909 still below the level of 1907, whilst the value of the exports of United States products and manufactures, which in 1908 was approximately the same as in the previous year, fell heavily in 1909, and showed only a moderate improvement in 1910. The coal, iron, and steel industries recovered very rapidly from the very sharp depression of 1908, but experienced a set-back in 1911, after which year the upward movement set in again. The wheat and cane sugar crops were poor in 1910, and especially 1911, whilst the maize crop, which was very large in 1910, fell heavily in the following year. The cotton crop is always subject to violent fluctuations; it was very small in 1909, and reached the highest level yet recorded in 1911.

This slowness of recovery, in spite of the tariff revision of 1909, combined with the rising cost of living in the United States—a phenomenon not restricted to that country—and the growing hostility to the great industrial combinations, many of which had been particularly active during the passage of the Tariff Act and were held generally to be largely responsible for the upward movement of prices, to affect unfavourably the political

[1] Compiled from the *Statistical Abstract for the United States*, 1918.

position of the Republicans, who had been in power uninterruptedly since 1897 and in spite of President Roosevelt's attitude were widely regarded as favourable to the combinations and were definitely identified with the policy of high protection. The elections of the late autumn of 1910 gave the Democrats a substantial majority in the House of Representatives, though the Republicans still retained control of the Senate by a narrow margin, and it rapidly became apparent that the tariff question was to be the chief, though not the only, issue at the next Presidential election. The Democratic majority passed through the House of Representatives bills to reduce substantially the duties on cotton goods, wool and woollens, iron and steel products, and various other commodities; some of these made no further progress, others actually passed the Senate, with various modifications, only to be vetoed by President Taft. The Republicans generally admitted that a further and even markedly downward revision of the tariff was inevitable, even if only as a matter of political expediency, but they urged that no action should be taken until the Tariff Board set up under the Act of 1909[1] had reported. That Board was actively at work; it was undoubtedly competent and, despite its Republican origin, as nearly impartial as possible; but the fact that the Republicans, who had passed two important tariff laws during their long tenure of office, had never recognised the necessity for any scientific consideration of the problem until they saw their power slipping from them, led many electors to regard the appeal to the Board as a mere device for delaying revision. In 1912 the House of Representatives failed to make any financial provision for the work of the Board, which accordingly came to an end. The failure of the negotiations in 1911 for reciprocity with Canada undoubtedly seriously damaged the prestige of the Republicans, and their prospects were made hopeless by the dissensions in their own ranks which caused the formation of the Progressive party and the nomination

[1] See note on p. 246 *supra*.

ECONOMIC PROGRESS, 1909–1913.

	1909.	1910.	1911.	1912.	1913.
Agriculture:	Million Winchester Bushels.	Million Winchester Bushels.	Million Winchester Bushels.	Million Winchester Bushels.	Million Winchester Bushels.
Production of wheat	737·2	635·1	621·3	730·3	763·4
Production of maize	2772·4	2886·3	2531·5	3124·7	2447·0
	Million Bales.	Million Bales.	Million Bales.	Million Bales.	Million Bales.
Production of cotton	10·0	11·6	15·7	13·7	14·2
Production of sugar—	Million Lbs.	Million Lbs.	Million Lbs.	Million Lbs.	Million Lbs.
(1) Cane	828·8	750·4	710·1	721·7	325·1
(2) Beet	851·8	1024·9	1020·3	1199·0	1385·5
Production of rice	606·6	680·8	637·0	695·9	715·1
Industry:	Million Tons.	Million Tons.	Million Tons.	Million Tons.	Million Tons.
Production of coal	411·4	447·9	443·2	477·2	508·9
Production of iron ore	51·2	56·9	41·4	57·1	59·6
Production of pig-iron	25·8	27·3	23·6	29·7	31·0
Production of crude steel	24·0	26·1	23·7	31·3	31·3
	Million Lbs.	Million Lbs.	Million Lbs.	Million Lbs.	Million Lbs.
Production of tin plates	1,371	1,619	1,756	2,157	1,845
	Tons.	Tons.	Tons.	Tons.	Tons.
Production of copper	488,000	482,000	490,000	555,000	547,000
	Short Tons.	Short Tons.	Short Tons.	Short Tons.	Short Tons.
Production of lead	352,000	375,000	392,000	393,000	412,000

Industry:					
Production of petroleum	Million Gallons. 7,693	Million Gallons. 8,801	Million Gallons. 9,259	Million Gallons. 9,363	Million Gallons. 10,425
Cotton spindles employed	Millions. 28·0	Millions. 28·3	Millions. 29·5	Millions. 30·6	Millions. 31·5
Shipbuilding (vessels built and added to Register)	Thousand Tons. 513·6	Thousand Tons. 178·2	Thousand Tons. 277·4	Thousand Tons. 174·7	Thousand Tons. —
Transport:					
Railways	Miles in Operation. 244,084	Miles in Operation. 249,992	Miles in Operation. 254,732	Miles in Operation. 258,033	Miles in Operation. 261,036
Shipping—	Gross Tons.	Gross Tons.	Gross Tons.	Gross Tons.	Gross Tons.
(1) Foreign trade	887,505	791,825	872,671	932,101	1,027,776
(2) Lake, river, and coasting trade	6,501,250	6,716,257	6,766,119	6,782,082	6,858,775
Foreign Trade—[1]					
Imports for home consumption—	Million £.	Million £.	Million £.	Million £.	Million £.
(*a*) Total	267·0	322·3	318·3	342·3	368·0
(*b*) Manufactured and partly manufactured articles[2]	108·7	136·0	135·3	136·2	157·3
Exports of domestic produce—					
(*a*) Total	341·3	356·3	419·5	452·1	505·9
(*b*) Manufactured and partly manufactured articles	139·9	159·8	189·1	212·6	246·5

[1] The foreign trade statistics relate to the twelve months ended on the 30th of June of the years given.

[2] Including a very small value of goods re-exported.

of Mr. Roosevelt as its candidate in opposition to the official party nominee, the retiring President. The elections of November, 1912, not only secured the Presidency for the Democrats, in the person of Dr. Woodrow Wilson, but gave them control of both the House of Representatives and the Senate, in the former case by an overwhelming majority.

One international question bearing on the general commercial policy of the United States was bequeathed by the Republican administration to its successor. The construction of the Panama Canal was approaching completion, and in August, 1912, Congress had passed the Panama Canal Act, which provided for the administration of the canal zone, and authorised the President to fix, within certain limits, the tolls to be paid by vessels using the canal, but stipulated that no tolls should be levied upon ships engaged in the coastwise trade of the United States (which is reserved to United States vessels), and that the tolls for ships of commerce should not exceed a certain maximum per net registered ton, nor be less, other than for vessels of the United States and its citizens, than the estimated proportionate cost of the actual maintenance and operation of the Canal. The British Government, both before and after the passage of the Act, had taken exception to these stipulations on the ground that they conflicted with the provisions of the Hay-Pauncefote Treaty of 1901, which laid down that "the Canal shall be free and open to the vessels of commerce and of war of all nations," complying with certain rules "on terms of entire equality, so that there shall be no discrimination against any such nation, or its citizens or subjects, in respect of the conditions or charges of traffic, or otherwise. Such conditions and charge of traffic shall be just and equitable." The British Government contended that the words "all nations" clearly included the United States, that consequently British vessels using the Canal would be entitled to equal treatment with those of the United States, and the same tolls must be charged for both classes, and further, that unless the whole volume of shipping making use of the Canal were taken into account there could be no guarantee that the vessels which actually paid toll would not have to bear more than their fair share of the cost of upkeep—that is, that the tolls would not be other than " just and equitable." The United States Government argued that there was nothing in the Hay-Pauncefote Treaty which prevented any Government from giving assistance by way of subsidy, or in any other manner, to the ships of its nationals which might make use of the Canal; and that consequently the United States Government was free to assist its own shipping, and could do this by remitting tolls or charging them only to refund them. And as regards other than coastwise shipping, they urged that the tolls in fact fixed by the President did not discriminate between United States and other shipping, and that the British Government had no ground of complaint unless and until such discrimination was in fact practised. The British Government rejoined that as regards the subsidy question, they did not dispute the right of the United States to give such support to their shipping or any part of it, but they still contended that the Treaty provisions did debar the United States from giving a subsidy in a particular way, the effect of which would be to impose upon British or other foreign shipping an unfair share of the burden of the upkeep of the Canal; that coastwise trade could not be so completely circumscribed that benefits conferred upon it would not affect vessels engaged in the foreign trade—especially as there was nothing in the United States laws to prevent a ship from combining foreign and coasting trade; and that they were entitled to protest so soon as the rights of British vessels were threatened by the establishment of the principle of discrimination, even though it was not made operative. They accordingly pressed for the reference of the whole question to arbitration.[1]

[1] The diplomatic correspondence was issued by the Foreign Office as *Miscellaneous*, No. 12 (1912), Cd. 6451; No. 2 (1913), Cd. 6585; and No. 5 (1913), Cd. 6645.

The controversy had reached this stage when the Democrats took office in March, 1913. The new President quickly came to the decision that the position taken up by his Republican predecessor was untenable, and urged Congress to repeal the obnoxious provisions of the Panama Canal Act. But the fact that this course could be represented as due to foreign pressure aroused strong opposition. The President persisted, but it was not until June, 1914, that after prolonged Congressional discussion an Act was passed amending the Panama Canal Act so as to cancel the exemption accorded to United States coastwise shipping and the power accorded to the President to discriminate, in respect of other shipping, between United States and foreign vessels: and the amending Act contained a proviso—which was indeed the price of its enactment—that nothing in it should be construed as a waiver or relinquishment of any right which the United States might have under the Hay-Pauncefote Treaty to discriminate in favour of its vessels using the Canal, or its right to regulate the conditions or charges of traffic as it thought fit.

Meanwhile a far-reaching revision of the customs tariff had been carried through. The tariff issue had played a very large part in the Presidential election of November, 1913, and the Congressional elections which preceded and accompanied it. The Ways and Means Committee of the House of Representatives, under the leadership of Mr. Underwood, had been at work preparing a bill during the session which ended in March, 1913, and the new President immediately on assuming office convoked a special session to deal with the matter. The Democratic majority remained solid; the President himself took definitely the leadership: the bill passed the House of Representatives early in May, and though there was delay subsequently in the Senate, which made many amendments, generally going still further than the lower House in the direction of the reduction of duties, and in the discussions between the two Houses, the bill was finally passed in October, 1913, and became immediately operative. It represented the most complete reversal of tariff policy which the United States had witnessed for half a century.[1] The principle of maximum and minimum rates of duty which had played such a part in the Tariff Act of 1909 was abandoned. A clause did appear which provided for a discount of 5 per cent. on all duties in the case of goods imported in vessels admitted to registration under the laws of the United States, but with the proviso that this should not be construed so as to abrogate or in any manner impair or affect the provisions of any treaty between the United States and any foreign nation. As many countries, including the United Kingdom and Germany, had treaties with the United States which provided that there should be no discrimination against their goods or shipping, and the United States Treasury ruled that in these cases the clause was inoperative, its effect was negligible. The tariff classification was recast radically, the minute subdivisions of many classes of goods (especially textiles and metal wares) being swept away; *ad valorem* rates of duty were largely substituted for specific rates; and the reductions and even abolitions of duties were numerous and far-reaching.

The most striking change made by the new Act was in the case of wool and woollen manufactures. Under the tariff of 1909 the duties on raw wool ranged from 4 to 11 cents per lb.: a short period of grace was now given, but as from December 1st, 1913, the duties were abolished. Woollen yarns and other goods were subject to *ad valorem* rates of duty, ranging from 35 to 55 and (in the case of clothing) 60 per cent., and also to specific duties imposed to compensate the manufacturers of woollens for the duties on wool. The abolition of the wool duties removed such justification as there was for these "compensatory" specific duties, and they were

[1] The full text of the Act, and a statement showing the old and new rates of duty, are given in *United States of America—New Customs Tariff Act* (issued by the Board of Trade as Cd. 7128, 1913).

swept away; and at the same time the *ad valorem* rates were reduced so that only in a limited number of cases did they exceed 40 per cent., being thus generally lower than under the short-lived tariff of 1894, when raw wool had last been free. Tops were to be charged 15 per cent., and yarns 20 per cent. The combination of *ad valorem* and specific rates under the previous tariffs had resulted in the actual incidence of the total duties being extremely heavy—in some cases the rate was well over 100 per cent.: it had in fact been almost prohibitive, and sweeping as was the reduction now made it was doubtful if it would result in any considerable competition from abroad with United States manufacturers.[1] In the case of cotton yarn and manufactures the very elaborate classification and specific duties of the 1909 tariff disappeared, and were replaced by a comparatively simple schedule of *ad valorem* duties, ranging in the case of yarns from 5 to 25 per cent. (according to fineness of counts), and in the case of cloth, not bleached, dyed, or mercerised, or printed, from 7½ to 27½ per cent., with an additional duty of 2½ per cent. when it had undergone any further process. On ordinary hosiery the rate of duty was reduced from 30 to 20 per cent.; on cotton gloves the reduction was from 50 to 35 per cent. But in the case of cotton manufactures, as of woollen goods, it was unlikely that the lowering of the tariff barrier would do more than allow competition in the finest quality products. Silk goods had been subject under the tariff of 1909 to minimum rates of 45 and 50 per cent.; the rates in most cases were now left at 45 per cent., this high level being maintained, in spite of the fact that the industry had long been very successful and encountered little competition, largely because silk goods were regarded as luxuries, and therefore suitable subjects for taxation for revenue purposes. The duties on yarns of jute, flax,

[1] The inquiries of the Tariff Board, in its Special Report on Wool and Manufactures of Wool (1912), and further inquiries had led to the conclusion that a duty of 35 per cent. would correspond roughly to the least difference in cost of production between American and foreign manufacturers (Taussig, p. 431).

hemp, or ramie were substantially reduced, as were also those on manufactures thereof.

Turning now to metals and manufactures thereof, iron ore, pig-iron, spiegeleisen, wrought iron, ferro-manganese, iron in slabs and blooms, and steel ingots, blooms and slabs (of other than special alloy steels) were placed on the free list, as were barbed and galvanised wire of the kinds used for fencing, steel rails, all agricultural machinery and implements, cash registers, sewing machines, linotype and type-setting machines, shoe machinery and certain other classes of machinery. In all these cases, however, United States manufacturers were in an extremely strong position, and had little, if anything, to fear from the abolition of the protective duties. On beams, girders, joists, and similar products the specific duties were replaced by a rate of 10 per cent. *ad valorem*; in the case of boiler plates and sheets the rate was to be 12 per cent.; on iron and steel plates and sheets (including tinplate) 15 per cent.; on steel bars 8 per cent., and on steel ingots, blooms, slabs and billets 15 per cent. The rates on ferro-alloys were reduced from 25 or 20 to 15 per cent. The duties on penknives, pocket knives, razors, scissors, and shears were reduced, but still remained at a high level—55 per cent. in the case of penknives, etc., valued at more than 1 dollar per dozen, 35 per cent. for penknives, etc., valued at not more than 1 dollar per dozen, and 30 per cent. in the case of the other articles mentioned. Throughout the metal schedule generally *ad valorem* rates were substituted for the specific duties or the combinations of the two forms which were common in the old tariff.

An important change was made in respect of sugar, which since 1897 had been subject to a duty of 1⅔ cents per lb., with a reduction of ⅕ for Cuban sugar: the duty was now to be 1¼ cents (with the same proportional rebate for Cuba) until May 1st, 1916; thereafter sugar was to be free. The postponement of the change was intended partly to give the sugar producers time to adapt themselves to the new conditions, but partly also to enable the Government's new internal taxation scheme (the establishment of an income tax) to become operative and make good the large loss of revenue consequent upon the repeal of the sugar duties.

Some other changes made by the Act of 1913 may be noticed briefly. Cement, hitherto subject to duties of 8 or 7 cents per 100 lbs., was made free; so were coal and coke, which had paid 45 cents per ton, flax (not hackled or dressed), hemp and hemp tow, leather and boots and shoes, printing paper (other than hand-made), soda ash and nitrate of soda, certain tanning materials, wood and timber, and wood-pulp. Of foodstuffs buckwheat and buckwheat flour, maize and maize meal, wheat, wheat flour and semolina, rye and rye flour, eggs, meat, milk and cream, cattle and sheep, and salt were added to the free list. The rates of duty on barley and rice were halved, and that on oats reduced by three-fifths. The rates on earthenware and china were lowered, but still left at a high level; under the tariff of 1909 they had been 55 and 60 per cent. *ad valorem*, they were now to be 35 and 40 per cent. on the cheaper grades and 50 and 55 per cent. on the higher qualities. Finally, it may be observed that the policy of free materials for industry did not extend to such commodities as lead ore and pig-lead, zinc ore and zinc in pigs, blocks, or sheets, and nickel and nickel oxide, all of which were left subject to substantial duties, whilst coal-tar dyestuffs remained dutiable at 30 per cent. *ad valorem*, and coal-tar distillates (including benzol and toluol) and a large class of other coal-tar products were removed from the free list and made dutiable at rates of 5 and 10 per cent. respectively.

As regards tariff administration, the extensive substitution of *ad valorem* for specific duties made necessary a revision and strengthening of the machinery for the assessment of values and the prevention of fraud, and in this connection the Secretary of the Treasury was empowered in cases where persons selling, shipping, consigning, or manufacturing goods exported to the United States refused to submit their books to the inspection of an accredited United States official—for example, a consul in the country of production—to levy on such goods an additional duty of 15 per cent. *ad valorem.* Provision was continued for the imposition of countervailing duties on bounty-fed goods, and also for the payment of drawbacks in the case of exported goods manufactured or produced in the United States by the use of imported materials or goods subject to duty, such drawbacks being equivalent to the amount of the duty paid in respect of such materials, less 1 per cent. A curious new provision laid down that "the President shall cause to be ascertained each year the amount of imports and exports" under the various tariff headings, "and cause an estimate to be made of the amount of the domestic production and consumption of said articles, and where it is ascertained that the imports" under any head "amount to less than 5 per centum of the domestic consumption of the articles enumerated he shall advise Congress as to the facts and his conclusion by special message, if deemed important in the public interest." Finally, the President was empowered "for the purpose of readjusting the present duties on importations into the United States and at the same time to encourage the export trade," to negotiate reciprocity agreements, subject to the approval of Congress.

The summary given in the preceding paragraphs will have indicated sufficiently the general character of the new tariff. The changes which it made, extensive as they were, were probably important less in their effect upon the industry and trade of the United States than as indicative of a feeling that the high protection which had been inaugurated by the McKinley Tariff of 1890, and after a temporary setback in 1894 was firmly established in 1897, had served the purposes of even its strongest advocates, and that United States industry had reached a stage of development at which it had little cause to fear foreign competition, except in a few special cases. No real opportunity, however, was afforded for the new tariff to be tested; before it had been in operation for a year the great European War began, and the whole world-conditions of commerce and industry underwent a series of dramatic and sweeping changes. The energies of the great industrial competitors of the United States were diverted almost entirely to the supply of munitions of war; Germany was deprived of access to the American markets; and ultimately the United States entered into the war. In these circumstances the tariff could have little influence on the course of United States manufacture and trade.

A BRIEF BIBLIOGRAPHY

TAUSSIG, F. W. *Tariff History of the United States.* Sixth edition. 1914.

TAUSSIG, F. W. *State Papers and Speeches on the Tariff.* 1893.

TAUSSIG, F. W. *The Tariff Debate of* 1909 *and the New Tariff Act* (in *Quarterly Journal of Economics*, November, 1909).

RABBENO, U. *The American Tariff Policy.* Second edition. 1905.

TARBELL, IDA M. *The Tariff in our Times.* 1911.

WRIGHT, C. W. *Wool-Growing and the Tariff.* 1910.

STANWOOD, E. *American Tariff Controversies in the Nineteenth Century.* 2 vols. 1904.

BOLLES, A. S. *Financial History of the United States.* 3 vols. 1886.

DEWEY, D. R. *Financial History of the United States.* 1903.

HILL, W. *The First Stages of the Tariff Policy of the United States* (Publications of the American Economic Association, vol. viii., No. 6).

GOSS, A. D. *History of Tariff Administration* (Columbia College Studies).

YOUNG, EDWARD. *Special Report on Customs Tariff Legislation* (House Executive Documents, 42nd Congress, 2nd Session, No. 109).

Reciprocity and Commercial Treaties (United States Tariff Commission, 1919).

MAYO-SMITH, R., and SELIGMAN, E. R. A. *The Commercial Policy of the United States* (in *Die Handelspolitik der wichtigern Kulturstaaten*, published by the *Verein für Sozial-Politik*, 1892).

CONNOR, J. E. *Industrial Causes affecting American Economic Policy since the Civil War* (in *Annals of the American Academy of Political and Social Science*, vol. xxiii., No. 1).

OSBORNE, J. B. *Reciprocity in the American Tariff System* (in *Annals of the American Academy of Political and Social Science*, vol. xxiii., No. 1).

WILLIS, H. P. *The Tariff of* 1909 (in *Journal of Political Economy*, November, 1909, and January, 1910).

FISK, G. M. *The Payne-Aldrich Tariff* (in the *Political Science Quarterly*, March, 1910).

PATTEN, S. N. *The Economic Basis of Protection.* Second edition. 1894.

LOW, A. MAURICE. *Protection in the United States.* 1904.

WRIGHT, CARROLL D. *The Industrial Evolution of the United States.* 1897.

HART, A. B. *Formation of the Union*, 1750–1829 (in *Epochs of American History*).

WILSON, W. *Division and Reunion*, 1829–1889 (in *Epochs of American History*).

BRYCE, J. *The American Commonwealth.* Third edition. 2 vols. 1895.

Statistical Abstract of the United States (published annually).

Twelfth Census of the United States (vols. vii.-xi., "Manufactures").

British and Foreign Trade and Industry (Board of Trade, Cd. 4954. 1909).

Tariff Acts passed by the Congress of the United States from 1789 *to* 1895 (54th Congress, 1st Session, Senate Document No. 219).

Return respecting the Customs Tariff of the United States (Board of Trade, Cd. 7579. 1894).

Imports and Exports, 1894–1907 (60th Congress, 2nd Session, House Document, No. 1504).

United States of America—New Customs Tariff (Board of Trade, Cd. 4856. 1909).

United States of America—New Customs Tariff Act (Board of Trade, Cd. 7128. 1913).

PART III

FRANCE

CHAPTER I

FRENCH COMMERCIAL POLICY, 1789 TO 1830

THE Revolution of 1789 first gave economic unity to France. Until that time internal commerce was hampered by innumerable tolls and feudal dues, by the right of the various provinces to impose customs duties against each other, by the prohibition of the movement of commodities, particularly of foodstuffs, from one part of the country to another, and by the diversity of the provincial tariffs upon foreign products. The transit of goods through the country was so costly as to be almost impossible.[1] The Constituent Assembly swept away all these obstacles; in 1790 it abolished the internal tolls and the provincial tariffs, and it established one common and uniform tariff against foreign countries in 1791. The new duties were fairly moderate; they ranged from 5 to 15 per cent. (or in a few cases 20 per cent.) on manufactured articles, and admitted free most raw materials (such as hides, wool, flax, and iron) and foodstuffs, such as corn and cattle. It is true that there were a number of prohibitions of import, but very few were of any economic importance;[2] and the prohibition of exports, to any considerable extent, only came when war was inevitable, and could be justified as a war measure.

But this was not the whole of the economic reform made by the Constituent Assembly. It abolished such serfdom as still existed among the rural population, and arranged for the cessation of the remaining feudal dues; it reformed taxation by making all classes of the com-

[1] Levasseur, i. p. 34.

[2] Amé, i. p. 53.

munity liable; it suppressed the industrial privileges of the guilds, and threw all trades and professions open to everyone that cared to enter them; it made an end of trading privileges both at home and abroad;[1] and on the whole it gave France the opportunity of the fullest and freest development of her industrial and commercial resources.[2] But in 1792 war broke out, and gradually the tariff policy of France became more and more restrictive. All existing commercial treaties, especially the one made with Great Britain in 1786, were annulled, and the prohibition of the export of commodities was extended; and then the National Convention, recognising that Great Britain was its most dangerous foe, entered on the attempt to cripple her by destroying her foreign trade. In March, 1793, the entry into France of certain commodities coming chiefly from Great Britain was prohibited, and in October of the same year, as that measure did not suffice, the import, sale, and use of all commodities made or manufactured in the United Kingdom or in the British Empire were forbidden under extremely heavy penalties. Yet even this enactment fell very far short of attaining the desired end,[3] and the Directory found it necessary to go still further. It ordered that a large number of commodities, whatever their place of origin, should be *reputed* to be British produce, and should be liable to be seized as such wherever found. But this extreme measure also proved insufficient; certainly by 1802 the customs revenue had fallen

[1] The privileges enjoyed by the Indian Company were abolished (Levasseur, i. 42).

[2] "Elle avait trouvé le cultivateur censitaire, corvéable, ou meme en quelques lieux serf, la terre chargée de droits féodaux; elle fit l'un et l'autre libres. Elle avait trouvé l'industrie gênée par les maîtrises et jurandes, par la multiplicité des impôts indirects, par les privilèges; le commerce entravé par les compagnies privilégiées, par les barrières de douanes; elle supprima les obstacles et déblaya la carrière devant l'industrie et commerce. La loi du 2–17 Mars 1790 émancipa l'industrie; celle du 7 Janvier 1791 constitua la propriété des inventeurs; celle du 2–15 Mars 1791 fonda sur un tarif modéré et uniforme les relations commerciales de la France avec l'étranger" (Levasseur, i. p. 46).

[3] Amé, pp. 36–7.

to 42 million francs (of which 11 millions were swallowed up by the cost of collection), but an enormous smuggling trade had arisen, and the French Government, in spite of its efforts, could not prevent the constant influx of British goods.

Under the Consulate, with Napoleon holding practically supreme power, the same policy was pursued, but its further application was delayed for a time by the negotiations which preceded the Treaty of Amiens, and the signature of that treaty in March, 1802. Though Napoleon declined to accept the contention of the British ministry that the signature of the treaty of peace restored the commercial relations of the two countries to their position under the agreement of 1786, he showed himself willing to make a fresh arrangement, and negotiations commenced, only to be brought to an abrupt end by the renewal of war in May, 1803. After Trafalgar, Napoleon, now become Emperor, began his supreme effort to break Great Britain's industrial and commercial power by isolating her from Continental Europe. The Berlin Decrees of November, 1806, with their sequel, the Milan Decrees of 1807 and 1808, prohibited all commercial relations between the countries under Napoleon's control (that is, the greater part of Europe) and Great Britain, announced that that country was in a state of blockade, and declared all vessels which had touched at British ports to be lawful prize. Meanwhile, the French tariffs were steadily rising; there had been a great increase in the duties on colonial produce in 1806, and in February and August, 1810, they were raised to an extraordinary height.[1] There were advances also on manufactured goods, but in spite of this and the prohibitions the manufacturers were constantly asking for yet more protection.[2]

The disorders of the early years of the Revolution

[1] Thus in 1806 the duty on sugar was 100 francs per 100 kilogs.; by the end of 1810 it was 400 francs. In the same period the duty on coffee rose from 150 to 400 francs; on cocoa from 200 to 1,000 francs.

[2] Amé, i. pp. 57, 59, and 61.

had almost destroyed the good effect of the liberating work of the Constituent Assembly; up to 1799 trade and commerce in France rather declined than advanced. With the rise to power of Napoleon, who really cared for industrial progress, and with the re-establishment of internal order, conditions began to improve, but the Exhibitions of 1801 and 1802 showed that, despite this improvement, industry had not yet risen again to the level which it had reached before the Revolution.[1] But between 1802 and 1806 there was distinct, if gradual, progress under the fostering care of Chaptel, the Minister of the Interior; and at the Exhibition of 1806 the Government could point to the fairly prosperous condition of French manufactures, particularly those of woollen and cotton goods. It could boast also of the increase of coal-mining (though this was chiefly in the Belgian provinces), of the commencement of the steel works at Creusot, of the improvement of the highways and canals. The upward movement continued for some years after 1806, and the Napoleonic period may be said to have witnessed the commencement of the industrial revolution in France: it is true that machinery came in only very slowly, and in this respect France lagged far behind Great Britain, chiefly because fuel was dearer and manual labour cheaper than in the latter country; but, nevertheless, there were many improvements in industrial methods. The output of the smelting works increased from 1,058,000 cwt. in 1789 to 1,623,000 in 1812, whilst the production of bar-iron rose from 723,000 cwt. to 1,155,000 in the same period. There was a considerable growth in the textile industries, in spite of the way in which the cotton manufacturers were hampered by the blockade of raw materials; in the productions of the chemical and tanning industries under the stimulus of new scientific processes; in the manufacture of glass and porcelain; and in sugar refining, encouraged by high prices and bounties. Foreign trade increased up to 1806, but after that date, with the extension of the

[1] Levasseur, i. p. 455.

"continental system," it rapidly declined. The following table gives the movement of foreign trade for the whole period of Napoleon's government of France:—[1]

Year.	Imports.	Exports.	Year.	Imports.	Exports.
	Million £.	Million £.		Million £.	Million £.
1799 ..	10·1	12·0	1807 ..	15·7	15·0
1800 ..	12·9	10·9	1808 ..	12·8	13·2
1801 ..	16·6	12·2	1809 ..	11·5	13·2
1802 ..	18·6	13·0	1810 ..	13·6	14·6
Average, 1799–1802	14·5	12·0	Average, 1807–1810	13·4	14·0
1803 ..	17·2	13·9	1811 ..	12·0	13·1
1804 ..	17·6	15·2	1812 ..	12·3	16·8
1805 ..	19·7	15·0	1813 ..	10·0	14·2
1806 ..	19·0	18·2	1814 ..	9·6	13·8
Average, 1803–1806	18·4	15·6	Average, 1811–1814	11·0	14·5

But there was a reverse side to this industrial progress. The development was essentially artificial; it was the outcome, not so much of the enterprise of French manufacturers, as of the compulsion laid upon consumers to have recourse to them, and their undisturbed sway in the home market. Except in a few cases there was no considerable improvement in their methods, and "after being kept apart for a quarter of a century from all regular contact with the products of the British manufacturers, we [*i.e.*, the French] found ourselves at the establishment of peace even further behind than was the case prior to the war; whilst machinery had gradually developed in England, in France it had made very little progress."[2] Moreover, there was much over-speculation in France, followed by extensive monetary difficulties, and the bad harvest of 1811 made thing worse. The result was a commercial crisis in the years 1811 to 1813. Napoleon recognised that his attempt to destroy the economic basis of Great Britain's power had failed, and that the "continental system" had resulted only in

[1] Based on Levasseur, i. p. 493.

[2] Amé, i. p. 67.

considerable disaster to the French ports. He tried, therefore, in 1813 to improve matters by granting licences enabling certain goods needed for French manufactures, such as cotton, tobacco, lumber, to be brought in ships so licensed at a duty of only 50 per cent., on condition that the same ships took an outward cargo of French products.[1] But it was too late to save the situation; the commercial disorder and general collapse discredited Napoleon's statesmanship, as the disastrous Russian campaign did much to destroy his military reputation.

The Restoration Monarchy was called on to deal with an extremely difficult problem. The economic policy of Napoleon had brought into existence a small but powerful class of iron-masters and textile manufacturers, who were bent on maintaining their monopoly of the French market, and dreaded the threatened invasion of British goods. The landowners were anxious to keep up the high price of grain. In April, 1814, the Comte d'Artois, acting as Lieutenant-General of the realm, issued an edict greatly reducing the duties on coffee and sugar, and practically abolishing those on raw cotton. The merchants holding stocks of colonial produce, and the cotton-spinners, who also thought that the value of their stocks would consequently be depreciated, were at once aroused, and, by representing the Government's action as the first step towards the abandonment of Protection, the opponents of the new policy were able to carry all the manufacturers with them. In a petition to the King in 1814, the Chamber of Commerce of Rouen went so far as to declare that "prohibition is the outcome of political and social rights. From the manufacturer who has made use of all his financial resources in order to establish a factory, down to the workman who

[1] "Pour cette année (1813) ne pouvant plus espérer la paix de la détresse de l'Angleterre, et n'ayant à l'attendre que des batailles qui allaient se livrer en Allemagne, voulant de plus rendre aux villes de Bordeaux, de Nantes, du Havre, de Marseilles, quelque activité commerciale, Napoléon avait accordé une quantité de licenses telle qu'on pouvait considérer comme presque rétabli le commerce avec l'Angleterre" (Thiers, quoted by Amé, i. p. 48).

finds there the means of existence for himself and his family—all demand, with perfect reason, the right to be the sole source of supplies for home consumption."[1] Though inclined to give up the system of prohibition, and convinced that the economic progress of France could only be secured by allowing foreign competition,[2] the new Government was not able to resist the pressure. Absolute prohibition was maintained in a great many cases, and with regard to others high Protection was adopted, and the record of the economic policy of the Restoration monarchy is simply the story of a Government attempting to hold the balance between the party which favoured commercial liberty and the various well-organised groups representing particular interests, and forced again and again to go much further in the direction of Protection than it desired. The Tariff Act of 1816 made it perfectly clear that, for a very long time, France would adhere to the commercial policy which she had adopted during the war.[3]

It would serve no useful purpose to describe the tariff legislation of the Restoration Monarchy in detail; it will suffice to give some illustrations of the manner in which the policy of Protection was carried out. To take the most conspicuous example: in 1814 it was estimated that iron from abroad could be delivered in France at from 30 to 40 per cent. below the French cost of production, and the Government, in order to help their own manufactures, proposed a specific duty on bar-iron of

[1] Quoted in Amé, i. pp. 68–9.

[2] Saint-Cricq, the Director-General of Customs and the real guide of the economic policy of the Restoration Monarchy, wrote: "Nous aurions moins de progrès à faire si une trop longue interruption dans nos relations commerciales n'eût constitué une prohibition à l'abri de laquelle on a pu négliger, sans danger, des moyens de perfectionnement qu'une heureuse rivalité n'aurait pas manqué de développer."

[3] The Napoleonic Wars exercised the same influence upon subsequent commercial policy in France as the Civil War in the United States. In both cases a system of high Protection was called into existence (though for different reasons) by war, and the interests to which it gave rise, and the manner in which people became accustomed to it by its long duration, secured its continuance in time of peace.

15 francs plus 10 per cent. (=16 francs 50 centimes) per 100 kilo., which was calculated to be about 50 per cent. *ad valorem.* The manufacturers were not satisfied —they desired prohibition—but they accepted the proposal, and in spite of the opposition of the seaports it was carried. The ministry intended it to be merely a temporary measure to offset the disadvantages under which the French iron-masters laboured, and to give them time to improve their works; and the duties, it was thought, should therefore be gradually reduced.[1] But by 1822 the invasion of British iron, produced by better methods than the Russian and Swedish products with which France had been supplied up to 1814, had greatly reduced prices, and the average had fallen from about 36 francs (duty free) per 100 kilo. in 1814 to 22–23 francs in 1822. The French manufacturers asserted that they still could not compete; and in 1822, in spite of the facts that the imports were falling and that the native industry had admittedly made much progress, the Government was compelled to increase the duty to 24 francs plus 10 per cent. (=26·4 francs) per 100 kilo. The net result was a duty on foreign bar-iron of about 120 per cent. *ad valorem ;* and a little later there was a slight further increase.[2] The imports of British iron fell from 1,463 tons in 1823 to 330 tons in 1825.[3] In 1820 there had been increases in the duties on steel and various kinds of steel goods; and in 1826 there were further advances on iron plates, cast-iron, and wire.

Another, and even more important, example was furnished by the agricultural duties, to which the various Governments of France had always paid considerable attention. In spite of the advocacy of Turgot, it was not until the French Revolution that the free movement of grain from one part of France to another had been permitted.[4] Originally in 1814 it was proposed to prohibit the export of corn and allow its free import, but in September of that year, in order to prevent prices

[1] Brandt, p. 74.
[2] Amé, i. pp. 145–7.
[3] *Ibid.*, p. 149 n.
[4] *Ibid.*, p. 105.

at home from falling too low because the producers were compelled to sell it within the French borders, the whole country was divided into three zones, and export was permitted when the prices there had fallen respectively to 23, 21, and 19 francs per hectolitre. In 1816 this principle was retained, but a small revenue duty on imports was established. By 1819, however, the reactionary royalist party was rising to power and seeking to base its political position upon the support of the agrarian interests: and it secured a reversal of the policy. The price of corn in that year was lower than it had been for some time, though not lower than the average for the period 1800–14;[1] the farmers feared the growing invasion of Russian grain, stimulated by the bounties given by the Government from November, 1816, to September, 1817, to meet the distress caused by the war of the Hundred Days and the second military occupation of France. So in 1819 the three-zone system was continued, but the importation of corn was made subject to a fixed duty and a surtax varying according to the amount by which the home prices fell below a certain level; and finally importation was to be prohibited altogether when the price in the three zones fell to 20, 18, and 16 francs per hectolitre. But this did not satisfy the ultra-royalist agrarian party, and in 1821, finding themselves in a strong majority in the Chamber, they forced on the ministry a law which raised the limit at which the surtaxes on imports were to commence, divided France into four zones, and raised the points at which prohibition should come into force to 24, 22, 20, and 18 francs respectively.[2] Another concession was made to the agrarians in the case of wool. In 1814 the Government had proposed an export duty of 30 francs per 100 kilo. on the better kinds of washed wools and 15 francs on the same qualities of unwashed wools—whilst imports

[1] The average price for 1801–14 was 21·34 francs per hectolitre; in 1816 it was 28·31 francs, and in 1817, 36·16 francs. In 1818 it had fallen to 24·65 francs.

[2] Brandt, pp. 79–82.

were to be free, or rather subject only to a small weighing-duty; there was a sharp conflict between the manufacturers of woollens, desiring the free import and prohibited export of wool, and the wool-growers, whose wishes were naturally to the contrary effect, but ultimately the Government plan was carried.[1] But by 1820 political conditions had changed; the export duties on the better kinds of wool were accordingly reduced, the prohibition hitherto maintained of the export of the commoner kinds was abolished, and import duties were imposed of 60 and 20 francs (according to kind) per 100 kilo. on the finer sorts, and 15 and 5 francs on the commoner qualities. After 1819 imports declined, but in 1822 the duties on the cheaper wools were again increased; there were further advances with a more detailed classification, made for all kinds in the next three years, and completed and confirmed in an Act of 1826.

These instances may suffice to show the general trend of commercial policy during the Restoration period—many other industries could tell the same story. It was a policy of Protection continued from the Napoleonic era, originally in the interests of the manufacturers; but as the reactionary and agrarian party gained the upper hand in Parliament, the system was generalised,[2] and extended particularly to serve the purpose of agriculture,[3] though some compensation was offered to manufactures in the form of bounties on exports, and draw-

[1] Amé, i. pp. 76–9.

[2] An example of care for native industries is furnished by the Commission of 1820, which asked for the prohibition of dye-stuffs made from woods, so that the French merchant marine might get the extra amount of freight involved in carrying the wood instead of extracts, which represented only 2 or 3 per cent. of the weight of the "matière première" (Amé, i. p. 129).

[3] The Act of 1822 increased the rates of duty on cattle for food purposes, common wool, flax, olives, and other agricultural products, in the interests of the French producers, and on rice because it competed with wheat as a foodstuff. Subsequently the woollen duties were increased by a series of royal ordinances; these were consolidated by the Act of 1826, which also increased the rates on cattle and hops.

backs.[1] The culminating point was reached in the Tariff Act of 1826, which completed the whole scheme of Protection, and seemed intended to make France almost entirely self-contained.

But there are two other points in connection with French commercial policy after 1814 which should be noted. The first of these relates to sugar. Under the law of 1816 the colonial possessions of France enjoyed a considerable advantage, in respect of rates of duty, for the sugar which they sent to her, and in 1819 they supplied 34 million kilo. out of a total of 39 millions imported. But they were still not content, and asked for a reduction in the rate of duty on colonial sugar and the prohibition of all other kinds; the Government would not go so far, but gave the colonies a further preference of 5 or 10 per cent., according as the foreign sugars were or were not imported in French vessels. This almost destroyed the non-colonial importation, but, as the colonies still complained, there were further increases on foreign sugars so as to raise the price of the whole supply in the home market, and after the legislation of July, the rate of duty on colonial sugar was only one-half of that levied on other kinds. An incidental effect of the high prices was a stimulus to the beet-sugar industry.[2]

The other noteworthy point is the treaties made with the United States in 1822 and Great Britain in 1826. The Restoration Monarchy had commenced with the idea of developing the commercial relations of France with the other Powers by means of a series of treaties,[3] but in face of the strong protectionist movement this was felt to be impossible, and, in fact, there were sharp

[1] These were in respect of sugar, wool and woollen yarn, manufactures of lead and copper, dressed hides, straw hats, and soap.

[2] Amé, i. p. 130.

[3] In 1814 the Ministry wrote to the Chambers of Commerce: "Nous sommes à la veille de reprendre avec les peuples qui nous environnent nos anciennes relations. . . . Ne perdez pas de vue que tout est réciproque ici; que nous n'avons rien à exiger des autres nations; qu'il ne peut être question que d'avantages mutuels à negocier et stipuler" (quoted by Levasseur, i. p. 563).

conflicts with Prussia, Russia, Sweden and the Netherlands. In 1820 the United States replied to some French tariff changes by increasing the dues payable by French vessels; France replied in the same way, and also by granting bounties on the importation of cotton in French bottoms. The two parties then, in 1822, came to an agreement, which put their shipping on equal terms. The same arrangement was made with Great Britain in 1826, with results on the whole disadvantageous to the French carrying trade.[1]

The following table gives the movement of French foreign trade between 1816 and 1830. The figures for the earlier years are for the whole of the imports and exports; it was not until 1827 that the "special trade" (*i.e.*, imports for French consumption and exports of French produce) was distinguished, and in fact it is only from that year that there are statistics on which any real reliance can be placed.[2]

Year.	General Trade.		Special Trade.	
	Imports.	Exports.	Imports for Home Consumption.	Exports of French Produce.
	Million £.	Million £.	Million £.	Million £.
1816 ..	9·7	21·9	Not available	Not available
1817 ..	13·3	18·6		
1818 ..	13·4	20·0		
1819 ..	11·8	18·5		
1820 ..	13·4	21·7		
1821 ..	16·0	16·2		
1822 ..	17·0	15·4		
1823 ..	14·5	15·6		
1824 ..	18·2	17·6		
1825 ..	21·4	26·7		
1826 ..	22·6	22·4		
1827 ..	22·6	24·0	16·6	20·3
1828 ..	24·3	24·4	18·2	20·4
1829 ..	24·6	24·3	19·5	20·2
1830 ..	25·4	22·9	19·6	18·1

Towards the end of this period there came a distinct reaction. There had always been a considerable body of opposition to the policy of extreme restriction, and

[1] Brandt, pp. 85–6.

[2] Foville, pp. 266 *seq.*

this increased in vigour as manufacturers felt the disadvantages of all-round Protection, and as the interests of particular groups exercised too evident an influence upon legislation. The Ministry of Martignac was conscious of the turn of public feeling, and appointed in 1828 a commission of inquiry, which reported that in the conditions of French industry a policy of "reasoned Protection" was desirable, but that great care should be taken to prevent the aid given to one industry from damaging another.[1] St. Cricq, now Minister of Commerce, prepared a scheme of reform, but its consideration was prevented by the political confusion which ended in the overthrow of the throne of Charles X. Surveying the economic policy from 1814 to 1830 as a whole, few students will be inclined to dissent from the judgment of Levasseur, that it is not so much the theory of Protection adopted by the Restoration Monarchy that is to be condemned—for it was the outcome of the particular conditions of France and Europe, and of a particular habit of thought—but the aggravation and elaboration of the resultant policy for twelve years at the dictation of private and sectional interests.[2]

[1] Levasseur, i. p. 591.

[2] *Ibid.*, i. p. 594.

CHAPTER II

THE MONARCHY OF JULY

THE new monarchy set up by the Revolution of July, 1830, was not likely to make any radical changes in the now almost traditional economic policy of France. Under the influence of the reaction against the extreme Protection of the last years of the Restoration Monarchy, Louis Philippe and his advisers were themselves prepared to make some amendments to the tariff; but they had been placed in power by the middle classes, who desired, above all things, to avoid the disturbance likely to be caused to trade and commerce by the more drastic political changes advocated by the republicans. The Government boasted of its origin; it accepted the task imposed upon it by its creators; and it deliberately endeavoured to administer the country in their interests.[1] It is true that the Parliamentary franchise was lowered, but in the existing economic conditions of France this tended only to strengthen the control exercised over the Legislature by that section of the middle class which was chiefly interested in trade and commerce, and, whilst not unwilling to see the protection given to the land-

1 "La politique que nous soutenions et pratiquions ainsi avait son principal point d'appui dans l'influence prépondérante des classes moyennes: influence reconnue et acceptée dans l'intérêt général du pays, et soumise à toutes les épreuves, à toutes les influences de la liberté générale. . . . Les classes moyennes, sans aucun privilège ni limite dans l'ordre civil, et incessamment ouvertes, dans l'ordre politique, au mouvement ascendant de la nation tout entière, étaient, à nos yeux, les meilleurs organes et les meilleurs gardiens des principes de 1789, de l'ordre social comme du gouvernement constitutionnel, de la liberté comme de l'ordre, des libertés civiles comme de la liberté politique, du progrès comme de la stabilité" (Guizot, *Mémoires*, vol. viii. pp. 522–3, ed. 1867).

owners reduced, was quite resolved not to allow any tariff changes likely to endanger its own position. Throughout the whole period 1830–48 there were few substantial modifications of the customs duties—though there were important changes for the better in the administrative arrangements of the customs service—and the Legislature almost always showed itself much less liberal than even the Executive.

The earliest enactments under the Monarchy of July were concerned chiefly with the transit and entrepôt trade. In 1831 and 1832 the restrictions upon the transit of foreign merchandise through France were mitigated, and the system of bonded warehouses re-arranged and developed. The Chamber reduced the number of ports at which the Ministry recommended that these warehouses should be permitted, but the main conflict arose over the proposal to authorise the establishment of similar warehouses at certain internal trading centres—Paris, Lyons and Strassburg. They had existed there before, but that did not prevent the seaports from making a determined opposition to the system, since they believed that their own trade would thereby be reduced. However, the Government scheme was carried.[1]

The next reform suggested by the Ministry did not secure even so limited an acceptance. The corn laws were working in a very unsatisfactory manner; the zones were badly arranged, and the selection of the markets whose average prices were to determine the opening or closing of the ports to foreign grain was open to many objections; the constant changes and resulting uncertainty hampered merchants; there were great inequalities of price between the various parts of the country; and although the average home production of corn was slightly higher in 1827–31 than in 1822–26, yet the average price showed a very considerable increase.[2] The Govern-

[1] Amé, i. pp. 181 *seq.*

[2] The average production of corn was about 57 million hectolitres in 1822–26, and 58 millions in 1827–31. The following

ment, therefore, proposed that the absolute prohibition (in certain cases) of the import of grain should be abandoned, and replaced by an extension of the sliding scale of duties; that the country should be divided into two great districts instead of four zones; that the price of bread should be taken as an index instead of the price of corn; and that in cases of scarcity the surtax on grain imported in foreign vessels should be suspended. But friends and foes alike had come to regard the grain duties as the corner-stone of the whole protective system;[1] the manufacturers made common cause with the agrarians, and only the first of the proposals was adopted. But its application was postponed until 1833; by that time prices were falling, as a result of the particularly good harvest of 1832;[2] the application of the law was then adjourned until "the revision of the tariff," and as that event did not take place, the corn laws of the Restoration Monarchy were still in force in 1860.[3]

This experience discouraged the Ministry (or rather the various short-lived Ministries of the years 1830–40) from attempting any more elaborate legislation for some time. A number of schemes were prepared in 1832 for the removal of the prohibitions on certain qualities of

table gives the average prices in francs per hectolitre (Brandt, p. 230):

Year	Price	Year	Price
1822	15·5	1827	18·2
1823	17·5	1828	22·0
1824	16·2	1829	22·6
1825	15·7	1830	22·4
1826	15·8	1831	22·1

In the first three of these years, and again in 1826 and 1827, there was a considerable surplus of exports over imports; in the other years the position was reversed.

[1] "Ma conviction profonde est que le jour ou la Chambre et le gouvernement auront abandonné la protection de l'industrie agricole, ce jour-là sera la veille de celui ou ils abandonneront la protection de tous les produits industriels" (St. Cricq, in debate on the proposed law).

[2] The production of wheat rose sharply from 56·4 million hectolitres in 1831 to 80·1 millions in 1832; the average price fell from 21·8 francs in 1832 to 15·6 in 1833. The average annual production for the next three years (1833–35) was 66·9 million hectolitres; the average price was in 1834 and 1835, 15·25 francs, and in 1836, 17·3 francs per hectolitre.

[3] Amé, i. p. 188.

cotton thread, on cashmere shawls and Russian leathers, and reductions in the rates on silks and cattle; and in 1834 for the free admission of more qualities of cotton thread, iron cables, and rum, and the reduction of the rates of duty on certain wools and iron bars; but none of these came before the Chamber, and the only successes were a few unimportant changes made by royal ordinance. The proposals of 1834 are chiefly interesting because made by Thiers, who was then for a brief period Minister of Commerce. As he was destined to exercise later a great influence on French economic policy, it is interesting to note his opinion at this time that, "employed as a means of retaliation, the system of restriction is disastrous; as a means of preference, it is improper (*abusif*); as an encouragement to an 'exotic' industry which cannot be brought here, it is powerless and futile. If used to protect a home industry which is likely to succeed, it is good, but only temporarily so; it ought to come to an end when the industry has completed its education, when it has become an adult."[1] Thiers' successor (and predecessor), Duchâtel, held even more radical views, but could accomplish nothing; he appointed in 1834 a commission to consider how far the maintenance of prohibition was necessary in the case of certain specified commodities (particularly textiles, over which there was a fierce conflict between the spinners and weavers), but the appointment only called forth a great agitation on the part of the threatened interests; and practically the matter dropped.

In 1836, however, the Chamber showed a more liberal tendency, partly because of the influence of the wine-growing districts. The duties on some kinds of wrought-iron, coal, linen, and cotton, were reduced; and the prohibitions of the import of some qualities of cotton yarn, cashmeres, Russian leather, and manufactures of copper, and of the export of such commodities as soap, hides, and timber suitable for shipbuilding, were abandoned. Moreover, the free admission of raw materials

[1] Quoted in Amé, i. p. 191.

was allowed on condition that within six months an equivalent amount of goods manufactured from them was exported. The result was that the Protectionists were alarmed, the manufacturers and agrarians again drew together, and a distinct reactionary tendency became apparent in the legislature,[1] though without producing any important changes (the agrarian influence was strong enough to secure the rejection of a Government proposal for a reduction of the cattle duties, in view of the decline of meat consumption in France). Finally, in 1841, there came the last noticeable enactment of the July Monarchy. The duty on sewing needles, which had remained at 2 francs per 100 kilo. since 1814, was quadrupled, with the result that whilst the import of British needles (which had an average value of 60–70 francs per 100 kilo.) was almost unaffected, the import of the cheap German needles (with an average value of 5–15 francs) collapsed altogether.[2] This brought France into conflict with the Zollverein, but the retaliatory measures adopted by the Germans had little effect. The law of 1836 had reduced the duties on cashmeres about 33 per cent.; but, on the other hand, the duties on flax and hemp products were now increased. This was due chiefly to the extremely rapid advance in the imports from the United Kingdom, where great improvements in production had been made about 1830, and which consequently took the place of Belgium as the chief competitor with the French industry. The weaving industry in France was rising, and the imports of foreign linen were falling; the French weavers desired the free or nearly free admission of linen thread, and higher duties on the manufactured article. The spinners, however, were undoubtedly in difficulties owing to the new competition, and they combined with the agricultural

[1] "Le tarif était soumis à des oscillations où les hasards des influences individuelles se manifestaient plus souvent qu'une pensée d'ensemble bien arrêtée, ce qui fit dire à M. Glaiz-Bizoin: 'La plupart de nos industries reçoivent une protection, non en raison de leur importance, mais en raison de l'importance des personnes qui les exercent'" (Amé, i. 206).

[2] Brandt, pp. 104–5.

producers of the raw material to demand higher rates on thread; and they were sufficiently strong to obtain their desire, whilst the rates of duty on linen textiles were also increased. Finally, the Act made some changes in regard to machinery. The shipbuilders complained that the duties on foreign machinery (especially steam-pumps, which were subject to the highest rates) hampered their industry; and they now secured the free admission of machinery intended for ships to be engaged in foreign trade. But the home manufacturers were given a bounty of 33 per cent. on all such machinery that they made; and as a further compensation, the duties on other kinds were increased in 1844. On the whole, then, the legislation from 1840 onward (the period of the Ministry of Guizot) did not depart to any notable extent from the old lines.

But during these years a series of events occurred which were important less in their immediate effects than as a foreshadowing of a revolutionary change which was to come later. Ever since Belgium had broken away from the kingdom of the Netherlands in 1830–1 attempts had been made by France to establish closer relations with the newly independent state. There can be no doubt that Louis Philippe desired, but did not dare, to authorise the acceptance of the crown offered to his son;[1] but it is also clear that there was strong opposition from the French manufacturers, who believed that such action would be followed by tariff changes which would expose them to the powerful Belgian competition. After the question of the succession was settled, proposals for a customs union with France were put forward tentatively from Belgium, which had shown extraordinary industrial productivity, was eager for large markets, and believed that the newly formed Zollverein might close Germany against it. But there was little enthusiasm on either side; the French manufacturers were hostile, and many Belgians feared that

[1] Guizot, *Mémoires*, ii. pp. 424–8.

commercial union might mean the loss of their newly acquired political independence. The negotiations continued at intervals, but nothing was done until 1842, when a treaty was signed which gave Belgium some preferences on iron, coal, and textiles, and secured for France reductions of the Belgian rates of duty in respect of silk manufactures, salt, and wine. Probably had the matter been decided by economic considerations alone the French Chamber would not have ratified the treaty, for the manufacturers were uneasy, and the value of the Belgian concessions was lessened by their immediate extension to the Zollverein; but ultimately the treaty, with some modifications, was ratified in 1845 for six years, mainly owing to political reasons and the desire to counteract any movement of Belgium towards the Zollverein.[1] In 1843 also a treaty with mutual reductions of duties was made with Sardinia for four years, and also approved by the Chamber chiefly on political grounds; and there were a number of other treaties of no great importance, mainly with non-European powers. Guizot had at one time some hopes of securing a treaty with Great Britain, and sounded some of the British Ministers on the subject; but though they were not unfavourably inclined, the scheme was felt to be impracticable at the moment; and political complications prevented a renewal of the proposal.

At this point it will be convenient to set out the figures of French foreign trade from 1830 to 1848 (see p. 289).[2]

The figures for 1848 show the marked effects (particularly in regard to the import trade) of the revolutionary troubles of that year, and this affects adversely the average for the last six-year period; but it will be seen that foreign trade as a whole showed throughout the

[1] Amé, i. pp. 219–27.

[2] The table is based on that in the *Annuaire Statistique de la France*, 1907, p. 77*. The French term, translated "manufactured goods" in this and subsequent tables, is "objets fabriqués," and includes partly-manufactured goods.

eighteen years of the Monarchy of July a steady upward tendency. Perhaps the most striking feature of the table is the relative insignificance of the imports of manufactured goods. It will be observed also that from 1831 to 1836 the value of the exports of domestic produce

IMPORTS AND EXPORTS OF MERCHANDISE, 1831–1848.

Year.	Imports of Merchandise for Home Consumption.		Exports of Domestic Produce.	
	Total.	Manufactured Goods.	Total.	Manufactured Goods (including Parcel Post).
	Million £.	Million £.	Million £.	Million £.
1831	15·0	1·0	18·2	13·5
1832	20·2	1·1	20·3	14·4
1833	19·4	1·4	22·4	16·2
1834	20·2	1·5	20·4	14·5
1835	20·8	1·6	23·1	17·0
1836	22·6	2·1	25·2	18·2
Average, 1831–1836	19·7	1·5	21·6	15·6
1837	22·8	2·1	20·6	14·5
1838	26·2	2·3	26·4	18·9
1839	26·0	2·2	27·1	19·5
1840	29·9	2·0	27·8	20·4
1841	32·2	2·2	30·4	22·5
1842	33·8	2·3	25·8	18·3
Average, 1837–1842	28·5	2·2	26·3	19·0
1843	33·8	2·1	27·5	20·4
1844	34·7	2·2	31·6	24·0
1845	34·2	2·3	33·9	25·5
1846	36·8	2·3	34·1	26·6
1847	38·2	2·0	28·8	21·2
1848	19·0	0·9	27·6	18·2
Average, 1843–1848	32·8	2·0	30·6	22·6

was always in excess of that of the imports for home consumption; but that the reverse was the case from 1840 onwards, the excess of imports becoming comparatively large.

The Monarchy of July was not an heroic Government; it clung too much to its "policy of resistance"; its views were short and its horizon narrow. But it did give France order for a time long enough to enable the necessary changes in industrial organisation to be completed; it took an intelligent and active part in the promotion and extension of railways, highways and canals; it brought the national finances into order; it passed a good deal of useful legislation;[1] and it did very much for primary and secondary education. Its great weakness was that it failed to recognise the social changes arising from the new economic conditions. It ignored the new force—the workmen—and these turned to the new doctrines of socialism. Its faults were due not so much to itself as to the conditions under which it had to work; and its greatest misfortune was that the merest accident brought about its fall at the time when a movement was in progress which might have enabled the Monarchy of July to carry out the reforms contemplated at the outset of its career.

During the eighteen years since the accession of Louis Philippe the industries of the country had made marked progress. The total consumption of coal in 1830 was 2,492,000 metric tons, and the home production 1,863,000; in 1847 the total consumption was 7,425,000 metric tons, the home production being 5,153,000.[2] The amount of pig-iron produced increased from 229,000 metric tons in 1831 to 592,000 tons in 1847.[3] Textiles showed a similar development: it is estimated that in 1834 there were 1,500,000 cotton spindles employed in France, and in 1844, 3,500,000.[4] The amount of cotton consumed rose steadily from 28,216 metric tons in 1831 to 63,952 in 1846 (there was a sharp falling off in the next two years).[5] The value of the raw wool consumed in France is estimated to have averaged about £640,000 in the latter years of the Restoration Monarchy, but had risen to £1,200,000 by 1847 (there are no statistics

[1] See the list of enactments given by Guizot in the last chapter (vol. viii.) of his *Mémoires*.

[2] *Annuaire Statistique*, p. 103*.

[3] *Ibid.*, pp. 47–8*.

[4] Levasseur, ii. p. 125.

[5] *Annuaire Statistique*, p. 112*.

of quantities); in linen and silk there was the same kind of upward movement. In regard to agriculture, the yield of corn averaged about 67,000,000 hectolitres for the years 1831–5, and, in spite of a comparatively very poor harvest in 1846, 80,000,000 for 1844–8.[1] The quantity of sugar manufactured rose with remarkable rapidity; it was 6,000,000 kilo. in 1830, and 53,000,000 in 1847.[2]

In view of this general progress of French manufactures and agriculture alike, the policy of extreme protection hitherto employed seemed no longer necessary. A considerable part of the trading community, particularly in Paris and the seaports,[3] began to advocate the adoption of a less restrictive policy; and they were supported by the wine-growers and the farmers of the Gironde.[4] The new movement received a great stimulus from the success of the English Free Trade agitation, as expounded to the French people in Bastiat's work entitled *Cobden et la Ligue;* and soon a Free Trade Association was founded in France, and gave expression to its doctrines in its newspaper, *Le Libre Exchange*, and more scientifically in the *Journal des Economistes*, which had been established in 1841. The manufacturers, and the agriculturists who took their side, in reply formed a counter-association, and issued *Le Moniteur Industriel* to present their case to the public.[5] The question was eagerly debated, and the Ministry—though hampered by the popular suspicion that Guizot was unduly favourable to Great Britain—believed that it could at last take action in the direction which some of its members had long desired. A Bill was prepared, which proposed to make a large number of important reforms in the tariff by abolishing prohibitions of import in respect of seventeen commodities, placing 113 articles on the free list absolutely and 185 others on the free list if imported in French vessels or (in some instances) by

[1] Brandt, p. 230. [2] Noël, p. 96.
[3] The lead was taken by Bordeaux.
[4] Noël, p. 83. [5] Amé, i. pp. 244–7.

land, reducing a number of other duties and admitting free materials necessary for the construction and equipment of ships. But the Bill encountered strong opposition from the Protectionists, in spite of the fact that many of the changes were of small importance, and none of them threatened any French interests at all seriously; and it was still only in the discussion stage when the revolution of February, 1848, brought about the overthrow of the Monarchy of July.

CHAPTER III

THE SECOND REPUBLIC AND THE SECOND EMPIRE—THE COMMERCIAL TREATIES

THE brief career of the Second Republic brought no change in the economic policy of France. In fact, even the Socialists, who at first shared the government with the more moderate Republicans, were inclined to make common cause with the manufacturers and landowners for the defence of the protective system;[1] they seem to have believed that its maintenance was necessary for the success of those sweeping economic changes which they were bent on accomplishing under the leadership of Louis Blanc. Their attempts ended in disaster, and intensified the alarm felt by the commercial and industrial classes, already sufficiently harassed by the disorders caused to business by the prolonged political confusion; and after a sharp struggle the Socialist leaders were ousted from the Government. The Republicans were free to arrange a new constitution; they decided upon a single Chamber and a President of the Republic—both to be elected by universal suffrage. Now, the grant of universal suffrage gave the decision into the hands of the peasantry, and the immediate result was the election of Louis Napoleon, partly because his name represented for France internal order and external renown.[2] The subsequent transition

[1] " Le suffrage universel ne fut pas plus favorable, tout d'abord, que le suffrage restreint au principe de la liberté commerciale . . . une sorte de réaction violente contre les tendances libérales des derniers jours du régime de Juillet se manifesta parmi les couches que la Revolution venait de faire surgir " (Noël, pp. 100–1).

[2] Seignobos, *Histoire politique de l'Europe contemporaine*, p. 152.

of Napoleon from President to Emperor presented few difficulties.

The tariff changes made during this period were few. The Constituent Assembly increased for a time the drawbacks and bounties given in respect of certain textiles, in order to help the manufacturers to meet some temporary difficulties.[1] Later the Legislative Assembly made shipping agreements with Belgium and some of the smaller American republics (Guatemala and Costa Rica); and it renewed the treaty of 1843 with Sardinia, obtaining important reductions of the Sardinian duties upon brandy and wines, reductions in respect of some other commodities, and the advantage of the reductions in customs duties made by Sardinia in consequence of her subsequent treaties with the United Kingdom, Belgium and Prussia, and giving in return some concessions as to goods brought over the land frontier—rice and fresh fruit. The tariff question was not directly raised until December, 1850; in that month Sainte-Beuve brought forward a series of resolutions which proposed the abolition of the protective duties on food and raw materials, the abandonment of all prohibitions, the reduction of the duties on iron after four years to a merely nominal figure, the establishment of maximum duties of from 10 to 20 per cent. on all manufactured goods, and the cessation of all shipping and colonial privileges. The resulting deficit in the national revenue was to be met by the imposition of an income tax.[2] The proposals gave rise to an animated debate in 1851, and, although their introduction was ill-timed, the fact that they secured the votes of one-third of the Legislative Assembly[3] showed that there was a considerable Free Trade party in the country. The opposition to them was led by Thiers, who based his case chiefly on the higher cost of production in France than in England, and the vital

[1] Amé, i. p. 256.

[2] *Ibid.*, pp. 267–8.

[3] 428 votes were given against further consideration of the proposals, 199 for.

importance to the French manufacturers of maintaining control of the home market.[1]

But with the establishment of the Empire a change began. Napoleon III. was a close student of English affairs; he had been much impressed by the reforms of Sir Robert Peel, and was not unwilling to attempt to imitate them in France. At the very outset of his reign the Foreign Minister drew the attention of his colleagues to the fact that the reform movement was not confined to Great Britain; and the Emperor and his ministers soon resolved on sweeping changes. It would have been extremely difficult to secure the concurrence of the Legislature, so it was determined to make use of the powers conferred on the Executive Government by laws of 1814 and 1836. The former empowered the Government to suspend the duties on foodstuffs and raw materials in case of emergency, subject only to the approval by Parliament of the decrees issued for that purpose; and the law of 1836 authorised the free admission (by decree) of goods intended to be still further worked up in France.[2]

The task was taken vigorously in hand. Between 1853 and 1855 the rates on coal, pig-iron, iron, steel, wool, dye-woods, cotton and other materials were reduced; under the stimulus of a sharp rise in prices the rates on cattle, meat, wines and other foodstuffs were lowered, and in 1853 the sliding scale regulating the movement of grain was suspended; free admission was granted to materials for shipbuilding; and the restrictions on foreign shipping were greatly reduced. These various decrees were confirmed by the Legislature in 1856, but not without considerable hesitation.[3] The Government now went still further, and in June, 1856, it proposed to the Legislature an enactment which abolished all the existing prohibitions,[4] and replaced

[1] Brandt, pp. 112–3.

[2] Devers, pp. 132–3.

[3] Amé, i. p. 271.

[4] There were still a large number of these, dealing with all kinds of commodities—woollen and cotton yarn and cloth, clothing, leather goods, certain classes of metal goods, refined sugar,

them by protective duties ranging from 30 per cent. *ad valorem* to double that amount. At once there was a violent agitation against these very moderate proposals for reform; the manufacturing towns—Roubaix, Lille, Rouen, Lisieux, Elbœuf—were particularly active in their hostility;[1] and the Government deemed it advisable to withdraw the scheme and to promise not to renew it before 1861. The Imperial policy met also with a bad defeat in the case of grain. In 1853, in consequence of a sudden rise of price, the sliding scale had been suspended, and as prices continued to rise until 1856, the suspension continued also; but when, in 1857, a rapid fall commenced and the Government made no attempt to re-establish the scale, the farmers were aroused, and, in spite of the opposition of ministers, the old conditions were restored in 1859.[2] By that time the attention of Napoleon and his advisers was concentrated on the Italian War, and the grave European complications which it brought in its train; and for a time it seemed probable that no further economic reforms would be attempted. In spite of some failures, Napoleon had made considerable breaches in the protective policy of France, and he and his minister, Rouher, could point to the statistics of French foreign trade as evidence of marked national progress under their regime. The movement of exports was particularly satisfactory; the following table gives the figures from 1849 to 1860:[3]

---

chemicals, drugs, etc.; many of them were purely accidental, being remnants of the "continental system." Few could be considered of any real importance to French industry (Amé, i. pp. 287–8).

[1] Amé, i. pp. 273–6.

[2] The following are the average prices in francs per hectolitre, 1851 to 1859 (Brandt, pp. 230–1):

Year	Price	Year	Price
1851	14·5	1856	30·7
1852	17·2	1857	24·3
1853	22·4	1858	16·7
1854	28·9	1859	16·7
1855	29·3		

[3] *Annuaire Statistique*, 1908, p. 77*.

IMPORTS AND EXPORTS OF MERCHANDISE, 1849–1860.

Years.	Imports for Home Consumption.		Exports of Domestic Produce.	
	Total.	Manufactured Goods.	Total.	Manufactured Goods.
	Million £.	Million £.	Million £.	Million £.
1849	29·0	1·2	37·5	25·9
1850	31·6	1·6	42·7	29·9
1851	30·6	1·6	46·3	30·7
1852	39·6	2·1	50·3	33·6
1853	47·8	2·5	61·7	41·3
1854	51·7	2·0	56·5	37·4
1855	63·8	3·0	62·3	43·2
1856	79·6	3·4	75·7	51·5
1857	74·9	2·8	74·6	51·9
1858	62·5	2·5	75·5	46·5
1859	65·6	2·5	90·7	56·1
1860	75·9	2·4	91·1	57·1

Towards the end of 1859 Napoleon's position in international politics had become extremely difficult. France was practically isolated in Europe: the events of the Italian War had made friendly relations with Austria impossible, without creating any particular feeling of gratitude on the part of Italy; the acquisition of Savoy and Nice had alarmed the European Governments, who habitually over-estimated the political ability and military strength of Napoleon, and made them believe that the Second Empire would endeavour to emulate the deeds of the First; the relations between France and her ally of the Crimean War were severely strained. The Emperor was anxious to put an end to this isolation, he was desirous of convincing the world that his aims were absolutely pacific, and he readily welcomed the suggestion that he should give the best possible evidence of this by making a commercial treaty with the United Kingdom. The idea was not new, for, as we have seen, it had been put forward long before by Guizot, and suggestions in the same direction had been made in 1852;[1]

[1] Amé, i. pp. 300–1.

but it was now taken up with energy, at first unofficially by Michael Chevalier, Cobden, and others of their school, and then by the Governments. Ministers on both sides, however, were only gradually convinced of the possibility of the scheme;[1] and on the French side it was necessary that the negotiations should be carried on in secrecy. It was quite true that tariff changes made in consequence of a treaty, and as part of that treaty, would not need the approval of the French Legislature, and an agreement with Great Britain would therefore be a way of accomplishing some of the tariff reforms which Napoleon III. and some at least of his advisers desired; but, though there was a not insignificant Free Trade party in France, the Protectionists were much more powerful, and, as they had shown in 1856, could cause the Government much inconvenience even if they could not entirely thwart the scheme. It was not until the negotiations were complete that Napoleon made his views public in a letter to one of his ministers, in which he announced his conviction that unless there is a constant growth of international exchange trade cannot flourish, that industry not subject to competition remains stationary, and that in the absence of growing industries agriculture itself will remain undeveloped. He therefore advocated the abolition of the duties on cotton and wool, the gradual reduction of those on sugar and coffee, the improvement of means of transit, the abandonment of all prohibitions, and commercial treaties with foreign Powers. There was a great outcry from the protected classes in France, stimulated by the favourable reception given to the Emperor's proposals by some of the British manufacturers, chiefly in Lancashire; but the treaty with the United Kingdom was signed on January 23rd, 1860. The final reasons on both sides were political.[2]

[1] For a detailed account of the negotiations, see Morley, *Life of Cobden*, chap. xxix.

[2] For the evidence of this on the French side, Morley, *loc. cit.*, pp. 720–728 (ed. 1903). On the British side Gladstone wrote: "A

The treaty did not do much more than indicate the general lines of the arrangements to be made; the details of the rates were left to be settled by subsequent consultations. Both parties guaranteed "most favoured nation" treatment to each other; both were left absolutely free to extend the same reductions to other Powers if they thought fit, and indeed it was understood from the first that the United Kingdom would do so; both reserved the right to impose additional customs duties equivalent to the excise which might be levied on any commodity; both agreed not to prohibit the export of coal. As to actual reductions of duties, the British Government undertook to recommend certain abolitions and diminutions to Parliament in Gladstone's forthcoming budget, and France undertook to abolish all prohibitions and to levy instead specific duties not exceeding 30 per cent. *ad valorem* up to October, 1864, and after that 24 per cent. The actual specific duties were to be fixed by joint agreement. The treaty was to hold good for ten years, and could be continued, unless one year's notice of its termination was given by either party, for another ten years.

The customs changes proposed by the British Ministry were accepted by Parliament—Gladstone's budget of 1860 reduced the number of commodities liable to duty from 419 to 48. As far as imports from France were concerned the most important diminutions were in respect of wines: the old duty was slightly more than 5*s.* 10*d.* a gallon; after January 1st, 1861, this was to be replaced by graduated duties ranging from 1 to 2 shillings. The French calculated that on their wines

---

French panic prevailed as strong as any of the other panics that have done so much discredit to this country. For this panic, the treaty of commerce with France was the only sedative. It was in fact a counter-irritant; and it aroused the sense of commercial interest to counteract the war passion. It was and is my opinion, that the choice lay between the Cobden Treaty and not the certainty, but the high probability of a war with France" (quoted in Morley, *Life of Gladstone*, ii. p. 23).

this meant a change from 159 francs per hectolitre to 27·5 francs. The duty on brandy was reduced 30 per cent.

On the French side the tariff changes were far more numerous and important. Only the specific duties on iron and coal were fixed by the original treaty; and in order to obtain guidance for the settlement of the remainder, the French Government appointed a commission to investigate first the average prices in France of the commodities now to be admitted, and secondly the specific equivalents of the *ad valorem* duties which should be imposed within the limits prescribed by the treaty.[1] The commission took a great amount of evidence of all kinds, and the net result of its deliberations was a report to the effect that whilst mechanically the French industries were in many cases far behind the British, yet they were sufficiently well established to meet competition, and probably would be likely to make radical changes in their equipment and organisation only if compelled to do so by that competition. Consequently the French Government did not think it advisable to impose duties up to the maximum indicated by the treaty—which in many cases would have been practically prohibitive.[2] They reached the 30 per cent. *ad valorem* limit only for some metal products; on linen, cotton, and woollen cloths the average was only about 15 per cent.; on tools 10–12 per cent.; on cutlery 20 per cent.; on glassware 10 per cent.; on china and earthenware 10 per cent.; on chemicals 10–15 per cent.[3] This action of the French negotiators did much to remove the reproach made in Great Britain against the original treaty that it was too one-sided, since under it Great Britain was

[1] The efforts of the commission were directed, in accordance with the desires of the French Government, largely to an attempt to determine the difference between the cost of production of each class of goods in France and foreign countries respectively; this was to decide the amount of the customs duties to be imposed.

[2] Amé, i. pp. 310–15.

[3] An elaborate discussion of all the duties, and the reasons for them, is given by Amé, i. pp. 317–468.

bound to abolish duties whilst France had only to reduce them, and might still leave them at almost a prohibitive height.

Napoleon and his advisers had hoped from the first that once Great Britain had set the example of a treaty, other nations would not be slow to follow it. The expectation was justified; and, indeed, the industrial powers had no alternative if they did not wish Great Britain to enjoy marked advantages over them in the French market. Negotiations were immediately set on foot by various Governments, and it was natural that the first completed arrangements should be with Belgium. That country granted to France reductions in the rates of duty on wines, silks, and leather goods; and in return was given the advantages of the "conventional" tariff established by France for Great Britain, with the addition of some changes in the rates on linen goods and prepared hides. Both contracting parties guaranteed "most favoured nation" treatment to each other. This was, in fact, the general policy pursued by France in all its treaties; it granted in each case the conventional tariff rates settled by the British treaty, and generally added one or two more reductions in respect of commodities in which the other contracting party was especially interested; then these additional reductions (which probably would only benefit to any appreciable extent the country to which they were first given) were extended to all the contracting Powers under the "most favoured nation" clauses. In return France secured from the Zollverein in 1862 (thus closing a long quarrel) reductions in respect of wines, textiles, and some miscellaneous commodities—though the arrangement was not ratified by the various German states until 1865; from Italy (1863) small reductions (for the Italian tariff was not very protective) in the rates of duty on silks, chemicals, glassware, and prepared hides; from Switzerland (1864) reductions in respect of wines, brandy, glassware, earthenware and chemicals. In 1865 treaties on similar lines were made with Sweden and Norway, the Hanse towns, Spain, and the Netherlands; in 1866 with Austria; and in 1867 with Portugal.[1]

Whilst an elaborate conventional tariff was being formed in this way, changes were being made in the general tariff, and the principles underlying French tariff policy generally. In 1860 and the following years, either by legislative enactment or Imperial decree, the duties on a large number of raw materials—skins, wool, cotton, dye-stuffs, jute, flax, hemp, coal, chemicals, and many others—were either greatly reduced or abolished; prohibitions of exports came practically to an end; bounties on exports were abandoned, and at the very commencement of the reform (in 1861) the French Government abolished the sliding scale for grain, and replaced it by freedom of export and a very moderate duty on imports.[2]

Important and far-reaching changes were also made, particularly in 1866, in respect of matters of navigation. The exclusion from the coasting trade of France of all but French ships, and the *surtaxes d'entrepôt* levied on non-European goods imported into France from European countries were maintained; but the preferential treatment of French vessels in regard to certain shipping dues and the trade between France and the West Indies or Algeria were abolished, as was also the system of surtaxes on goods imported into France not in French vessels or vessels of the country in which the goods originated. The prohibition of the importation of foreign vessels was replaced by simple duties at rates of 5 to 10 per cent. *ad valorem*, the French shipbuilders being granted the right to the duty-free admission of materials for the construction and equipment of ships.

Clearly the result of these extensive changes was an absolute break with all the traditions of French commercial policy; what was the effect on the industrial

[1] Details in Amé, ii. pp. 1–36.
[2] Devers, pp. 139–41.

development of France? It must not be supposed that the opponents of the Emperor's action were ever brought to approve it; the Legislature gave its formal assent to changes made often without its knowledge, but the new policy was to the end accepted only reluctantly and with disapproval by the larger part of those classes who exercised political influence. By 1868, when the power of the Emperor had been severely shaken by failures in foreign policy, whilst the effects of the commercial crisis of 1864 had not yet ceased to be felt, and political events in the United States and the Germanic Confederation had harassed trade, and the time for the extension or abandonment of the British treaty was approaching—by that year the forces which favoured Protection had recruited their strength, and a demand was made for an inquiry into the effect of the whole treaty system and the changes which it had brought in its train. The conflict continued for some time, but finally the Ministry gave way, and two commissions were appointed in 1870, only a very few months before the outbreak of the Franco-German War and the collapse of the Empire.

It is always arguable that the industrial and commercial progress of France between 1860 and 1870 might have been greater and more rapid if a higher tariff wall had been maintained; or that progress was certain in any case, and that tariff changes exercised little influence upon it. But this is mere speculation, and all the evidence goes to show that during the period from 1850 to 1860, when moderate reforms were being made, France commenced a rapid advance, which quickened considerably with the introduction of more radical changes of policy after 1860. First as to foreign trade. The figures of the imports and exports of merchandise (*Special Trade*) for the period 1849–1860 have already been given: the following table gives them for the next ten years.[1]

[1] *Annuaire Statistique*, 1908, p. 77*.

IMPORTS AND EXPORTS OF MERCHANDISE, 1861–1870.

Year.	Imports for Home Consumption.		Exports of Domestic Produce.	
	Total.	Manufactured Goods.	Total.	Manufactured Goods.
	Million £.	Million £.	Million £.	Million £.
1861	97·7	4·5	77·1	47·2
1862	87·9	6·1	89·9	54·4
1863	97·1	5·8	105·7	59·6
1864	101·1	6·2	117·0	68·2
1865	105·7	6·9	123·5	67·0
1866	111·7	8·3	127·2	68·6
1867	121·6	9·2	113·0	61·2
1868	132·3	9·5	111·6	59·4
1869	126·1	10·9	123·0	65·6
1870	114·7	11·6	112·9	57·0

The figures of French trade with the chief treaty-states are also instructive. In 1857 British exports to France were valued at £11,327,000; they showed a marked decline in the next two years, but in 1860 rose to £12,701,000; in the next year they were £17,427,000, and they rose steadily to £26,597,000 in 1866; after that there was a decline, due in part to a general commercial depression. Our imports from France were £11,965,000 in 1857, and in 1860 £17,774,000; they reached in 1866 £37,017,000, and after that declined for a time.[1] With the Zollverein French exports remained almost stationary, with the exception of 1866, when there was a drop—they were valued at 8·4 million pounds in 1862, and 8·6 millions in 1868; her imports, however, rose from 5·2 millions to 10·6 millions. With Switzerland the value of the exports rose from 5·5 million pounds in 1862 to 10·4 millions in 1868, and the imports from 2·3 millions to 5·3 millions. The value of the total trade with Belgium increased from 13·8 million pounds in 1860 to 24·4 millions in 1869.[2]

The expectation that industry would receive a great

[1] *Statistical Abstract for the United Kingdom*, Nos. 13 and 27.
[2] Noël, pp. 238–9.

stimulus from the opening of foreign markets and competition at home was amply justified; and the development was aided by the growth of means of transit and transport. In 1850 there were 3,010 kilometres of railways in France; by 1860 there were 9,439; by 1870, 17,440.[1] In 1850 the merchant shipping of France (2 tons and upwards) was returned at about 680,000 tons; by 1860 the amount had reached 996,000 tons, and by 1870, 1,072,000 tons.[2] The home production of coal averaged 5·2 million tons for the five years 1850–4; for 1860–4 the average was 9·8 million tons, and for the next quinquennial period it amounted to 12·4 million tons; the total consumption increased in almost the same proportion, from an average of 8·1 million tons for the period 1850–4 to one of 19·2 millions of 1865–9.[3] The annual production of pig-iron averaged 552,000 tons in the years 1850–4; for the period 1865–9 it amounted to 1·3 million tons.[4] In 1849 only 9,000 tons of steel were manufactured, as against 23,000 in 1859, and 110,000 in 1869.[5] The cotton industries were naturally affected by the American Civil War, and the consequent temporary cessation of supplies, but, nevertheless, the consumption of raw cotton in France averaged 78 million kilo. for the period 1857–9, and 90 million kilo. for 1867–9.[6] Between the same two periods the average consumption of imported raw wool grew from 36½ million kilo. to 93 million kilo.[7] In the case of linens, on the other hand, the surplus of imports over exports rose from an average of 25 million kilo. in 1857–9 to an average of 45 million kilo. in 1867–9, in spite of a very large growth in French exports; the chief cause of this condition of affairs seems to have been the slowness of the French manufacturers to make use of jute.[8]

[1] *Annuaire Statistique*, 1908, p. 55*.

[2] *British and Foreign Trade and Industry*, 1903, p. 386.

[3] *Annuaire Statistique*, 1908, pp. 46* and 103–4*. Metric tons have been converted.

[4] *Annuaire Statistique*, p. 48*, and *British and Foreign Trade and Industry*, 1909, p. 168.

[5] Amé, ii. p. 404.

[6] *Ibid.*, p. 422.

[7] *Ibid.*, p. 415.

[8] Amé, pp. 425–6.

In agriculture it was natural that the wine-growers should reap the greatest benefit. The production is, of course, subject to fluctuations due to natural causes, and the statistics of particular years are scarcely an adequate indication of the movement of the industry; but it may be pointed out that the estimated output of wine was 45 million hectolitres in 1850, 15 millions in 1855, 39 millions in 1860, and 69 millions in 1865.[1] The exports of brandy and spirits amounted to 173,000 hectolitres in 1858, 224,000 in 1863, and 333,000 in 1867; after that there was a decline.[2] The manufacture of home-produced sugar was 132 million kilo. in 1859; after being stationary for some years it leaped up to 210 millions in 1865, and reached 242 millions in 1869.[3] The quantity of wheat grown, which had averaged 82 million hectolitres for the years 1845–9, reached 98 million for the years 1865–9,[4] in spite of poor harvests in 1866 and 1867. The one discouraging fact was the very slow rate of increase in the population, which in 1849 was estimated at 35,690,000, and twenty years later at only 38,390,000, in spite of the fact that the acquisition of Savoy and Nice had added 689,000 persons to the inhabitants of French territory in 1860.[5] The proportion engaged in agriculture diminished considerably; in 1851 the rural population numbered 6,146 out of every 10,000 of the whole, whilst by 1866 the number had fallen to 5,119.

It is evident, however, that on the whole (except in respect of population) France had made very substantial progress in the twenty years of Napoleon's rule. By 1870 she had become a great industrial power; her commerce had expanded largely, her manufactures were firmly established, her agriculture was flourishing; and her economic strength was revealed to an astonished Europe by the ease with which she bore the burdens cast upon her by the war.

[1] Foville, p. 161. [2] Noël, p. 236. [3] *Ibid.*, p. 236.
[4] Brandt, p. 231. [5] Foville, pp. 9–10.

CHAPTER IV

COMMERCIAL POLICY, 1870–81

THE Government of the Third Republic was called upon at the close of the war to deal with a financial situation of hitherto unparalleled difficulty. Thiers, who had been entrusted with the conduct of the Executive Government, estimated that to provide for all necessary expenditure (including the great debt-charges caused by the war indemnity) the annual amount raised by taxation must be increased by 556 million francs, or 22 million pounds sterling—an increase absolutely unprecedented.[1] By various forms of internal taxation he could raise, he thought, about 350 millions; and for the rest he resolved to have recourse to the customs. His own economic views had become frankly protectionist, but his main anxiety at this time was to secure revenue. He proposed in 1871 to increase the duties on sugar and coffee; to subject a number of raw materials—silk, wool, hides and skins, wood, etc.—to the duties from which they had been freed by the reforms of Napoleon III.; to re-establish some export duties; to impose harbour dues, and to renew the surtaxes on commodities imported in vessels other than those of France or the country in which the goods originated.[2] Manufactured commodities it was not possible to touch to any great extent, since most of the treaties made under the Empire would continue in force for a number of years.

The proposals had a varied reception in the National Assembly. The additions to the revenue duties on

[1] Thiers, *Notes et Souvenirs*, pp. 186–92.
[2] Devers, p. 147.

sugar and coffee were approved at once, and extended to those on tea, cocoa, pepper and some other commodities. On the other hand, the proposed export duties were dropped without the Government making any strenuous effort to retain them—the anticipated yield was very small. The import duties on vessels built abroad were greatly increased; the shipping surtaxes were imposed, and also the harbour dues; but in this connection difficulties were caused by the commercial treaties. Goods brought direct from the country of origin were exempted from the surtax if carried in the ships of treaty states (with the comparatively unimportant exception of Spain); and even if brought indirectly they were exempt if carried in Austrian, Belgian, Dutch, Italian, Swedish, German, or Portuguese vessels. The Austrian Treaty of 1866 (*i.e.*, subsequent to the shipping legislation of that year) had expressly given Austrian shipping practically complete equality with that of France, and this had been extended to the shipping of the other contracting states by virtue of the "most favoured nation" clause; the earlier treaties had given vessels of the contracting states national treatment in respect only of direct trade. For the proposed changes to be productive of much revenue they must apply to all shipping, but this was possible only if Austria would consent to abandon its rights under the treaty of 1866. It might have done so, since it was interested only in the Mediterranean trade, and the French Government was willing to meet its wishes so far as that was concerned; but it was subjected to strong pressure from Prince Bismarck, and ultimately refused to grant the French request.[1] The proposals of Thiers in regard to shipping remained then ineffective, except in the case of the harbour dues, which affected foreign and French vessels alike.

But the great problem was the imposition of import duties on raw materials. The Ministry proposed to subject silk, wool, cotton, flax and jute to a duty of

[1] Amé, ii. p. 318 *seq.*

20 per cent. *ad valorem;* and hides, timber, oil-seeds, etc., dye-stuffs, and all other raw materials hitherto exempt, to various duties not to exceed 20 per cent.[1] Clearly this would hamper the manufacturers, and the President (who made himself responsible for the new scheme, which was, in fact, his work) proposed to remedy this first by the grant of drawbacks, and secondly by imposing on imported manufactured goods a compensating surtax presumed to be equivalent to the amount of the duty on raw materials.[2] But it was evident that the calculation and arrangement of the drawbacks would be a task of very great administrative difficulty, and the Budget Commission proposed, as an alternative scheme, the abandonment of the high duties and drawbacks, and the substitution of a uniform rate of 3 per cent. on raw materials, and an equivalent surtax on manufactured goods. It was estimated that this arrangement would produce some 60 million francs; the Government had counted on obtaining 165 millions. There was a long parliamentary conflict; the manufacturers (especially those of Lyons) resisted the President's proposals fiercely; and finally the matter was referred to a new commission, which was directed to investigate the probable effect of the proposed taxation, and it was definitely stated in the resolution that the National Assembly would adopt duties on raw materials only if it proved impossible to provide adequate revenue in any other way. Thiers resigned, but was persuaded to retain office.[3]

In May, 1872, the Commission reported. It recommended duties of 5 per cent. on cotton (with a drawback), and $2\frac{1}{2}$ to 2 per cent. on silk, wool, flax, hemp, and jute (without drawbacks); and its plans were adopted. It was an unsatisfactory proposal from the point of view of a Government anxious to obtain revenue, since until

[1] Devers, p. 150.

[2] The right of France to do this had been recognised in the commercial treaties.

[3] For his own account of these events see Thiers, *Notes et Souvenirs*, pp. 259–62.

the expiration of the treaties the new taxes would yield only some 42 million francs—a comparatively unimportant sum. Moreover, it was resolved that no duties should be imposed on raw materials unless a corresponding surtax was imposed on manufactured goods; and, whatever the actual powers of the French Government under the existing treaties may have been, the practical result was to render the new tariff law useless until the revision of the treaties or the establishment of an entirely new set.[1]

Already negotiations had commenced, first with the United Kingdom. But there the French Government encountered many difficulties; the British ministers were unwilling to recognise the right of France to impose duties on imported raw materials unless the same commodities were taxed when produced at home, and they were not so favourable to the idea of commercial treaties as they had been in 1860. France had difficulties with Belgium also; and in March, 1872, she denounced both the British and Belgian treaties. Then fresh negotiations began, and in November, 1872, a new convention with the United Kingdom was signed. France pledged herself not to increase the taxes on raw materials imposed by the new tariff, and she abandoned some; she exempted British ships from the operation of the *surtax de pavillon*[2] up to 1879. In the following February a new arrangement was made with Belgium on similar lines.[3] Both of these were only to be in force till the middle of 1877. The numerous exemptions from the shipping surtaxes, and the practical impossibility of doing anything with the proposed duties on raw materials, at last brought the National Assembly to recognise the uselessness of the two enactments, and in July, 1873, both were repealed. Two months earlier, Thiers had abandoned

[1] Amé, ii. p. 297.

[2] *I.e.*, British shipping was to be on an equality with French vessels in respect of all goods imported in them into France, and not merely, as hitherto, in respect only of goods imported directly from the United Kingdom.

[3] Devers, pp. 155–6.

office; and of all his elaborate plans of 1871, only that unimportant part which concerned the harbour dues had been realised. The deficit was met by a number of new internal taxes of various kinds—excises, stamps, etc., and the taxation per head in France was higher than in any other country of Europe.[1]

It soon became necessary for the French Government to consider what policy it should adopt when the various treaties came to an end, and in order to obtain some guidance on this point the Ministry of Commerce invited, in April, 1875, an expression of opinion from the Chambers of Commerce and similar bodies. It asked three questions: Was the general tariff in need of revision? Was it desirable to continue the system of commercial treaties? Should the customs duties be specific or *ad valorem?* The great majority replied that the general tariff did need revision, and preferred specific to *ad valorem* duties; the larger number were in favour of the continuance of the system of commercial treaties, but a strong minority (including Rouen, Roubaix, and Turcoing—all textile centres) advocated the establishment of a simple autonomous tariff.[2] And it is noteworthy that even amongst the supporters of the commercial treaties, the greater part were opposed to the insertion in them of the "most favoured nation" clause. The task of preparing a new scheme of duties was entrusted to the Superior Council of Commerce, Agriculture and Industry—a body formed a few years previously, and composed of members of the Chamber of Deputies, presidents of Chambers of Commerce, representatives of agriculture, industry and banking, and some officials who, however, were not entitled to vote.[3]

The result was a scheme for a moderate tariff which reproduced almost without alteration the rates of duty

[1] Brandt, pp. 146–7.

[2] Devers, p. 157.

[3] The great work of Amé, who was Director-General of Customs, was published chiefly for the guidance of the council at the instigation of Léon Say, the Minister of Finance.

established by the conventional tariff already in force; almost the only increased rate of duty of any importance was in respect of woollen goods. It was thus admitted that the existing conventional rates would afford a satisfactory basis for negotiations, and could therefore be reduced without any resultant economic disadvantage to France. *Ad valorem* duties were abandoned almost entirely; whatever theoretical advantages they might have, experience had shown that they caused endless administrative difficulties.[1] At the time of the treaty with Great Britain in 1860 an attempt had been made to get rid of them; but considerations of time, and the difficulty of calculating the specific equivalents, had caused many of them to be retained. But disputes as to the valuations at the customs-houses were constant; and in spite of various administrative changes, frauds by under-valuation were frequent. The customs officials themselves were anxious to be freed from a complicated and irksome task.

The plan so elaborated was not discussed by the Chamber, owing to the constitutional crisis of 1877, but in the first month of the following year Teisserenc de Bort, the Minister of Commerce, brought forward a new scheme, though he had previously approved the Commission's plan with some modifications. It was much more protectionist than the previous proposals, since it increased the duties by about 24 per cent. on the average; so that whilst the council had practically recommended that the conventional tariff should become the general tariff, and be subject to reductions by treaty, the Ministry now proposed merely to retain the existing arrangements. But that did not satisfy the Legislature. There was a marked revival of the agitation in favour of Protection—just as in Germany in the same years; in both countries the campaign was led by the textile and iron industries, which were able to act the more effectively since they

[1] For German and American experience in this matter, see pp. 5, 155, 210-2.

were in the hands of a comparatively small number of powerful firms.[1] The silk industry alone was ranged with the commercial classes on the other side, and favoured the maintenance of the commercial treaties, to which the Protectionists were particularly hostile. In agriculture the wine-growers supported the policy pursued since 1860, but the great majority of the land-owners were with the opposition—they were alarmed by the growing invasion of American wheat and the continued low prices. The imports and exports of wheat into France fluctuate greatly; between 1861 and 1880 there was a surplus of exports over imports in five years, and in the other fifteen the surplus of imports over exports varied from 971,000 to 29,349,000 hectolitres.[2] The surplus of the imports of wheat over exports, which had never previously exceeded 14 million hectolitres, reached nearly 18 millions in 1878, more than 29 millions in 1879, and nearly 27 millions in 1880. The result was that prices did not rise, and even fell a little,[3] in spite of poor harvests (the cause of the large importations) in 1878 and 1879; and the French farmers became alarmed. They threw themselves into alliance with the manufacturers, and the agitation was helped by the commercial crisis which had commenced elsewhere in Europe in 1873, but did not make itself felt in France till some years later: it was marked, amongst other things, by a general fall in prices, due in part to the growth of means of transport and the fresh developments of mechanical power in industry. All over Europe and America industry was entering on a period of transition which tried manufacturers severely, and harassed commerce also. Yet, in spite of all these difficulties, French foreign trade continued to make steady progress—imports especially advanced with great rapidity in the years 1878–80; the following table gives the figures of the imports and exports of merchandise (*Special Trade*)

[1] Brandt, pp. 152–3. [2] *Ibid.*, p. 231.

[3] Average prices per hectolitre were: 1877, 23·4 francs; 1878, 21·2; 1879, 22·1; 1880, 22·2 (Brandt, p. 231).

from 1871 to 1880;[1] it must be remembered that prices declined very sharply after 1873.

IMPORTS AND EXPORTS OF MERCHANDISE, 1871–1880.

Year.	Imports for Home Consumption.		Exports of Domestic Produce.	
	Total.	Manufactured Goods.	Total.	Manufactured Goods.
	Million £.	Million £.	Million £.	Million £.
1871	142·7	15·0	114·9	61·8
1872	142·8	18·1	150·5	76·2
1873	142·2	12·6	151·5	79·4
1874	140·3	13·4	148·0	76·4
1875	141·5	15·4	154·9	78·0
1876	159·5	23·4	143·0	72·2
1877	146·8	21·7	137·5	69·5
1878	167·0	22·6	127·2	68·1
1879	183·8	22·3	129·3	67·0
1880	201·3	24·0	138·7	73·6

Nevertheless, the various circumstances mentioned above, and the example of Germany, made the Senate and Chamber of Deputies even more protectionist than the Ministry. The Senate appointed a commission to inquire into the commercial and industrial depression; and the Chamber sent the ministerial tariff proposals to a committee. Both held elaborate inquiries extending over nearly a year, and during that time the campaign in the country in favour of Protection was carried on by the *Société des Agriculteurs de France* and the *Association de l'Industrie française pour la Défense du Travail national;* the Free Trade party started a counter campaign, but without conspicuous success. Under the guidance of Méline the commission of the Chamber made radical changes in the proposals submitted by the Government. It declared that special advantages should be given to those national industries which employed most labour;

[1] *Annuaire Statistique*, 1908, p. 78*, and *British and Foreign Trade and Industry*, 1909, pp. 60–1. Owing to changes in classification, the figures for the imports of manufactured goods before and after 1876 are not precisely comparable.

it asserted that the treaties of commerce had clearly failed, since in the seventeen years after 1860 the total imports had exceeded the total exports by about 11 million pounds in value, thus adopting an elementary fallacy; it drew especial attention to the "American peril"; and it abandoned the hitherto avowed and moderate object of the protective policy—the possibility of French manufacturers competing with foreigners on equal terms—and advocated the purest Protection. It accepted the Government's recommendations in a number of cases, but it made substantial additions to the rates of duty proposed in respect of woollen yarn, and on behalf of the agrarians it increased the proposed rates on hides, cheese, cattle, etc. The Ministry stood firmly by its original proposals, and the new Minister of Commerce, Tirard, announced that the commercial treaties must be made; that they had promoted the economic progress of France; that the chief industries, particularly the cotton and metal trades, were quite able to stand alone, with only the moderate help given them by the conventional tariff; and that the difficulties of agriculture were due chiefly to inclement seasons. The leader of the Commission, Méline, urged that its proposed duties were not intended to be universally applied—that, in fact, the increases were intended to facilitate the work of the French diplomatists in the negotiation of the new commercial treaties, which he and his friends recognised must be made.[1] There was a long parliamentary struggle, but the Ministry had its way, helped by the want of unity between the industrial and agricultural sections of the protectionist forces; nearly all the additions and changes recommended by the Commission of the Chamber were rejected, and the agrarians secured only the imposition of duties on certain animals imported for food. There were more difficulties in the Senate, which was favourably inclined to protection for agriculture; but ultimately the original ministerial proposals,

[1] See the lengthy summary of the debates in Devers, pp. 162–72.

with only slight modifications, became law in May, 1881. The new tariff was far more elaborate and detailed than any of its predecessors.

On the whole, it was a victory for the supporters of greater freedom of trade. The new general tariff on manufactured goods exceeded the previous conventional rates by an average of 24 per cent., but this was intended only as a basis for negotiations; coffee, sugar, cocoa were taxed for revenue purposes only; raw materials and foodstuffs were free, or subject only to small duties, and some articles had been added to the free list; *ad valorem* rates were almost entirely abolished. The new system was much more moderate, in the amount of protection which it gave to native producers, than the one adopted a little earlier in Germany; and unlike the German Government, the French ministers were prepared to continue the policy of international commercial agreements, subject to the approval, in each case, of the Legislature. They laid down three principles for their own guidance in the negotiations: (1) The concessions to be made should not exceed as a whole 24 per cent. on the general tariff; (2) specific duties alone should be imposed; (3) cereals and cattle should not be included, since it was desirable for the Government to have a free hand in cases of emergency.[1] The negotiations began immediately, first under the guidance of Rouvier, and later of Tirard. Treaties were made in 1881 with very little difficulty with Belgium, Italy, Portugal, and Sweden and Norway, and in 1882 with Spain and Switzerland;[2] in 1883 an agreement with Austria-Hungary secured reciprocal "most favoured nation" treatment, and this was extended to Russia and Turkey, to Germany under the terms of the Treaty of Frankfurt, to Servia in 1883, and to Holland in 1884. With the United Kingdom no treaty involving reciprocal reductions could be made,

[1] Devers, pp. 171–2. It seems probable, however, that the last principle was dictated partly by the desire to give agriculture, which was admittedly in difficulties, as much help as possible.

[2] A treaty with the Netherlands was refused ratification by the Dutch Legislature.

partly because that country would not reduce the wine duties, and for financial reasons would not guarantee that they should not be increased; and partly because no agreement could be reached on the question of *ad valorem* and specific duties—the United Kingdom was desirous that *ad valorem* rates should continue to be levied on certain products.[1] But a treaty signed in 1882 gave the United Kingdom "most favoured nation" treatment in all matters relating to trade and commerce other than customs duties, and national treatment in matters of navigation, subject to certain limitations (as, for instance, exclusion from the coasting trade, which France reserves to native vessels); and by legislative enactment at the same time France admitted the United Kingdom to the benefits of the minimum tariff.[2]

The net result of the treaties was that the new conventional tariff included some 1,200 articles on which the rates of duty were either reduced or "conventionalised"—*i.e.*, made unchangeable so long as the treaties should be in force—whilst 300 (including those on grain and cattle) remained subject in all cases to the rates of the general tariff. All the treaties provided for the equal treatment of French and foreign shipping; but as the French mercantile marine was far from prosperous (it amounted to 996,124 net tons in 1860, rose to 1,072,048 in 1870, and fell steadily to 919,298 in 1880),[3] and the free import of materials for shipbuilding had not apparently been of much service, it was decided in 1881 to give State bounties to shipbuilders, and to owners for long-distance voyages.[4] In the ten years 1881–90

[1] The British Government was pledged not to enter into any treaty which included in respect of any important article of British trade rates of duty higher than the conventional rates of 1860. There were some instances in which the maximum reduction which the French Government could make on the new general tariff rates would have left the rates of duty above this level.

[2] For full details of those negotiations, see Rausch, pp. 186 *seq.*

[3] *British and Foreign Trade and Industry*, 1909, pp. 114–5. The figures are for vessels of two net tons and upward.

[4] The bounties ranged from 60 francs per gross ton on steel ships to 10 francs per gross ton on wooden vessels of less than

rather more than one million pounds were paid in bounties on shipbuilding alone, and the mercantile steam shipping increased from 356,636 to 747,512 gross tons.[1]

---

10 tons. On machinery and boilers 12 francs per 100 kilo. were paid. The bounty on voyages was 1½ francs per net ton for every 1,000 miles of journey; on vessels bought from abroad the bounty was half this amount. *Vide infra*, pp. 419–21.

[1] Franke, p. 137. But the net tonnage of mercantile shipping rose only from 919,000 to 944,000 (*Report on British and Foreign Trade and Industry*, p. 376). For a detailed discussion of French shipping and the bounty system, see Franke, pp. 122–39. See also pp. 342 seq., *infra*.

CHAPTER V

PROTECTION FOR AGRICULTURE—THE FRANCO-ITALIAN TARIFF WAR—SUBSEQUENT ECONOMIC PROGRESS

THE agricultural classes had been disappointed by the tariff of 1881; they had made considerable efforts to secure an extension of Protection to their own particular interests, but without success except in a few almost unimportant instances. Yet they were the most numerous section of the community; in 1882 the number of persons concerned with agriculture was over 18 millions, as against about 9 millions for industry and 4 millions for trade.[1] Nearly one-half the total population (actually 48·8 per cent.) were dependent on agriculture in one way or another. Moreover, the great number of small holdings made agricultural prices a subject of immediate and keen interest to a much larger class in France than anywhere else; in 1882 there were 5,530,000 holdings of 100 acres or less, and of these 4,803,000 did not exceed 25 acres.[2] And there is no doubt that, in particular, those farmers who were engaged in wheat-growing were not in a very prosperous condition during the period from 1881 to 1890; in the first five years of that decade prices fell rapidly. The following table gives the average prices of wheat for the quinquennial periods 1871–5 and 1876–80, and for the several years from 1881 to 1890:[3]

[1] Brandt, p. 168.
[2] *Ibid.*, p. 168.
[3] *British and Foreign Trade and Industry*, 1909, p. 194.

WHEAT PRICES, 1871–90.

Period.	Price per Imperial Quarter. s. d.
Average, 1871–5	55 4
Average, 1876–80	51 0
1881	51 8
1882	44 11
1883	44 3
1884	41 4
1885	38 3
Average, 1881–5	44 1
1886	38 6
1887	41 2
1888	43 9
1889	42 1
1890	44 1
Average, 1886–90	41 11

Average prices between 1881 and 1890 were on the whole considerably lower than those for the period 1861–70, and very much lower than those for 1871–80, and the average production per acre had increased only slightly,[1] partly because of the smallness of the holdings and the lack of capital necessary for improvements; on the other hand, taxation had greatly increased since 1860, and especially since 1870, whilst it was estimated that the average wages of agricultural labour had increased 20 per cent.[2] The cattle-rearing industry was in a much better position, but the wine-growers and silk-producers, hitherto large exporters and therefore ranged on the side of the Free Traders, were now entering on a period of grave difficulties owing to the ravages of phylloxera and other diseases. The production of wine, which had reached in 1875 the exceptionally high figure of 84 million hectolitres, sank to 34 millions in 1881, and 25 millions in 1886; as a natural consequence the imports, which were insignificant in 1876, reached

[1] See the tables in Brandt, p. 231. [2] Foville, pp. 98–9.

8 millions in 1881 and 11 millions in 1886.[1] In the case of silk, the growing competition of China and Japan made itself felt acutely at the time when the French producers were struggling to recover from their disasters. The sugar-producers of Northern France complained of the ineffective character of the surtaxes on beet sugar, which did nothing to check the influx of the bounty-fed sugar of Germany and Austria-Hungary.[2] For all these various reasons the agriculturists were distressed and dissatisfied; they were ready to follow the leadership of Méline in his energetic campaign in favour of the extension of Protection to agriculture; and the characteristic feature of the tariff history of France, as of Germany, in the decade 1881–90 is the development of Protection in this particular direction.[3] The various agricultural interests were no longer hostile; they combined, and, as in Germany, were able to force their policy upon the country,[4] in spite of the activity of the "Ligue anti-protectioniste," led by Léon Say.

It will suffice to sketch the growth of this legislation very briefly. In 1881 the importation of American pork was forbidden on sanitary grounds, though there was some opposition to this from the seaports. In 1884, as the result of strong pressure from Northern France, the surtax on beet sugar was raised from 3 to 7 francs, and various excise changes made in order to encourage the home producers. In 1885 the rates of duty on animals imported for food were raised—on oxen from 15 to 25 francs, on cows from 8 to 12, on calves from 1½ to 4, on pigs from 3 to 6, on sheep from 2 to 3. At the same time rye, barley and oats which had been duty free since 1861, were subjected to a tax of 1½ francs per 100 kilo., and the rates on flour were raised from 1·2 to 6 francs. In 1887 the duty on oxen was raised to 38 francs, on cows to 20, on calves to 8, on sheep to 5; the duty on flour was advanced to 8 francs, and on oats to 3 francs.[5]

[1] Devers, pp. 183–4.
[2] *Ibid.*, p. 176.
[3] For a hostile criticism of French agricultural protection see Meredith, *Protection in France*, chaps. iv. and v.
[4] Devers, p. 184.
[5] *Ibid.*, pp. 176–9.

In this latter year the customs duty on alcoholic liquors was raised to 70 francs per hectolitre of pure alcohol; this was at first intended as a temporary measure to deal with some passing difficulties created by German tariff legislation, but ultimately in 1888 the tax was continued indefinitely. In 1890, in order to give such help as was possible to the wine-growers, an excise was imposed on the manufacture of certain "wines" from raisins; additional customs duties could not be imposed owing to treaty obligations.

In the case of wheat, the first new enactment was in 1885. Under the tariff of 1881 the duty was 60 centimes per 100 kilo.; the growers now asked that the amount should be raised to 5 francs. The Government, with Méline at the Ministry of Agriculture (established in 1881), was not unfavourable, but the Chamber of Deputies was not prepared to make so sweeping a change, and contented itself with fixing the duty at 3 francs. But the Protectionists regarded this merely as the first step, and immediately began to call for a fresh increase. They urged that the prices realised in the home market were not sufficient to cover the cost of production, which amounted to from 19 to 20 francs per hectolitre; prices were actually considerably below this, although the import declined rapidly after the new corn law came into effect. In March, 1887, the duty was raised to 5 francs, but the Government was empowered to suspend the law at any time by simple proclamation.[1] The following table shows the production and consumption of wheat in France, and the average prices, for the years 1886 to 1890.[2]

Year.	Production.	Consumption.			Average Price per Imperial Quarter.
		Home-Grown.	Imported.	Total.	
	Million Cwt.	Million Cwt.	Million Cwt.	Million Cwt.	s. d.
1886 ..	158·1	157·8	14·6	172·4	38 6
1887 ..	165·7	165·5	18·2	183·7	41 2
1888 ..	145·5	145·2	23·1	168·3	43 9
1889 ..	159·6	159·2	23·3	182·5	42 1
1890 ..	172·2	172·0	21·6	193·6	44 1

[1] Franke, p. 13.

[2] *British and Foreign Trade and Industry*, 1909, pp. 177 and 194.

On the whole the duties seem to have raised prices, but not considerably. But probably the best view as to the effect of the new duties is obtained by a comparison with English prices. In 1883 and 1884 the import duty on wheat in France was 1s. 1d. a quarter; in the first year the amount imported was 21·1 million cwt., in the second it was 22·1 millions; but whilst in 1883 the price per imperial quarter in France was only 2s. 8d. more than in England, in 1884 it was 5s. 8d. In 1886, after the duty had been raised from 60 centimes to 3 francs, and when imports amounted to only 14·7 million cwt., the French price was higher than the English by 7s. 6d. per quarter, but the average price in France was still lower than in 1884, and very much lower than in any previous year since 1865. In 1888, 1889, and 1890, after the increase of the duty to 5 francs, the average prices in France rose somewhat, but the excess of French prices over English rose in the three years to 11s. 11d., 12s. 4d., and 12s. 2d. respectively.[1] It would seem, then, to be fairly clear that the effect of the duties was not so much to raise prices as to prevent a fall in France similar to that which took place in England, and to that extent doubtless the French corn-growers benefited by the tariff changes.[2]

The one considerable event in the history of French foreign commerce during this period is the tariff war with Italy. Economic relations with that country had been decidedly strained for some time past. Italy had entered in 1863 into the commercial treaty system established by Napoleon III.; but at the time her convention with France lapsed, in 1875, she was engaged in the preparation of a new general tariff, and there were difficulties in the way of the renewal of a commercial agreement. At last, in 1877, a treaty was signed, and promptly rejected by the French Chamber by a narrow majority. On July 1st, 1877, Italy's new tariff came into

[1] *Report on British and Foreign Trade and Industry*, 1903, p. 126. Probably some allowance should be made for difference in qualities.

[2] *Cf.* Franke, pp. 10–13.

force, and for some months the trade between that country and the French Republic was governed by the two "autonomous" tariffs; but neither party was content, and negotiations were soon renewed. An arrangement was quickly reached, and this in turn was superseded by the treaty of 1881, following on the new French tariff of that year. The new arrangements were to hold good until 1892, but there was provision for the termination of the treaty by either party in December, 1887; and a year before that date the Italian Government gave notice of its intention to use this power in the case of all treaties by which it was bound. The changed economic conditions of Italy, due to the completion of unity, the abolition of internal customs boundaries, and the growth of railways, had rendered it desirable in the judgment of the Italian Ministry that there should be a complete tariff revision—it was also in need of revenue; and the result of its deliberations was a strongly protective set of duties, which averaged nearly 60 per cent. *ad valorem.*[1] It had renounced the treaties in order to give itself a free hand in tariff matters, but at the same time it declared its readiness to enter into a new arrangement with France, and negotiations began in August, 1887. By this time, however, the Italians had been greatly annoyed by the increase of the French import duties on cattle, which had inflicted serious damage on an important part of the Italian export trade.[2] The French Government desired that the basis of discussion should be furnished by the treaty rates of 1881; Italy desired to start from its new general tariff, and summarily rejected the French suggestion. The diplomatic discussion was then transferred from Paris to Rome, and the Italians put forward their definite proposals. They would consider only 89 articles out of the 272 on which they had made reductions in 1881;

[1] *Report on Tariff Wars*, p. 14.

[2] The value of the Italian export of cattle to France was £1,500,000 sterling in 1880, and only £240,000 in 1889 (*Report on Tariff Wars*, p. 15).

and on most of these 89, and especially silk and woollen goods, they intended to make substantial increases.[1] On the other hand, they desired from France the guarantee of "most favoured nation" treatment, and some reductions of duties, chiefly upon cattle. These demands were rejected by the French Government; an alternative proposal on its part proved inacceptable to Italy; and the negotiations came to an end in February, 1888.

From March 1, Italy intended to apply to French products her new general tariff; and as the rates thus levied were somewhat higher than the rates established by the French general tariff, France proceeded to impose surtaxes on a number of Italian products. Thus there was an increase on wines from 15 to 20 francs per hectolitre, on butter from 13 to 25 francs per 100 kilo., on eggs from 10 to 20 francs, on dried fruits from 6 to 15 francs; and such raw materials as silk, flax, hemp and skins, hitherto free, were subjected to small duties.[2] Italy replied by some further increases in her own tariff rates on goods imported from France; and each party imposed surtaxes on goods brought in its opponent's ships. Diplomatic discussion still continued, and in July Italy made fresh suggestions; it offered reductions of 50 per cent. on its new general tariff, without, however, getting near to the terms of 1881. The new scheme was not acceptable to France, and the conflict continued. It lasted till the end of December, 1889, when the Italian Parliament authorised the abandonment of the war tariff against France; but it was not until January, 1892, that the French Government dropped its surtaxes on Italian products. From that time on the two countries dealt with each other under their respective general tariffs until 1899.

The consequences of the war to the commerce between the two countries are unmistakable. The table on p. 326 shows the French exports to Italy and Italian exports to France for the five years preceding and five

[1] Franke, p. 18. [2] *Report on Tariff Wars*, p. 23.

years following the commencement of the war. It will be remembered, however, that practically, although the acute struggle was over by the beginning of 1890, the conflict continued to 1899, since until that year neither country would grant the other its best terms; the table shows that the trade had not even then recovered from the blow of 1888.[1]

The Italian Government admitted that the export trade in wine had suffered badly; that Spain and Portugal had replaced Italy in the French market. In 1887

Year.	Value of—	
	French Exports to Italy.	Italian Exports to France.
	Million £.	Million £.
1883	12·0	17·1
1884	11·3	14·7
1885	11·5	10·5
1886	12·4	12·4
1887	13·0	12·3
Average, 1883–7 ..	12·0	13·4
1888	6·2	7·2
1889	6·7	5·3
1890	6·5	4·9
1891	5·4	4·9
1892	6·7	5·3
Average, 1888–92 ..	6·3	5·5
1899	6·1	6·3

France took from Italy 2,782,000 hectolitres of wine, and in 1888 only 817,000; in the former year France took 78 per cent. of the total Italian export, and in the latter year 45 per cent. In that case there was a marked falling off in the Italian exports; in other cases there was no such decline, since either new markets were found, as in the case of some agricultural produce, or the goods went to the same destination by a different route. A striking illustration of this latter alternative is furnished

[1] *Report on Tariff Wars*, p. 24.

by silk: in 1887 Italy exported to France 28,178 quintals[1] of raw silk, and to Switzerland 7,300 quintals; but in 1888 France took only 9,188 quintals, whilst the amount sent to Switzerland rose abruptly to 29,621.

On the other side, France suffered in regard to her exports to Italy of colonial produce, silk and woollen manufactures, and a number of other commodities. The value of the woollen goods taken by Italy from France fell from 20 million francs in 1887 to 6·6 millions in 1888; silk goods dropped from 6·8 to 3·4 millions, cotton goods from 5·3 to 1·6 millions, yarns of all kinds from 3 to 1·7 millions.[2] On the whole, however, the total of French exports to all countries did not fall off, but, on the contrary, they showed an increase; so that France was able to recoup herself elsewhere (chiefly in the United Kingdom, and as regards woollen goods in Germany) for the loss of much of the Italian market. Italy suffered much more—her total exports declined considerably. The competitors of the two countries reaped the benefits of the struggle; to the combatants themselves it brought only difficulties and a great amount of damage.

The elections of 1885 and 1889 had greatly strengthened the parliamentary forces of the Protectionists, and they prepared to carry their policy into full practice. They had been able, owing to the agrarian difficulties, to rally the agricultural classes to their cause; and their first efforts in 1890 were, as we have already seen, on behalf of the wine-growers. In the same year, on the proposal of Méline, they secured increased duties on maize, rice and meal. The manufacturing classes had always been in favour of Protection, and their zeal for it was stimulated by the continued commercial depression after the crisis of 1882, and the fact that the chief industries of France were making only slow advances.

One of the main reasons for this was doubtless the very slight growth of the population, which numbered 36,103,000 in 1872, and 38,348,000 in 1892—an increase

[1] A quintal = 100 kilo.

[2] Franke, p. 20.

of only a trifle over 6 per cent. in twenty years. Consequently, in spite of the development of railways and the extension of the application of machinery to industry, the industrial output did not make very satisfactory progress.

The following table gives some summary figures indicating the industrial development of France during the two decades from 1870 to 1889:[1]

	Annual Averages.			
	1870-1874.	1875-1879.	1880-1884.	1885-1889.
	Million Tons.	Million Tons.	Million Tons.	Million Tons.
Production of coal	15·1 *	16·3	19·3	20·7
Production of pig-iron	1·2	1·4	1·9	1·6
Production of crude steel	0·13	0·3	0·4	0·5
	No.	No.	No.	No.
Spindles in use ..	3,580,000 (1872-1874)	3,776,000	3,887,000	4,240,000
Consumption of raw cotton	Million Cwts. 1·5	Million Cwts. 1·8	Million Cwts. 2·0	Million Cwts. 2·2
Consumption of raw (sheep and lambs') wool	Million Lbs. 330·0	Million Lbs. 379·3	Million Lbs. 409·5	Million Lbs. 467·5
Shipping built and added to register	Tons. 41,681 (1872-1874)	Tons. 28,642	Tons. 36,469	Tons. 24,538

* Including some lignite.

It will be observed that in no case was there any marked expansion; the cotton industry had not yet recovered from the blow caused by the transference of Alsace-Lorraine to Germany in 1871. The consumption of silk was estimated at 5·8 million kilo. in 1872;[2] it fluctuated greatly, and in 1891 was 6·8 millions (after being as high as 9·6 millions in 1888). In one industry alone—the manufacture of alkali and its kindred pro-

[1] *British and Foreign Trade and Industry*, 1909, pp. 118–9, 157–9, 164–71.

[2] Foville, p. 234.

ducts—was there marked success, mainly owing to the discovery of the ammonia-soda process by Solvay; the output increased from 525,000 tons on the average for 1874–8 to 1,023,000 for 1889–93.[1] Foreign trade was unsatisfactory; France was declining in comparison with her neighbours. The main statistics are given in the following table:[2]

IMPORTS AND EXPORTS OF MERCHANDISE.

Period.	Imports for Home Consumption.		Exports of Domestic Produce.	
	Total.	Manufactured Goods.	Total.	Manufactured Goods.
	Million £.	Million £.	Million £.	Million £.
1881	194·5	27·3	142·5	75·0
1882	192·9	31·0	143·0	75·5
1883	192·2	30·7	138·1	74·0
1884	173·7	27·9	129·3	67·6
1885	163·5	24·4	123·5	65·2
1886	168·3	23·4	130·0	69·8
1887	161·0	23·5	129·9	69·5
1888	164·3	23·2	129·9	68·3
1889	172·7	24·5	148·2	77·0
1890	177·5	26·0	150·1	80·0

There was growing dissatisfaction in France with the whole system of commercial treaties in the form which had prevailed since 1860. The agriculturists and manufacturers were inclined to high Protection, and were opposed to anything which mitigated it; and it was thought also that treaties made for a definite term of years tied the hands of the Government unduly, since no alteration could be made during the period, however much economic conditions might change. When at the end of 1889 the Superior Council of Commerce invited the opinions of the Chambers of Commerce and similar institutions on the subject, 96 out of 107 Chambers declared for the denunciation of the existing treaties, and 62 were opposed to any renewal. A substantial

[1] *Dictionnaire du Commerce*, ii. p. 1357.
[2] *British and Foreign Trade and Industry*, 1909, p. 61.

majority of the other organisations consulted gave similar advice.[1] On the other hand, it was felt to be undesirable to isolate France completely, and there was a general feeling in favour of the adoption of a suggestion of Méline—that there should be minimum and maximum tariffs, the former to be granted to those countries with which France made treaties, and the latter to apply to all countries not so favoured. This arrangement would differ from the system adopted by Germany at about this time in that the German " conventional " tariff was unchangeable so long as the treaties endured, whilst France would be able to raise her minimum tariff whenever she deemed it necessary. The " most favoured nation " clause was extremely unpopular.

The general arguments of the advocates of Protection were those with which we are already familiar in other countries. They emphasised the necessity of a policy of defence against growing competition, especially from the United States; they urged that a policy of Protection for agriculture, however much to be condemned in Germany, where it was adopted in the interests of the large landowners, was laudable in a country like France, with its great multitude of peasant proprietors; they put forward the doctrines of national self-sufficiency and security of the home market; and they argued that the restriction of imports would stimulate native industries, create an increased demand for labour and a consequent rise of wages.[2] The fears of some manufacturers that they would be further hampered by the taxation of raw materials were allayed by the promise of compensatory duties or drawbacks, and by the prospect of an enlarged home market owing to the renewed prosperity of the agricultural classes. But, indeed, argument was almost unnecessary; with the farmers and manufacturers combined the Protectionists were strong enough to overcome without difficulty all opposition.

[1] Franke, pp. 25–6.

[2] See the summary of debates in Devers, pp. 186–206. *Cf.* Brandt, pp. 182–5.

CHAPTER VI

THE TARIFF OF 1892 AND SUBSEQUENT DEVELOPMENTS

THE preparation of the new tariff was entrusted to the two Councils of Commerce and Industry, under the general guidance of the Ministry; and the resultant scheme was presented to the Chamber of Deputies in October, 1890. It adopted the plan of the maximum and minimum scales of duties; the former to be applied against all countries which in their rates of import duties differentiated in any way against the French products, whilst the products of countries which did not so differentiate were to be admitted at the minimum rates. The basis of the minimum tariff was declared to be not Protection, but simply an attempt to enable French industries to meet foreign competition on equal terms.[1] In most cases it was proposed to increase the old rates of duty, but the Government still declined to recommend taxation of those agricultural products which were raw materials for industry. The Chamber referred the plan to its standing commission for customs matters, which had been established at the commencement of the year at the instigation of Méline; and that commission, under Méline's guidance, proceeded to make radical changes—it increased the proposed rates considerably, in particular those on timber, wines, cattle and meat (in order to compensate the farmers for the free admission of wool and hides); it made some advances on manufactured goods; and it recommended the grant of bounties to the native growers of flax and silk, since those commodities

[1] Devers, p. 186.

were to be exempt from duty.[1] It urged also that the grant of the minimum tariff should not be made in such a way as to prevent France from increasing it at any time if she thought fit.

The discussions were long, not so much because of the strength of the opposition (though under the leadership of Léon Say that was able enough) as because of the resistance of the Ministry[2] to some of the proposals of the commission, and differences between the Senate and the Chamber—the former made 176 amendments, of which 148 were ultimately accepted. Some increases on agricultural products made by the commission were adopted, but, on the other hand, the Chamber rejected proposals for the taxation of silk-cocoons, and established instead bounties for six years to the silk-growers and weavers.[3] The commission had recommended higher duties on wine than the Ministry, and these were accepted; but its changes in regard to oil-seeds (in which the agriculturists were greatly interested) were rejected. The alterations made by the Senate were entirely in the direction of increased rates. The new tariff became law in January, 1892.

The new customs schedules dealt with 721 commodities, or groups of commodities, and were much more detailed and elaborate than those of any other continental tariff of the period. The minimum rates could be imposed on all products of countries which gave France similarly advantageous treatment; but non-

[1] "Votre Commission . . . a recherché pour chaque branche de production agricole ou industrielle le droit exact qui lui paraissait indispensable pour en assurer l'existence et le libre développement. Elle a considéré, comme le Gouvernement, que pour donner à nos tarifs leur veritable valeur et rendre à la production française courage et confiance, il importait avant tout de fixer le minimum des droits qui lui seront assurés, quoiqu'il arrive, *et au dessous desquels il ne sera pas permis de descendre a l'avenir.* C'est sur ce principe fondamentale que repose l'économie de notre tarif minimum" (*Report of M. Méline*).

[2] France was enjoying a period of ministerial stability under Freycinet. Jules Roche was Minister of Commerce all through the period of tariff discussion.

[3] Franke, p. 37.

European products coming from European countries and European products not coming directly from the country of origin were subject to surtaxes. Specific duties were employed almost solely; the only exceptions were in the case of chemicals. The new duties marked a very considerable advance of Protection; the average duty on agricultural produce was 25 per cent. *ad valorem* (the grain duties remained unaltered), and the following table shows some of the changes on manufactured goods.[1] The most noticeable advances were in respect of textiles. The new minimum rates of duty were very much higher than those of the conventional tariff created in the same year for Germany by the Caprivi treaties.

DUTIES IN FRANCS PER 100 KILOGRAMMES.

Articles.	Conventional Tariff before 1892.	Minimum Tariff of 1892.
	Francs per 100 Kilo.	Francs per 100 Kilo.
Linen yarns (unbleached)	13–100	16–100
Linen or hemp tissues[2] (unbleached)	22–375	24–500
Cotton yarns (unbleached) ..	15–300	15–310
Cotton tissues ,, ...	50–540	62–620
Silk tissues ,, ...	0	400
Pig-iron	1·50	1·50–3·50
Iron bars	6	5
Steel rails	6	6
Tin plates	7	7·50–10

[1] Brandt, p. 193.

[2] The rates given are the highest and lowest. The scale was highly complicated, as the following example (which is not exceptional) will show:

Duties on tissues of linen or hemp, unbleached, weighing from 10 to 40 kilo. per 100 square metres, and containing in warp and weft in a square of 5 millimetres each side, after division of the total by two,

6 threads or less	45 francs.
7 or 8 ,, ...	65 ,,
9 or 10 ,, ...	80 ,,
11 or 12 ,, ...	100 ,,
13 or 14 ,, ...	125 ,,
15, 16, or 17 ,, ...	140 ,,
18, 19, or 20 ,, ...	220 ,,
21, 22, or 23 ,, ...	300 ,,
More than 23 ,, ...	400 ,,

There were similar groups for goods weighing more than 40 or less than 10 kilo. per 100 square metres. For bleached cotton tissues there were seven divisions, and six of these contained four separate rates of duty, according to the number of threads in a

At the same time the Act establishing bounties for shipbuilding and subsidies to shipping was renewed, and bounties given for the growing of silk, flax, and hemp.

France was able, without encountering serious obstacles, to make arrangements with most of the European Powers, by which she granted them the advantages of her minimum tariff, and secured their lowest tariff rates in return. There were some difficulties with Spain, and against Portugal and Italy the maximum scale was adopted (in the latter case only for a time). But the most serious conflict was with Switzerland. That Republic had undertaken in 1890 the revision of its general tariff, partly in order to secure additional revenue for the Federal Government. When the tariff of 1892 was under discussion in France, the Swiss authorities intimated that they could not accept the French minimum scale as a return for concessions on their side, and consequently they asked for reductions on sixty-two articles, chiefly industrial products. The French Ministry was not unwilling to give way, on account of the importance of the Swiss market; but the protectionist element in France was too strong to permit such a concession, and the proposals of the Minister of Commerce were rejected by the Chamber. Consequently in January, 1893, the Swiss Government subjected French goods to its new general tariff, and imposed surtaxes on some 200 commodities. France in its turn levied its maximum tariff on Swiss goods, but its war rates were much lower than those employed by Switzerland.[1]

The war lasted for a little more than two years and six months. But both sides soon became weary of the struggle, and were alarmed at its effects. Negotiations began in the latter part of 1894; but Switzerland adhered to its refusal to accept the French minimum tariff in

---

square of the usual 5 millimetres. It is unnecessary to point out the trouble and cost of administration resulting from so elaborate a classification, which is, however, probably inevitable if the system of specific duties is to be satisfactory.

[1] Franke (p. 48) regards this as the chief cause of France's defeat.

return for its own conventional rates—it insisted on a number of special reductions, and as France was anxious to come to terms, she at last agreed to give Switzerland lower rates on twenty-nine commodities. In return she received the benefits of the Swiss conventional rates with the "most favoured nation" clause. Legislation in the two countries in July and August, 1895, confirmed the new arrangements, which remained, however, terminable by either party at any time, on due notice.[1]

The effects of the war were severe on both sides. France's export trade suffered most in the case of wine (which dropped from about £950,000 in 1891 and about £770,000 in 1892 to £70,000 in 1894), sugar (which was also almost entirely destroyed), cattle, and clothing. Switzerland, on its side, lost in silk and silk goods and cottons. But France lost much the more heavily, and the result of the war was so far a victory for Switzerland that she secured some preferences over other nations in the French market, without giving France any such preference in return. The following table shows the value of the French total exports to Switzerland, and of Swiss exports to France, for the four years preceding the war, and the four years after its commencement:

Year.	French Exports to Switzerland.	Swiss Exports to France.
	Million £.	Million £.
1889	9·2	4·1
1890	9·7	4·2
1891	9·4	4·1
1892	9·1	3·7
Annual average, 1889-92	9·35	4·025
1893	6·9	3·0
1894	4·4	2·7
1895	6·5	2·7
1896	7·2	3·0
Annual average, 1893-96	6·25	2·85

Subsequently the upward movement continued, but very gradually; it was not until 1899 that the Swiss

[1] *Report on Tariff Wars*, pp. 1–6, 77–85.

export trade to France returned to the dimensions of 1890, whilst in the case of the French export trade to Switzerland the recovery was not complete until 1903.

By 1908 the only European country whose products were subject to the French maximum rates was Portugal, and the advantages of the minimum tariff had been extended in whole or in part to Canada (under the Franco-Canadian Convention of 1893, which was amplified in 1907), the Argentine, Colombia, San Domingo, Ecuador, Mexico, Paraguay, Uruguay, Venezuela, Egypt, and Japan. With the United States of America an agreement was reached in 1898, whereby the concessions authorised by Section 3 of the Dingley Tariff Act were granted to France in return for the minimum rates on canned meats, various fruits, hops, timber, and a few other commodities.

The tariff thus established in 1892 remained in force, with some alterations, but in its essential features unchanged, for no less than eighteen years, and before we proceed to examine the causes which ultimately brought about its revision, it will be convenient to review briefly some of the indications of France's economic development during this period. First as regards foreign trade; the following table summarises the movement from 1890 to 1909:[1]

IMPORTS AND EXPORTS OF MERCHANDISE, 1890–1909.

Period.	Imports for Home Consumption.		Exports of Domestic Produce.	
	Total.	Manufactured Goods.	Total.	Manufactured Goods.
	Million £.	Million £.	Million £.	Million £.
Average, 1890–94	168·8	24·6	136·8	73·6
Average, 1895–99	163·7	25·2	144·3	79·5
Average, 1900–04	182·1	32·4	168·6	94·6
1905	191·2	34·8	194·7	109·9
1906	225·1	40·0	210·6	123·2
1907	248·9	46·9	223·8	133·7
1908	225·6	44·6	202·0	118·5
1909	249·8	47·2	228·7	128·0

[1] *British and Foreign Trade and Industry*, 1909, p. 61; and *Statistical Abstract for the Principal and Other Foreign Countries* (No. 39), p. 104.

It will be observed that the expansion of the foreign trade of France was only very gradual in comparison with that of her chief European rivals, and that the development was much more pronounced in the case of exports than in the case of imports; comparing the averages for the quinquennial periods 1890–4, and 1905–9, exports advanced 55 per cent. and imports only 35 per cent.

But France is mainly an agricultural country, and inasmuch as the tariff of 1892 was intended primarily for the benefit of the agrarian interests, it is to the agricultural development during this period that attention must mainly be directed. And first it may be pointed out that there was a heavy fall in the imports of articles of food and drink; the average value for the years 1890–4 was 54·1 million pounds, for 1895–9 it was 44·2 millions, for 1900–4 it had fallen to 33·6 millions; and though there was some increase in the next four years, the average for 1905–8 was only 37·4 millions. The following table shows the consumption of wheat in France for the period 1880–1909, with the shares contributed by home production and imports respectively.[1]

Period.	Consumption of Wheat.			Consumption per Head of Population.
	Home-Grown.	Imported.	Total.	
	Million Cwts.	Million Cwts.	Million Cwts.	Lbs.
Annual average, 1880–84	157·5	27·1	184·6	548
Annual average, 1885–89	157·8	18·5	176·4	516
Annual average, 1890–94	154·0	29·1	183·1	534
Annual average, 1895–99	171·1	13·4	184·5	535
Annual average, 1900–04	168·6	5·3	173·9	499
1905	173·3	3·9	177·3	506
1906	167·7	6·3	174·0	496
1907	195·1	7·5	202·6	579
1908	163·9	1·7	165·6	473
1909	183·4	2·9	186·3	531
Annual average, 1905–09	176·7	4·5	181·2	517

[1] *British and Foreign Trade and Industry*, 1909, pp. 177 and 194; and *Statistical Abstract for the Principal and Other Foreign Countries* (No. 39), p. 511.

The tendency towards the independence of France from foreign supplies of wheat was very marked, and though there was a slight downward movement of consumption per head of population, though the fluctuations were very marked,[1] it does not appear that this was due to any upward movement of price in France itself.[2]

The production of wine averaged 35·2 million hectolitres in the quinquennial period 1890–4, and 36·8 millions for 1894–9; subsequently it rose very rapidly, averaging 53·3 millions for 1900–4, and 58·8 millions for the four years 1905–8. This increase in production was accompanied by, and was largely a cause of, a heavy fall in prices, which caused much economic disorder in the vine-growing regions.[3] The production of sugar (expressed as refined) advanced very rapidly also between 1889 and 1902, but after that date there was a decline; the average seasonal production, which was 587 million kilo. for the period 1889–90 to 1893–4, and 687 millions in the following quinquennium, rose to 893 millions for the period 1899–1900 to 1903–4, but dropped to 722 millions for the next four years.[4] The surplus of the

[1] The Customs Commission of the French Chamber viewed the general result with much satisfaction: "Notre production sera bientôt suffisante pour l'alimentation totale de la population française, qui tend malheureusement à demeurer stationnaire, ainsi que pour la réserve des semences destinées à produire le récolte de l'année suivante. Nous deviendrons à notre tour exportateurs de blé, et ce ne sera pas la moindre conséquence du régime douanier en vigueur" (*Rapport par M. Morel*, 1908, p. 13).

[2] The Customs Commission of the French Chamber of Deputies estimated the average price per hectolitre for the eight years 1884–91 at 18·26 francs, for 1892–9 at 16·65 francs, and for 1900–7 at 16·71 francs (*Rapport*, p. 13). The official average annual prices of wheat in the five years (1900–4) ranged from 32s. 7d. to 38s. 7d. per Imperial Quarter; in the period 1905–9 the range was from 39s. 1d. to 40s. 7d., but the average consumption per head was greater in the later period. The questions of the relation between the price of wheat in France and the price elsewhere, and of the comparative movements of the prices, are more complicated, owing to the facts that there is an undoubted difference in respect of quality between French and such wheats as are sold in the United Kingdom, for example, and that the French demand for imported wheat is in some years (owing to abundant harvests) practically insignificant.

[3] *Annuaire Statistique de la France*, 1908, p. 44*.

[4] *Ibid.*, p. 50*.

exports of potatoes over the imports, which amounted on the average to 1,203 million quintals for the years 1890-4, and 1,022 millions for 1895-9, rose to 1,688 millions for the quinquennium 1900–4, and averaged 1,455 millions for the next three years.[1] The rearing of cattle developed, and for the supply of sheep France came to depend solely on her own production and that of Algeria. Finally, it may be observed that in the report of the Customs Commission of the French Chamber of Deputies, which considered the proposals for tariff revision in 1908, emphasis was laid on the fact that the average annual value of the imports of food of all kinds, which was 59·5 million pounds for the eight years 1884–91, declined after the tariff of 1892 to 46 millions for the period 1892–9, and to 35·4 millions for the period 1900–7; and the committee urged that nevertheless there had been during the same period a marked decline in the average prices of all important articles of general consumption.[2]

But it is necessary to point out that the rates of duty under the tariff of 1892 have been raised from time to time in the interest of the agrarians. Thus in 1894 the rate of duty on wheat was increased from 5 to 7 francs per 100 kilo., and there were corresponding advances in the rates on flour. The duties on live pigs and fresh pork were raised in 1898 and again in 1903, the total increases being from 8 to 15 francs per head in the case of pigs, and from 12 to 25 francs per 100 kilo. in the case of fresh pork. The duty on cattle was doubled in 1903 and that on sheep advanced from 15½ francs to 25 francs per head; in the same year there was a corresponding

[1] *Annuaire Statistique de la France*, 1908, p. 106.

[2] *Rapport*, pp. 11–17 and 317. They quote with approval a remark by M. Deschanel in the debate of 1891: "La solution définitive du problème agricole n'est pas dans la douane, elle est dans la science. Oui, mais la douane ouvre la porte à la science et lui permet de concourir ainsi à la cause du progrès. Elle est dans l'augmentation du rendement et le perfectionnement des méthodes. La douane, avec une protection moderée, ramène les capitaux à l'agriculture, à l'industrie, car le travail, à lui seul, ne suffit pas."

increase in the rates on imported beef and mutton. Owing to the fall in prices after 1893, the rate of duty on butter was raised from 6 to 20 francs per 100 kilo. in 1898 without checking the fall for long. Finally, the wine duties were rearranged and increased in 1899.

Turning now to industry, the following table summarises some of the statistics of the French development since 1890.[1]

	Annual Average.			1905.	1906.	1907.	1908.	1909.
	1890-4.	1895-9.	1900-4.					
Consumption of coal ..	Million Tons. 35·6	Million Tons. 39·8	Million Tons. 45·1	Million Tons. 48·7	Million Tons. 51·8	Million Tons. 55·1	Million Tons. 54·7	Million Tons. 56·4
Production of pig-iron ..	2·0	2·3	2·6	3·0	3·3	3·6	3·4	3·6
Production of crude steel	0·8	1·3	1·7	2·2	2·4	2·7	2·7	3·0
Shipping built and added to the Register	Tons. 22,224	Tons. 44,739	Tons. 95,713	Tons. 49,859	Tons. 32,132	Tons. 30,969	Tons. 77,023	Tons. 33,104
Cotton spindles employed ..	No. 4,430,000	No. 5,100,000	No. 5,940,000	No. 6,250,000	No. 6,500,000	No. 6,600,000	No. 6,700,000	No. 6,850,000
Consumption of raw cotton	Million Cwts. 3·0	Million Cwts. 3·2	Million Cwts. 3·6	Million Cwts. 4·0	Million Cwts. 4·0	Million Cwts. 4·5	Million Cwts. 4·6	Million Cwts. 5·1
Consumption of raw (sheep and lambs') wool ..	Million Lbs. 504·7	Million Lbs. 558·2	Million Lbs. 517·2	Million Lbs. 503·4	Million Lbs. 553·4	Million Lbs. 565·5	Million Lbs. 526·1	Million Lbs. 624·3
Consumption of raw silk	19·5	19·4	18·2	18·4	17·8	19·5	19·1	19·6

It will be apparent from this table that though there was real progress, it was nothing like so great as that which took place during the same period either in the two chief neighbouring countries, the United Kingdom and Germany, or in the United States. In the great industrial and commercial development of the last decade of the nineteenth and the first decade of the twentieth century, France had relatively little share; her coal and metal industries showed progress which was satisfactory only if the growth elsewhere were ignored; on her textile

[1] Statistics taken from *British and Foreign Trade and Industry*, 1909, pp. 152–173, and *Annuaire Statistique de la France*, 1908.

industries no more favourable judgment can well be pronounced. In this connection it is important to remember that the rate of growth of the population of France is extraordinarily slow—between 1890 and 1908 the total increase was only 887,000.[1] This was due to a number of causes, including doubtless the system of peasant holdings and the effect of the French law of succession;[2] but it is obvious that so long as such a condition endures, France must lose more and more ground in the industrial competition.

There are two other matters of importance in connection with French commercial policy which it will be convenient to notice in this place. The first of these is the arrangement in regard to the French colonial possessions.[3] Imports from Algeria are subject normally to the rates of duty of the French minimum tariff, but certain sugar products are admitted free, and a number of articles of " colonial produce " (such as cocoa, chocolate, coffee, tea, pepper, and nutmegs) are liable only to rates of duty lower, usually by one-half, than those of the minimum tariff. As regards Tunis, numerous products (including horses and cattle, wheat and other grains) are admitted free from that possession, either up to a specified amount, as in the case of horses and cattle, or without limit; and Tunis also enjoys some advantage in respect of the importation of wine into France. The remaining French colonies are divided into two groups—the first including Guadeloupe, Martinique, Réunion, French Guiana, Indo-China, Madagascar, New Caledonia, St. Pierre and Miquelon, Gaboon and Mayotte, whilst the second includes all other French possessions in Africa,

[1] Between 1890 and 1908 the population of the United Kingdom increased by 19 per cent., that of Germany by 28 per cent., that of the United States by 39 per cent., and that of France by only 2½ per cent.

[2] *Cf.* Coubertin, *L'Évolution française sous la troisième République*, pp. 392–7.

[3] See the return entitled *Foreign Countries* (*Preference to Colonies*), H.C. 296, 1909. As regards Corsica (which has its own Customs tariff) practically all its products are admitted into France duty-free, whilst the same treatment is accorded to French goods sent to the island under coasting-trade regulations.

with the "establishments" in India and Oceania. From all of the first groups sugar and other "colonial produce" may be imported at the same rates as similar produce from Algeria, subject (as in that case also) to the condition that they are imported direct.[1] The same treatment is extended to sugar and sugar products from the possessions comprised in the second group; their other products are liable as a rule to the rates of the French minimum tariff, but palm oil, building wood, and oxen from French West Africa, and bananas from French Guinea, are admitted free, whilst raw coffee from the Ivory Coast, French Congo and French Guinea, raw cocoa from French Congo, French Guinea and Dahomey, and vanilla from French Oceania, are admitted at rates considerably lower than those of the minimum tariff, subject in all cases to the condition as to direct importation, and, except palm oil and building wood, to a limitation of quantity (which is fixed annually for each colony). On the other hand, no duties are levied on French products (except sugar) imported directly into Algeria; there is a very long list of French products which are not liable to duty on importation into Tunis; and all French products are admitted free into the other colonies comprised in the first group indicated above (the Customs tariffs of these colonies are practically identical with that of France), and into most of those included in the second group. In Senegal, French Guinea, Upper Senegal and Mauritania a surtax is levied on imports not of French origin.

The other development of French fiscal policy which needs to be noticed is the system of bounties on shipbuilding and navigation, which was inaugurated in 1881, to take the place of the discriminating duties on goods carried in foreign ships.[2] Under a legislative enactment

[1] The carrying trade between France and Algeria is regarded as part of the coasting trade, and is therefore confined to French vessels.

[2] For detailed information on this subject see Meeker, *History of Shipping Subsidies*, pp. 43–83, and the Consular Report on the *French Mercantile Marine Laws* (Miscellaneous Series, No. 651).

of that year construction bounties were to be given according to a sliding scale on vessels and their machinery built in France (the highest rate being applicable to vessels built according to plans approved by the French Admiralty), together with navigation bounties—*i.e.*, a fixed sum for each thousand miles covered. Foreign-built vessels were accorded navigation bounties at half the rates allowed to vessels constructed in France. It is noteworthy that the construction bounties were officially stated to be given as "compensation for the increased cost which the customs tariff imposes on shipbuilders," and that the navigation bounties were compensatory "for the obligations imposed on the merchant marine in respect of recruiting and assisting the navy." The law was to be in force for ten years, and its results were not very satisfactory. The total sum paid in bounties during the period was about £4,900,000, of which about one-quarter was in respect of construction, and three-quarters in respect of navigation. The total registered French tonnage (sailing and steam), which was 914,000 tons in 1881, increased with some rapidity until it reached 1,034,000 tons in 1884; after that date it commenced to decline, and sank to 933,000 tons in 1889, after which year there was, for a time, a recovery. There was undoubtedly a stimulus to shipbuilding in the early years, especially as regards steam-vessels; in the years 1882–4, 110,300 tons of steam-shipping was built as compared with only 23,400 tons in the preceding three years.[1] In the next three years (1885–7), however, the total was only 30,500 tons—the fact being that in spite of the bounties on shipbuilding the cost of French steamships was so much greater than that of ships built abroad, that shipowners preferred to buy foreign ships, even though these earned smaller navigation bounties.[2] French-built iron and steel tonnage earning navigation bounties increased from 160,000 tons in 1882 to 191,000

[1] *British and Foreign Trade and Industry*, 1909, pp. 118–119.

[2] The French Minister of Marine estimated in 1893 that an ordinary steamship, which cost 300 francs per ton in the United Kingdom, would cost 420 francs in France.

tons in 1890; during the same period foreign-built tonnage increased from 44,000 to 91,000 tons; the tonnage of French-built wooden vessels earning navigation bounties declined heavily, whilst that of foreign-built wooden vessels increased, though it remained almost insignificant (9,800 tons in 1890).

By a law of 1893 the bounties on the construction of ships and their machinery were increased; the navigation bounties were modified, the half-bounties to foreign-built vessels being abolished, and higher rates being accorded to native-built sailing-ships than to steamships. Vessels engaged in the international coasting trade were to receive only two-thirds of the navigation bounties payable to ocean-going vessels (*navigation au long cours*). The law was to be in force for ten years, the navigation bounties being gradually reduced during that period. In the nine years 1893–1901 the amount paid by the State in construction bounties was £1,870,000, and in navigation bounties £4,170,000; and, nevertheless, the general effect of the law on French shipping was disastrous. The effect of the withdrawal of the bounties from foreign-built vessels, and the higher rates paid in respect of sailing-vessels, was to give a great stimulus to the construction of such vessels, and to check the building of steamships. In the ten years 1893–1902 there were built in France and added to the register 509,000 tons of sailing-vessels, and only 112,000 tons of steamships—this at a time when everywhere else steamships were displacing sailing-ships. Steamship-owners complained of a system which gave absolutely higher bounties to sailing-ships, and prevented them from buying vessels abroad; the shipbuilders asked for higher subsidies and the denial of registry to vessels built abroad; shippers were dissatisfied with their growing dependence, so far as French vessels were concerned, on slow sailing-vessels; and the continued relative decline of the French mercantile marine was a matter of general anxiety.[1] Con-

[1] *Cf.* the tables in *British and Foreign Trade and Industry*, 1909, pp. 116–7.

sequently, in 1902 there was fresh legislation. The construction bounties remained as under the law of 1893; but the navigation bounties were re-arranged to the advantage of steam-vessels, and a new equipment bounty was introduced in the form of an allowance payable on certain conditions for each day (not exceeding 300 in any one year) that a steamer should be in commission. This new bounty alone was applicable to foreign-built steamers, whilst French-built steamers could choose for each voyage between this equipment bounty and the navigation bounty. The total new tonnage to benefit by this law, in addition to the existing tonnage, was limited to 500,000 tons steam (of which two-fifths might be foreign built) and 100,000 tons sailing. The law was to be in force for fifteen years, and the bounties were to be reduced automatically so as to come to an end with the expiration of the period; and a maximum sum of £6,600,000 was to be expended. This amount, however, would have been quite insufficient for the 600,000 tons of new shipping which the law also contemplated (it was estimated that it would not suffice for more than 280,000 tons). The result was an amendment of the law in 1906, which increased the construction bounties, and modified the equipment bounty.

In spite of all these various efforts and the mail subsidies, French shipping remained in an unsatisfactory condition. It is true that the tonnage on the register increased with some rapidity after 1902—it reached its minimum in 1895 with 887,000 tons, and had risen to 1,403,000 tons in 1907; but as against this increase of 516,000 tons, British shipping increased by 2,497,000 tons, and German shipping by 1,288,000 tons. The share of French shipping in the foreign trade of France (the coasting trade, including that between France and Algeria, is reserved to it) averaged 33 per cent. in the five years 1880–4, and had sunk to 25 per cent. on the average for the three years 1905–7.[1] There was a real impetus given to the building of steamships in the years

[1] *British and Foreign Trade and Industry*, 1909, p. 107.

1903–5, when 128,000 tons were built and added to the register; but in the next two years the total was only 41,000 tons. The judgment of the Commission of the French House of Representatives in 1906, after twenty-five years of Government subsidy, that the bounties alike to builders and shipowners must be maintained if French shipbuilding and the French mercantile marine were to continue to exist, is a sufficient indication of the purely artificial character of the whole shipping industry of France, and of the unsuccess of the policy which has been adopted in regard to it.

CHAPTER VII

THE TARIFF OF 1910

THE customs tariff which came into force in January, 1892, remained substantially unchanged for eighteen years. As indicated in the previous chapter, some modifications of the rates of duty upon agricultural products were made from time to time, and there were also a few alterations in respect of manufactured goods; but these were all of relatively small importance. The tariff was soon felt to be, on the technical side, unsatisfactory from many points of view; some sections of French industry began early to call for increased protection; but in spite of the fact that the absence of conventional rates of duty fixed for a definite period rendered it possible for revision to be undertaken at any time, it was not until the middle of the year 1906—that is, not until after the new tariffs of the states of Central and Eastern Europe had come into operation—that the reconstruction of the French tariff was taken seriously into consideration. It is important to remark, however, that the movement did not originate with the Government, but with the Customs Commission of the Chamber of Deputies and although the Government put no obstacle in the way of the inquiries which the Commission proposed to undertake, with a view to the revision of the tariff, it did not at first show any particular sympathy. Later this policy was modified to some extent, but the Government constantly declined to put forward any proposals of its own, and maintained an independent and critical attitude towards the legislative proposals which, in default of Governmental action, were introduced by individual members of the Customs Commission and ultimately welded into a single Bill.[1]

The need for some measure of revision was generally recognised. In the first place, industry had undergone great changes since 1892. New manufactures had arisen, such as those of automobiles, artificial silk, some electrical industries, typewriters and phonographs, synthetic perfumery, and machinery and mechanics' tools of all kinds, in response to the needs of new technical developments. There had been important changes in manufacturing methods also, the most conspicuous, perhaps, being the mercerisation of cotton goods, the mineral tanning of hides and skins, numerous electro-technical processes, and the production of special alloy steels by the utilisation of such metals as tungsten and molybdenum. New natural products, such as quebracho (a dyeing extract), had made their appearance in French markets. Hitherto the customs administration had been compelled to deal with the products of new industries or methods by assimilating them as well as they could to the products already specified in the tariff schedules to which the resemblance seemed closest; but it had long been apparent that nothing short of a thorough revision in respect of both classification and nomenclature would be satisfactory.

A further justification for the demand for revision was found in the changes which had been made in 1903 and the following years in the customs tariffs of other European states. These had all aimed at greater specialisation, both in response to the facts of industry and as an improved means of giving tariff favours without unduly generalising them, and it was thought to be necessary for France to do the same. And in this connection the relation between the French minimum and maximum rates of duty called for reconsideration, the fact being that the conditions in regard thereto had become totally different from those anticipated in 1892.[2]

[1] *Rapport Général*, par M. Jean Morel, pp. 39–40 and 49.
[2] *Rapport Général*, pp. 60–1.

The rates of duty of the maximum tariff were on the average about 15 per cent. higher than those of the minimum tariff, and the assumption had been that the maximum tariff would be the rule and the minimum tariff the exception, the rates of the latter being applied only in a few cases or to the products of a few countries. In practice, however, the very opposite came to be the fact; the advantages of the minimum tariff were extended to all European countries except Portugal, and to numerous non-European countries also. The result was that the protection afforded to French industry by the tariff was very much less than its authors had intended, whilst the difference between the maximum and minimum scales was too small to render the threat of the imposition of the higher rates a very effective weapon in commercial conflicts. It was, therefore, believed to be necessary to raise the level of the duties of the minimum tariff, and, at the same time, in order to strengthen the hands of the French Government in commercial negotiations, to increase the difference between the minimum and maximum rates.

It will be observed that there was no suggestion of any change in the commercial policy of France, which followed the example of the United States rather than that of the German Empire and other states of continental Europe. France, as the United States, had established two scales of duty; the lower scale to be applied, in whole or part, to the products of countries which did not discriminate unfavourably against French products, and the higher scale to be applied against countries which did so discriminate. Unlike Germany, she had declined as a general rule to enter into treaties which should fix these minimum rates for any definite time, and consequently she had retained her autonomy in tariff matters undiminished. There was now in France no controversy whatever as to the desirability of continuing this arrangement and the other characteristic features of French tariff policy, such as colonial preference and the *surtaxes d'entrepôt*; the revision was to be, in consequence, solely a revision of the rates of duty.

The Customs Commission of the Chamber of Deputies held an elaborate inquiry, and produced its report, together with the draft of a law amending the existing tariff, towards the end of 1908. The general lines on which it proceeded have already been indicated—they were the increase of the general tariff (that is, of the maximum rates of duty), and the increase in numerous instances of the minimum tariff also; the greater differentiation between the maximum and minimum rates (the former were to be generally 50 per cent. in excess of the latter); the inclusion of new tariff headings; and a highly developed specialisation.[1] The revision was predominantly in the interests of industry, thus contrasting strongly with the latest revision of the German tariff, which had been dictated largely by regard for agriculture. No changes were proposed in respect of the duties on such products as grain, live and dead meat, butter, margarine, lard, milk, hard cheeses, eggs, wine, cider and vinegar.[2] The rates of duty on "colonial produce" (sugar, molasses, coffee, cocoa, chocolate, pepper, pimento, nutmegs, cloves, vanilla, tea and tobacco) remained unaltered. No changes were made in regard to coal, coke, anthracite and wood charcoal. The policy of allowing the duty-free admission of practically all raw materials, and of compensating the French producers of similar commodities for the absence of protection, by the grant of bounties or in other ways, was also maintained.[3] Very few changes were proposed in the schedules relating to chemical products, dyes and colours, woollen yarns and other woollen goods, and manufactures of wood.

The most sweeping changes proposed in regard to the minimum rates, which so far as most industrial nations

[1] A comparison of the proposed rates of duty with those of the 1892 tariff is contained in the *Proposed New French Tariff*, Cd. 4489, 1909.

[2] There is only one scale of duty for grains.

[3] *Rapport Général*, pp. 64–5.

trading with France are concerned are alone of importance, were in the schedules relating to metals, where the duties were increased especially as regards special steels; manufactures of metal, where there was a far-reaching reclassification and increases in the rates of duty on such classes of imports as steam-engines, pumps and ventilators, agricultural machinery, machine tools, mechanicians' tools, cables and wire, detached parts of machines, and watches and watch movements; and the textile schedules, owing (*inter alia*) to reclassification, the imposition of surtaxes for mercerisation and stamping (*gaufrage*), and the increase of the rates of duty on the highest counts of cotton and linen yarns. Other important increases related to mineral-tanned leather, some classes of boots, shoes, and gloves, elastic tissues, scientific instruments and apparatus, certain kinds of cotton hosiery, paper and furniture.

So soon as the Bill was laid before the Chamber of Deputies the French Government indicated its reluctance to accept a large number of the proposals, and after proceeding some way the debate was adjourned to enable discussion to take place between the representatives of the Government and the Customs Commission. As a result agreement was reached as to only a comparatively small proportion of the tariff numbers in dispute. As to all the more important schedules the difference of opinion still continued, the Government asking simply for the maintenance of the existing rates of duty. This, however, would clearly have defeated the whole object of the revision, and when consideration of the Bill was resumed in the Chamber of Deputies the Government gave way. It was, however, able to exercise a moderating influence, and ultimately the new classification of cotton and woollen tissues, and most of the increases of duty upon these and upon silks and silk ribbons of European origin, were dropped; and in a number of instances (such as special steels, iron and steel and wire thereof, tools, and boots and shoes) the changes were less drastic than those originally proposed.

The Bill passed the Chamber on December 29, 1909, and was referred by the Senate to its own Customs Commission, of which M. Méline was a prominent member. The Senate was undoubtedly much more protectionist in its sympathies than the Chamber of Deputies, and such alterations as it was possible to make in the limited time available for consideration and inquiry (for the Government was anxious that the new tariff, whatever its nature, should come into force at the commencement of April) were, as a rule, in the direction of a still further increase of the rates of duty.[1] Though the Government continued to object to a number of the proposed rates, and was able, as in the Chamber, to exercise a moderating influence, it does not appear to have made any very strenuous effort to assert itself. The Bill as amended by the Senate Commission and by the Senate itself was adopted by the Chamber of Deputies almost without debate by an overwhelming majority (416 votes to 92); it was promulgated on March 30, and came into force on April 1, 1910. The most striking thing in its history was the manner in which the various Ministries which were in office whilst the revision of the tariff was under consideration endeavoured apparently to divest themselves of responsibility for the decisions which might ultimately be taken. Such a course is natural, and even proper, in the United States, where the Constitution aims at the independence of the executive and legislative authorities; but it is remarkable in a country possessing a system of parliamentary government.

The general nature of the new tariff as compared with the old has already been indicated. Out of 654 tariff numbers, about 500 were revised, but in an appreciable proportion of cases only the maximum tariff rates were raised, or there was a simple alteration of nomenclature. A few increases were made in respect of agricultural products, especially hops, salted meat, lard, and some

[1] *Rapport fait au nom de la Commission des Douanes du Sénat*, par M. Noël, 1910, *passim*.

table fruits; but the great majority of the changes related to manufactured goods, and here the very extensive changes in classification and the advance in specialisation render it extremely difficult to estimate the extent of the increase, and practically impossible, in the absence of sufficiently detailed statistics, to form any judgment as to the effect of the new duties on the trade of various countries with France. The reductions of rates of duty were few in number, the most conspicuous being in respect of pure alpaca yarns (which were to be admitted free), soya and maize oils for soap-making, aluminium, sulphate of soda, indiarubber sheets and pure vulcanised threads. There were also instances in which increased specialisation involved a reduction of the rates on some classes of a particular commodity whilst increasing the rates on other classes.[1]

The system by which surtaxes varying in amount are levied on certain European goods imported into France from countries other than those of origin, and on all non-European goods (with a few exceptions) imported from European countries, was continued, the objects being, of course, to aid French shipping and secure for French ports some share of the distributing trade.[2]

The new law made no change in regard to the existing commercial relations between France and other countries; it simply substituted one set of rate schedules for another, and with two exceptions, Portugal and the United States, all important countries trading with France were already enjoying the advantages of the minimum tariff in whole or part. With regard to Portugal the position has not been modified, but the danger of a tariff war with the United States, which would have subjected France to

[1] A comparison of the old and new rates of duty is contained in the *New French Customs Tariff*, Cd. 5127, issued by the Board of Trade.

[2] This *surtax d'entrepôt* is not levied on raw wool from Australia, South Africa or India; raw cotton from India; jute, phormium tenax, and esparto; and plumbago from Ceylon. The rate varies on Colonial produce; on most other articles it is 3 fr. 60 per 100 kilo.

their new maximum tariff from April 1 had an agreement not been reached, was averted. A curious provision of the new French law authorised the Government (subject to legislative approval) "to maintain in force exceptionally and as a temporary measure the rates of the general [*i.e.*, maximum] tariff in force prior to the present law as regards all or any goods the produce of countries which do not subject French products to any differential treatment whatever." The exact purpose of this clause was not clear, unless it were to give the French Government the opportunity of establishing an "intermediate" tariff, following in this respect the example of Canada; but it was immediately utilised in an agreement with the United States. Under this arrangement, which was confirmed by the Legislature on the same day as the new tariff was enacted, the United States obtain the new minimum rates on a large number of commodities, including, however, some (such as those on coffee, cocoa, pepper, tea, and coal) in which they are not specially interested and not including any of the rates in the textile schedules, and the old general tariff rates are continued in respect of certain of their exports, such as preserved fruits, fine cutlery, some classes of boots, iron and steel tubes, common brushware, and various other articles.

The new French tariff was accepted by the countries with which French manufacturers were in competition, if not with equanimity at least without active protest, except on the part of Germany and Belgium. Only in the latter case was there any threat of reprisals, and even there the suggestion of the manufacturers that some French imports into Belgium, especially wines, should be subjected to increases of duty, by way of retaliation, though it found some official support, was not adopted.

The tariff came into force on April 1, 1910, and the following table shows the movement of French foreign trade from 1910 to 1913, the last complete year before the Great War:

Year.	Imports for Home Consumption.		Exports of Domestic Produce.	
	Total.	Manufactured Goods.	Total.	Manufactured Goods.
	Million £.	Million £.	Million £.	Million £.
1910	286·9	56·6	249·4	137·8
1911	322·6	60·8	243·1	140·4
1912	329·2	64·6	268·5	156·7
1913	336·9	66·3	275·2	167·3

During these four years the production of pig-iron rose from 4·1 million tons to 5·2 million tons; the consumption of raw cotton rose swiftly from 3·1 million cwt. in 1910 to 5·4 million cwt. in 1912, receding slightly in the following year; the consumption of raw wool declined from the high level of 1909 and remained practically stationary at from 590 to 602 million lbs., though it dropped to 567·8 million lbs. in 1912: the consumption of raw silk fell very heavily, and in 1913 reached the lowest point recorded for many years. There was some progress made in the commerce and industry of France during the four years from the enactment of the tariff of 1910 to the outbreak of the European War, but it was in no way comparable to the development shown by her great industrial competitors on the west and on the east.

A BRIEF BIBLIOGRAPHY

AMÉ. *Étude sur les Tarifs de Douane.* 2 vols. 1876.

ANNAUNE, P. *Le Commerce Exterieur et les Tarifs de Douane.* 1911.

BRANDT, A. VON. *Beiträge zur Geschichte der französischen Handelspolitik.* 1896.

DEVERS, A. "La Politique Commerciale de la France depuis 1860" (*Verein für Socialpolitik.* Vol. l. 1892).

RAUSCH, E. *Französische Handelspolitik vom Frankfurter Frieden bis zur Tarifreform von 1882.* 1900.

FRANKE, B. *Der Ausbau des heutigen Schutzzollsystems in Frankreich.* 1904.

AUGIER, C., and MARVAUD, A. *La Politique Douanière de la France.* 1911.

LEVASSEUR, E. *Histoire des Classes Ouvrières et de l'Industrie en France* (1789 *à* 1867). 2 vols.

LEVASSEUR, E. *Histoire du Commerce de la France de* 1789 *à nos jours.* 1912.

MEREDITH, H. O. *Protection in France.* 1904.

NOËL. *Histoire de Commerce Extérieur de la France.* 1879.

PIGEONNEAU. *Histoire du Commerce de la France.* 2 vols. 1889.

MORLEY, J. *Life of Richard Cobden.* Popular edition, 1903.

WOLOWSKI. *La Liberté Commerciale et les Résultats du Traité de Commerce de* 1860. 1869.

BUTENVAL. *Politique Économique et Négotiations Commerciales du Gouvernement de la République Française,* 1871–73. 1874.

FUNK-BRENTANO et CHARLES DUPUIS. *Les Tarifs Douaniers et les Traités de Commerce.* 1895.

MEEKER, R. *History of Shipping Subsidies.* 1905.

Report on Tariff Wars. (Cd. 1938. 1904).

Foreign Countries (*Preference to Colonies*). (H.C. 296. 1909.)

FOVILLE, A. DE. *La France Économique.* 1890.

RAMBAUD, A. *Histoire de la Civilisation contemporaine en France.* 5th edition. 1898.

British and Foreign Trade and Industry. (Cd. 4954. 1909.)

Annuaire Statistique de la France.

Rapport Général fait au nom de la Commission des Douanes de la Chambre des Députés, par M. Morel. 1908.

Rapport Général fait au nom de la Commission des Douanes du Sénat, par M. Noël. 1910.

New French Customs Tariff. (Cd. 5127. 1910.)

INDEX